Privacy

Privacy

The Architecture of Forgetting

Jeremy McEntire

CAGE & MIRROR PUBLISHING

Published by Cage & Mirror Publishing
Oklahoma City, Oklahoma

ISBN 979-8-9940343-9-2

First Edition

Printed in the United States of America

For Buffer and Proxy, who never consented to being tracked.

Foreword

Six questions run through this book, each one deceptively simple, each one revealing—when pursued to its structural root—an architectural failure that no amount of policy, regulation, or corporate goodwill can repair. Why does logging into a website hand the identity provider a complete map of everywhere you go online? Why does every database store data in a form the operator can read, ensuring that every breach, every subpoena, and every insider threat exposes everything? Why does proving you are human require a system that tracks everything you do? Why does every message you send create a permanent record of who you talked to, when, and how often—even when the content is encrypted? Why does a purchase require trusting five intermediaries with your complete transaction history? Why does installing software require permission from a gatekeeper who can be pressured into saying no?

These are not policy failures. They are architecture failures. The systems were built this way not out of malice but because surveillance was the path of least resistance—logging is easier than not logging, storing everything is cheaper than deciding what to store, and tracking is more profitable than not tracking. The economics pointed one direction, the engineers followed, and the result is an infrastructure where privacy is not violated by bad actors exploiting good systems but by good systems functioning exactly as designed.

This book describes what to build instead. Six components, each addressing one structural failure, each independently adoptable, each closing gaps the others leave open. The architecture is the argument. If the components work as described, the questions answer themselves. The reader will judge whether they do.

Contents

Preface

This book describes a six-component privacy architecture for the internet. Each component addresses a specific failure in current infrastructure: identity systems that track users across sites, databases that expose data when breached, accountability mechanisms that require surveillance, communication systems that log metadata, multi-party workflows that leak information to intermediaries, and software distribution channels controlled by gatekeepers who can be pressured into censorship.

The components are independently adoptable. Most readers will implement one or two, not all six. Each provides value on its own. Together, they close each other's gaps.

The book is organized into paired chapters. Each pair begins with a problem chapter—what fails and why—followed by an architecture chapter—what to build instead. The architecture chapters include pseudocode, threat models, and an honest assessment of what each component does not protect against. Two synthesis chapters examine how the components compose and what building them requires. The final chapters address the political economy of the transition and why forgetting matters.

Who this book is for. Software architects and engineers building systems that handle personal data. Security engineers evaluating privacy architectures. Technical leaders making build-versus-buy decisions about identity, storage, and communication infrastructure. Anyone who wants to understand what a privacy-preserving internet would look like at the protocol level.

What this book assumes. Familiarity with basic cryptographic concepts (hashing, symmetric and asymmetric encryption, digital signatures). Comfort reading pseudocode. Understanding of client-server architecture and web protocols. No specific language or framework knowledge is required—the pseudocode is language-agnostic.

How to read this book. Sequentially for the complete picture. By component pair (Chapters 2-3, 4-5, 6-7, 8-9, 10-11, 12-13) for specific concerns. Chapter 14 for the composed architecture. Chapter 15 for implementation guidance. Chapters 16-17 for context on adoption and motivation.

The code in this book is illustrative, not extracted from production implementations. Translate to your stack. The architecture is the contribution, not the pseudocode.

CHAPTER 1

The Architecture of Forgetting

Consider what happens when you check your email. Your device connects to a server that logs the connection time, source IP address, and session duration. The email service has already scanned the contents—for spam filtering, but also for advertising keywords that reveal purchasing intent, travel plans, medical concerns, financial activity. The metadata is permanent: who you correspond with, how often, at what times. When you click a link in an email, the destination site receives your referrer header, correlates it with a tracking cookie it set months ago, and updates a behavioral profile that spans every site in its advertising network. When you then search for something mentioned in the email, the search engine logs the query, ties it to your account, and feeds it into a model that predicts your future behavior. When you message a friend about what you found, the messaging platform logs the relationship, the timing, and—in most cases—the content.

That sequence—email, click, search, message—took ninety seconds. It generated permanent records in at least four databases operated by at least three companies in at least two jurisdictions. None of these records will expire. Each can be subpoenaed independently. Together, they reconstruct not just what you did, but what you were thinking about, what prompted the thought, and who you shared it with. This is not a worst case. This is a Tuesday morning.

The question this book addresses is not whether this infrastructure can be reformed through policy, regulation, or corporate goodwill. It has been under reform pressure for over a decade, and the surveillance has intensified, not diminished. The question is whether the underlying architecture can be replaced—not with a single privacy tool, but with a set of structural changes that make the observation described above architecturally infeasible.

The internet was designed to share information. The surveillance came later, layered on top by services whose business models required knowing everything about everyone. What began as infrastructure for communication became infrastructure for observation—not through conspiracy, but through the path of least resistance. Logging is easier than not logging. Storing everything is cheaper than deciding what to store. Tracking is more profitable than not tracking.

The result is an internet where every interaction creates a permanent record. Every authentication event logs an identity. Every database stores readable data that can be breached, subpoenaed, or sold. Every message passes through servers that retain metadata about who contacted whom and when. Every multi-party transaction exposes its complete details to every intermediary. Every application is distributed through gate-

1

keepers who can revoke access under pressure.

The failures are not hypothetical. In 2017, the Equifax breach exposed the personal data of 147 million people[1]—Social Security numbers, birth dates, addresses, driver's license numbers. The data was encrypted at rest. The encryption was irrelevant because the application tier decrypted it for every query, and the attacker compromised the application tier. In the same year, an NSA contractor was identified and arrested within days,[2] not through any failure of content encryption, but through printer microdots, access logs, email metadata, and a postmark. In 2017, Apple removed all major VPN applications from its Chinese App Store[3] under government pressure, cutting off privacy tools for an entire population through a single gatekeeper decision. Each failure represents a different layer of the problem. Each has an architectural response.

This book describes those responses. Not a single system, but six independent components, each addressing a specific failure in current infrastructure. The components work alone and compose together. Adopt one for partial protection. Adopt all six and the gaps close.

The Scale of the Problem

The surveillance infrastructure is not a peripheral feature of the internet. It is the business model.

The global digital advertising market exceeds $600 billion annually.[4] That revenue depends on behavioral data—on knowing what users search for, what they buy, where they go, who they communicate with, and what content captures their attention. The data is collected through identity systems that track users across sites, through databases that store behavioral histories in readable form, through communication platforms that log relationship graphs.

The data is not merely collected. It is concentrated. A small number of companies hold behavioral data on billions of people. This concentration creates risk at a scale that no previous information architecture has faced. A single breach can expose hundreds of millions of records. A single policy change can alter the privacy posture of billions

---

1   Federal Trade Commission, "Equifax Data Breach Settlement," July 2019. The FTC's complaint documented that attackers exploited an unpatched Apache Struts vulnerability in Equifax's online dispute portal, gaining access to personally identifiable information of approximately 147 million consumers. Equifax agreed to a settlement of up to $700 million.

2   *United States v. Reality Leigh Winner*, Case No. 1:17-cr-00034-JRH-BKE (S.D. Ga. 2017). Winner was sentenced to sixty-three months—the longest sentence ever imposed for an unauthorized disclosure to the media under the Espionage Act. The forensic identification relied on printer steganography (Machine Identification Code dots), NSA audit logs, email metadata, and geographic correlation.

3   Apple Inc. removed VPN applications from its China App Store on July 29, 2017, following regulations from China's Ministry of Industry and Information Technology requiring government authorization for VPN services. Apple CEO Tim Cook addressed the decision on Apple's Q3 2017 earnings call (August 1, 2017): "We would obviously rather not remove the apps."

4   Global digital advertising spending exceeded $600 billion in 2023, with estimates ranging from $602 billion to $680 billion depending on market scope definitions. Sources: Statista, "Digital Advertising—Worldwide," 2024; eMarketer/Insider Intelligence, "Worldwide Digital Ad Spending Forecast," 2023.

of users overnight. A single government request can access the behavioral history of an entire population.

The concentration also creates power. The entities that hold behavioral data can influence elections, manipulate markets, discriminate in employment, and enable authoritarian control—not through malice necessarily, but through the structural capability that concentrated behavioral data provides. The capability exists regardless of whether any particular operator intends to abuse it.

The 2018 Cambridge Analytica disclosure illustrated both the concentration and the fragility. Facebook's data architecture permitted a third-party application to access not only the data of users who installed it, but the data of those users' friends—ultimately affecting 87 million profiles.[5] The data was not "stolen" in the breach sense. It was accessed through the platform's own API, operating within the rules as they existed at the time. The architectural capability preceded the policy failure. The data was accessible because the architecture made it accessible. The subsequent policy changes addressed the specific API endpoint; they did not alter the fundamental reality that a centralized platform holding behavioral data on billions of people will always present this surface.

The standard response to this concentration is regulation. GDPR in Europe. CCPA in California. Sector-specific rules in healthcare (HIPAA), finance (PCI-DSS, SOX), and education (FERPA). These regulations impose constraints on data collection, use, and retention. They create compliance obligations, notification requirements, and penalties for violations.

Regulation has not solved the problem. It has raised the cost of data collection without changing the underlying architecture. The data is still collected, still stored in readable form, still accessible to operators, still vulnerable to breach. Compliance departments manage the regulatory burden. Legal teams interpret the requirements. Fines, when imposed, are absorbed as a cost of doing business. The fundamental architecture—centralized, readable, permanent—remains unchanged because the regulations operate within it rather than challenging it.

The alternative is to change the architecture itself. Rather than regulating what operators do with data they can read, build systems where operators cannot read the data. Rather than requiring data minimization policies, build systems that architecturally minimize by construction. Rather than mandating breach notification, build systems where breaches yield nothing readable. This is the approach this book takes. It is not anti-regulation. It is complementary to regulation. But it operates at a different level—the level of what is structurally possible, not what is legally permitted.

---

5   Facebook disclosed the figure of "up to 87 million" affected profiles in an April 4, 2018 blog post by CTO Mike Schroepfer. The UK Information Commissioner's Office investigation resulted in a £500,000 fine against Facebook (the maximum under the pre-GDPR Data Protection Act 1998). The U.S. FTC imposed a $5 billion penalty in July 2019.

The Six Components

Component	Problem Addressed	Core Mechanism	Chapter Pair
Anonymous Identity	Cross-site tracking via stable identifiers	Hash-derived, site-specific tokens	2–3
Blind Database	Data exposure through breaches and subpoenas	Client-side encryption with server-side opacity	4–5
Proof of Human	Bot abuse and Sybil attacks	Logarithmic effort scoring without behavioral surveillance	6–7
HermesP2P	Metadata accumulation on communication servers	Peer-to-peer routing with onion encryption	8–9
Cryptogram/Delegator	Information leakage to workflow intermediaries	Per-recipient section encryption with blind routing	10–11
Chess	Gatekeeper control over software distribution	Self-validating executable documents	12–13

Each component replaces an architectural assumption that the current internet treats as given.

Anonymous Identity replaces the assumption that authentication requires a stable, cross-site identifier. Current SSO systems—"Sign in with Google," "Sign in with Facebook"—assign you a persistent identifier that follows you across every site that uses the provider. The identifier enables the provider to build a complete map of your online activity. Anonymous Identity uses a hash construction to derive site-specific tokens that serve the same authentication purpose without enabling cross-site correlation. The token you present to your bank and the token you present to a social network are cryptographically unlinkable—derived from the same master credential but distinct by construction.

Blind Database replaces the assumption that the server must be able to read stored data. Current databases store data in a form the operator can query, inspect, and produce on demand. A breach exposes everything. A subpoena yields everything. An insider can read everything. Blind Database uses client-side encryption—the client encrypts before upload, the server stores ciphertext it cannot decrypt. The server provides storage and availability. The server cannot read what it stores. A breach yields noise. A subpoena yields noise.

Proof of Human replaces the assumption that accountability requires surveillance. Current anti-abuse systems—CAPTCHA, behavioral biometrics, reputation scoring—rely on observing and tracking user behavior to distinguish humans from bots. Proof of Human accumulates signals that demonstrate humanness (email verification, payment instruments, activity history) and converts them to a single score, storing proofs that attestation occurred rather than the raw data. The score travels with the user. The behavioral data does not.

HermesP2P replaces the assumption that message delivery requires a central server that logs metadata. Current messaging systems route through servers that know who sent each message, who received it, when, and how often. Even with end-to-end content encryption, the relationship graph is fully visible. HermesP2P routes messages through a peer-to-peer network using onion encryption, where each relay knows only its immediate neighbor in the chain and no single node sees the complete path.

Cryptogram and Delegator replaces the assumption that workflow intermediaries must see the complete picture. When you make a purchase, the payment processor sees your financial identity, the store sees what you bought, the shipper sees your address. Each intermediary accumulates data far beyond what its function requires. Cryptogram fragments the workflow into sections encrypted for specific recipients. Each party decrypts only its designated fragment. The delegator routes the fragments without reading them.

Chess replaces the assumption that software distribution requires a gatekeeper. App stores, certificate authorities, and hosting providers all represent chokepoints where access can be revoked under pressure. Chess represents applications as self-validating documents—carrying their own code, state, and cryptographic proof of integrity. The document can travel through any channel. Verification happens locally. No gatekeeper is architecturally necessary.

Five Design Principles

Five principles run through every component. They are not aspirations. They are engineering constraints that the architecture satisfies.

1. Structural protection over policy protection. The server cannot read the data—not because policy prohibits it, but because the server does not hold the decryption keys. The communication network does not log metadata—not because a retention policy says to delete it, but because the architecture generates nothing to retain. Policy can be changed, violated, or secretly reinterpreted. A terms-of-service promise that "we will never share your data" can be revised quietly, overridden by acquisition, or nullified by a court order. A cryptographic guarantee that the server cannot read the data cannot be revised by anyone. The distinction between "will not" and "cannot" is the distinction between policy and structure. This architecture operates in the domain of "cannot."

2. Honest-but-curious operator assumption. Every server, every relay, every intermediary is assumed to follow the protocol correctly but to read anything it can access. The architecture removes access rather than trusting restraint. An operator who follows the protocol and simultaneously attempts to extract every bit of information from what it can observe will learn nothing useful—because the architecture ensures that what it can observe reveals nothing.

3. Independent adoptability. Each component provides value without requiring the others. An organization that deploys only Anonymous Identity gains cross-site unlinkability. An organization that deploys only Blind Database gains breach resistance. The components compose, but composition is not required. Each component used alone has an explicit gap—a limitation that another component closes. Those gaps are documented in each architecture chapter and mapped systematically in Chapter 14. The reader adopting a single component gets genuine protection with a known, bounded limitation—not a false sense of completeness. Most readers will adopt one or two components, not all six. Deploying all six requires a consortium-level effort that any individual reader is unlikely to undertake. The architecture is designed for this reality. A startup can adopt Anonymous Identity and Blind Database on day one with a small engineering team. Adding Proof of Human requires additional signal infrastructure. Adding HermesP2P requires peer-to-peer networking. Adding Chess requires ecosystem development that does not yet exist at production quality. The incremental adoption path is deliberate, not an afterthought.

4. Ephemerality as default. The default state of information in this architecture is gone. Messages disappear after delivery. Workflow state is destroyed after the workflow completes. Communication metadata is never created. Data persists only when someone deliberately chooses to retain it, and even retained data is encrypted with keys that can be destroyed. The architecture inverts the current default: remembering requires effort; forgetting is free.

5. User as cryptographic root of trust. The user holds the keys. The user derives the tokens. The user controls what is readable and by whom. The server is a custodian of ciphertext, not a gatekeeper of access. This principle is what makes operational blindness possible—the server's inability to read data is a consequence of the user holding the keys, not of any restriction imposed on the server.

The Perfection Fallacy

A predictable objection arises against any privacy architecture: it does not provide perfect protection, therefore it is worthless. The objection identifies a real limitation—no architecture defeats all adversaries in all scenarios—and draws an invalid conclusion.

The correct comparison is not between this architecture and an imagined ideal. The correct comparison is between this architecture and the actual status quo.

The status quo fails against data breaches. This architecture does not—the breached database contains ciphertext that is computationally unreadable without keys the attacker does not have. The status quo fails against metadata subpoenas. This architecture limits exposure—HermesP2P retains no communication metadata, and blind databases produce only ciphertext in response to legal demands. The status quo fails against cross-site tracking. This architecture does not—site-specific tokens are unlinkable by construction. The status quo fails against insider access. This architecture does not—the insider cannot read encrypted data any more than an external attacker can.

Both architectures fail against endpoint compromise—if an attacker controls your device, all bets are off. Both fail against a sufficiently resourced global adversary performing traffic analysis at network edges. Both fail against malicious authors distributing harmful software. These shared failures are the failures that no system can prevent.

They are not arguments for the status quo. They are the irreducible minimum of risk in any networked system.

The principle has a name in this book: the Perfection Fallacy. It appears whenever a critic attacks an improvement by pointing to remaining vulnerabilities as though the improvement created them. The pattern is rhetorical, not analytical. It takes the form: "Your system does not protect against X, therefore it is useless." The response is always the same: does the status quo protect against X? If not, the criticism is not an argument against the improvement. It is an argument against all systems, including the one the critic implicitly defends.

The Perfection Fallacy is particularly corrosive in security discourse because security improvements are always partial. No lock makes a house impenetrable. No encryption defeats every attacker. No architecture survives every threat model. If the standard for adoption is perfection, nothing is ever adopted, and the catastrophically inadequate status quo persists by default.

The correct standard is improvement. Does this architecture reduce the set of threats that succeed? Does it raise the cost of attack? Does it eliminate entire categories of vulnerability that the status quo exposes? By this standard, the architecture succeeds. It does not claim to solve everything. It claims to solve the things it solves, honestly identifies the things it does not, and invites comparison with the alternative—which is not some imagined perfect system, but the actual infrastructure that currently fails billions of people daily.

The Good Police Work Principle

A second predictable objection comes from law enforcement: privacy architecture makes investigation impossible. Here is the direct answer.

This architecture does not make investigation impossible. It makes mass surveillance impossible. The distinction is critical and frequently elided by those who benefit from mass surveillance.

Consider two investigative scenarios. In the first, an officer suspects that Alice is involved in a crime. The officer obtains a warrant, seizes Alice's devices, examines her local data, serves process on services she uses, and builds a case. This is targeted investigation. It requires prior suspicion of a specific individual. It operates through legal channels with judicial oversight. It is the kind of investigation that democratic societies have conducted for centuries. This architecture does not impede it. Alice's devices contain her keys. Her local data is decryptable with those keys. Her service providers can produce whatever they hold, which under this architecture is ciphertext—but the investigation proceeds through Alice's endpoint, not through the server.

In the second scenario, an officer has no specific suspect. The officer queries a centralized database: "Show me everyone who searched for X." "Show me everyone who communicated with phone number Y." "Show me everyone who visited location Z between 8 PM and midnight." These are mass queries against entire populations. They do not require prior suspicion. They operate as fishing expeditions—casting a wide net and examining what comes up. This architecture makes these queries unanswerable, because no centralized database holds the answers.

The architecture enforces a simple principle: investigation requires a hypothesis before it begins. You must know who you are looking for before you look. The question "Does suspect X visit site Y?" remains answerable—serve process on suspect X, examine their devices, check their tokens. The question "Who visits site Y?" becomes unanswerable—not because the answer is hidden, but because no centralized record exists that could provide it. The distinction is between targeted investigation (hypothesis first, then evidence) and mass surveillance (evidence first, then hypothesis). The architecture permits the former and prevents the latter.

This is the Good Police Work Principle: architecture should make mass queries computationally infeasible while preserving targeted investigation capability. The asymmetry is the feature. It aligns the cost structure of investigation with the due process requirements that democratic societies claim to value.

The principle is not anti-law-enforcement. It is pro-due-process. The Fourth Amendment prohibits unreasonable searches—wholesale queries against entire populations without particularized suspicion. The Supreme Court's 2018 decision in *Carpenter v. United States*[6] affirmed that this principle extends to certain digital records, though the precise boundaries of digital Fourth Amendment protections remain contested. Current internet infrastructure makes bulk queries trivially easy because the data exists in concentrated, queryable form. This architecture makes unreasonable searches architecturally impossible while leaving reasonable searches—targeted investigation of specific suspects with appropriate legal authorization—fully functional. The architecture enforces at the structural level what the Constitution requires at the legal level.

The enforcement is stronger than any legal constraint. A secret court order can reinterpret legal protections. A classified memo can expand surveillance authority. A compliant company can quietly hand over data while publicly denying it. An architectural constraint cannot be secretly reinterpreted. The server that does not possess the data cannot produce it regardless of what any authority demands. The protection is mathematical, not political.

Status Quo Comparison

The following table summarizes what changes between current infrastructure and this architecture across key scenarios:

Scenario	Current Infrastructure	This Architecture
Data breach	Readable records exposed; notification required; identity theft follows	Ciphertext exposed; computationally useless without keys

---

6   *Carpenter v. United States*, 585 U.S. ___, 138 S. Ct. 2206 (2018). The Court held (5–4) that accessing seven days of historical cell-site location information constitutes a search under the Fourth Amendment, requiring a warrant supported by probable cause.

Subpoena for user data	Operator produces readable records	Operator produces ciphertext it cannot decrypt
Cross-site tracking	Stable identifiers enable correlation by advertisers and data brokers	Site-specific tokens are unlinkable by construction
Communication metadata	Central servers hold complete relationship graphs	No central server; metadata distributed and ephemeral
Insider threat	Administrator or DBA can query all data	No god mode; operator cannot read stored data
App store censorship	Gatekeeper removes app; users lose access	Self-validating documents distribute through any channel
Bot/spam abuse	CAPTCHAs (increasingly ineffective); behavioral tracking	Proof of Human score makes abuse economically prohibitive
Multi-party workflow	Every intermediary sees complete transaction	Each party sees only its encrypted fragment
"Delete my data" request	Operational nightmare across backups, replicas, logs	Crypto-erasure: delete the key, data becomes noise
Endpoint compromise	All defenses fail	All defenses fail
Global adversary (traffic analysis)	Traffic analysis possible	Traffic analysis possible

The last two rows are identical. They represent the threats that no architecture can defeat. The preceding rows represent the threats where the architectures differ—and in every case, this architecture provides protection that the status quo does not.

The table is worth studying. Nine scenarios show improvement. Two show parity. Zero show regression. The architecture does not introduce new vulnerabilities. It eliminates existing ones while leaving the irreducible vulnerabilities unchanged.

Composition and Independence

The six components interact but do not depend on each other. This independence is architectural, not accidental.

Anonymous Identity alone provides cross-site unlinkability. But the User Service that issues tokens holds identity mappings. If the User Service is compromised, the mappings are exposed. Adding Blind Database closes this gap—the mappings are stored encrypted, unreadable even to the User Service operator.

Proof of Human alone filters bots and enables accountability. But the humanness score could serve as a cross-site identifier if attached to a global identity. Adding Anonymous Identity closes this gap—the score binds to site-specific pseudonyms that cannot be correlated.

HermesP2P alone eliminates metadata logging. But without identity stake, spammers flood the network with cheap pseudonyms. Adding Proof of Human closes this gap—public channels require minimum humanness scores, making spam economically prohibitive.

Each component has a gap. Each gap is closed by another component. The closure pattern is documented in Chapter 14. For now, the point is structural: partial adoption provides partial protection with explicit, known gaps. The reader can make an informed decision about which gaps to close and which to accept.

An organization that adopts Blind Database and nothing else protects its users against data breaches and insider access. It does not protect against identity correlation, metadata accumulation, or gatekeeper censorship. The protection it provides is real. The protection it does not provide is documented. The reader who understands both makes a better security decision than the reader who deploys a conventional system and assumes the regulatory compliance checklist constitutes protection.

Why Previous Privacy Attempts Failed

Privacy-enhancing technologies are not new. PGP email encryption dates to 1991. Tor anonymization dates to 2002. Various encrypted storage solutions have existed for decades. These technologies work—the cryptography is sound, the implementations are solid, the protections they provide are genuine. Yet the internet has become more surveilled, not less, in the years since these technologies appeared.

The failure is not technical. It is architectural. Previous privacy technologies addressed individual layers in isolation. PGP encrypts email content but does nothing about metadata—the server still knows who emailed whom and when. Tor anonymizes web browsing but does not address identity, storage, or software distribution. Encrypted databases protect data at rest but expose it to any application with query access. Each technology solves its specific problem and leaves every other problem untouched.

The most instructive example is Signal, the end-to-end encrypted messaging application. Signal's cryptography is excellent—the Signal Protocol is the standard against which all other messaging encryption is measured. Yet Signal requires a phone number for registration. The phone number is a stable identifier, linkable to a civil identity through carrier records. The content is protected. The identity is not. The metadata—who communicates with whom, when, how often—is shielded from Signal's servers by design, but the initial registration creates an identity anchor that the architecture cannot subsequently erase. Even the best encryption cannot compensate for an identity system that was not designed with the same rigor.

The result is a patchwork of protections with systematic gaps. A user who encrypts their email and browses through Tor is still tracked by login cookies, still has their data stored in readable databases, still communicates through messaging systems that log metadata, still depends on app stores that can be pressured into removing privacy tools. The individual protections are genuine. The aggregate protection is insufficient because the gaps between protections are where surveillance actually occurs.

This architecture differs from previous attempts in one fundamental way: it addresses all six layers simultaneously and designs for composition, each component aware of the others' existence and purpose. The components are independent—each provides value alone—but they are designed to close each other's gaps. Anonymous Identity prevents cross-site tracking, and Blind Database prevents the identity service itself from being a vulnerability. HermesP2P eliminates metadata logging, and Proof of Human prevents the resulting anonymity from enabling spam floods. Each component anticipates the gap it leaves and identifies which other component closes it.

How This Book Is Organized

The book follows a consistent structure. Each of the six components occupies a chapter pair: a problem chapter that examines what fails and why, followed by an architecture chapter that presents the solution with pseudocode, security analysis, and honest limitations.

Part I: Anonymous Identity (Chapters 2–3) addresses identity and tracking. Chapter 2 examines what SSO providers know, why centralization creates surveillance, and why alternatives fail. Chapter 3 presents the hash construction that produces unlinkable, site-specific tokens.

Part II: Blind Database (Chapters 4–5) addresses data storage. Chapter 4 examines why encryption at rest fails, how property-preserving encryption leaks structure, and what the encryption paradox actually is. Chapter 5 presents the client-side encryption architecture that achieves operational blindness.

Part III: Proof of Human (Chapters 6–7) addresses accountability. Chapter 6 tears down CAPTCHA, biometrics, reputation systems, and economic stake as accountability mechanisms. Chapter 7 presents the logarithmic effort scale and signal taxonomy.

Part IV: Ephemeral Communication (Chapters 8–9) addresses metadata. Chapter 8 examines what metadata reveals and why content encryption alone is insufficient. Chapter 9 presents onion-routed peer-to-peer messaging.

Part V: Zero-Trust Collaboration (Chapters 10–11) addresses intermediaries. Chapter 10 examines how multi-party workflows leak information. Chapter 11 presents the cryptogram document structure and blind delegator protocol.

Part VI: Censorship-Resistant Distribution (Chapters 12–13) addresses gatekeepers. Chapter 12 examines chokepoints in software distribution. Chapter 13 presents self-validating executable documents.

Part VII: Composition and Deployment (Chapters 14–17) synthesizes the components. Chapter 14 shows how they compose and presents the full threat model. Chapter 15 provides an implementation roadmap with recommended primitives and migration patterns. Chapter 16 examines the political economy of privacy. Chapter 17 reflects on why forgetting matters.

Each architecture chapter includes a "What This Does Not Protect Against" section. Every system has limits, and honesty about those limits is a prerequisite for trust. A system that claims to protect against everything protects against nothing, because the claim itself demonstrates either ignorance of the threat landscape or willingness to mislead.

The pseudocode throughout is language-agnostic and illustrative. It is not extracted from production implementations. No specific library or language bindings are assumed. The reader translates to their stack. The architecture is the contribution, not the pseudocode. The pseudocode makes the architecture concrete enough to evaluate and implement. The implementation details—choice of language, choice of framework, performance optimization—are the reader's decisions.

The cryptographic primitives referenced throughout are standard and well-studied. SHA-256 for hashing. Ed25519 for signatures. X25519 for key agreement. AES-256-GCM or ChaCha20-Poly1305 for symmetric encryption. HKDF for key derivation. These are not novel or exotic. They are the consensus recommendations of the cryptographic community, available through audited libraries like libsodium on every major platform. The architecture's novelty is in how the primitives are composed into systems, not in the primitives themselves.

The architecture is ready to build. Four of the six components—Anonymous Identity, Blind Database, Proof of Human, and Cryptogram/Delegator—are implementable today with existing cryptographic libraries and current infrastructure. HermesP2P is prototypable with current peer-to-peer networking patterns but requires engineering for production reliability. Chess requires ecosystem development—sandboxing environments, developer tooling, user expectations—that does not yet exist at scale. The readiness gradient is honest. Chapter 15 provides the implementation roadmap.

CHAPTER 2

The Identity Problem

The internet has an identity system. It was not designed. It emerged, incrementally, from a sequence of engineering decisions made under pressure to solve immediate problems. The result is an architecture in which a small number of companies authenticate the majority of the world's online population and, as a structural consequence of that authentication, maintain a comprehensive record of where those people go, what they do, and who they interact with. This is not a conspiracy. It is an architecture. The surveillance is a property of the design, not an intention of the designers.

Understanding how this architecture works, why it persists, and why the proposed alternatives fail is necessary before any replacement can be designed. The identity problem is not a lack of technology. Cryptographers have produced elegant solutions to every component of the problem in isolation. The identity problem is that no deployed system simultaneously provides the three properties that a working solution requires: convenience, privacy, and accountability. Every existing system sacrifices at least one. The sacrifices are structural, not incidental, and understanding why they occur is the prerequisite to building something that does not make them.

What SSO Providers Actually Know

Single sign-on (SSO) is the dominant identity architecture on the consumer internet. "Sign in with Google," "Sign in with Facebook," "Sign in with Apple" – these buttons appear on millions of websites and applications. The user clicks one, authenticates with the provider, and gains access to the third-party service. The interaction takes seconds. No new password to create, no account registration form to complete, no email verification loop to endure. The convenience is genuine, and it solved a genuine problem.

Before SSO, every website maintained its own user database, its own password storage, its own account recovery mechanism. Users accumulated hundreds of credentials, most of them variations on the same few passwords, all of them potential points of failure. The security was terrible. Password reuse meant that a breach on one site cascaded to every other site where the user had employed the same credentials. The credential management problem was real, and centralized identity providers addressed it by consolidating authentication into a few well-defended systems operated by companies with the engineering resources to do security properly.

The consolidation worked for security. It did something else for privacy. Here is what happens, at the protocol level, when you click "Sign in with Google" on a third-party website.

The website redirects your browser to Google's authorization server, passing along the website's identity and a list of requested permissions. Google authenticates you (or confirms that you are already authenticated in an active session). Google then redirects your browser back to the website with an authorization token. The website exchanges this token for your profile information – typically your name, email address, and a unique identifier.

At this point, Google knows that you have just visited this website. Not because the website reported your visit, but because the authentication flow requires Google's participation. The redirect passed through Google's servers. The token was issued by Google's infrastructure. The authentication event is logged because authentication events must be logged for security, fraud detection, and abuse prevention. Google knows which site you visited, when you visited it, and how you identified yourself there.

This is true for every site that uses Google SSO. Every authentication event creates a record in Google's infrastructure that links your identity to a specific third-party service at a specific time. If you use "Sign in with Google" across thirty websites, Google has a map of your activity across all thirty. The map updates every time you authenticate. Over months and years, this produces a detailed profile of your online behavior – which news sources you read, which retailers you shop at, which forums you participate in, which tools you use for work, which services you use for entertainment.

The profile is not incidental to the service. The profile is the business model. SSO authentication is free to both users and websites because the information it generates has commercial value. The user's browsing pattern, correlated across every site where they clicked the convenient button, informs the advertisements they see, the search results they receive, and the recommendations that shape their experience of the platform. The authentication is the product's input. The behavioral profile is the product's output. The user is the raw material.

Facebook's model is structurally identical. Apple's implementation differs in important ways – Apple generates unique per-site email addresses and limits profile data sharing – but the authentication event itself still flows through Apple's servers. The provider knows you authenticated. The architectural constraint is not specific to any company's privacy policy. It is inherent in the SSO protocol: if a third party vouches for your identity, the third party must be present at the moment of vouching, and presence implies knowledge.

The scale of this knowledge is worth stating explicitly. Google processes authentication for applications and websites that collectively serve billions of users. Facebook's SSO is embedded across millions of sites. These are not estimates of theoretical capability. They are descriptions of the operational reality. The identity providers that authenticate the internet's users have, as a structural consequence of performing that authentication, assembled the most comprehensive maps of human online behavior ever constructed. The maps were not the goal. The maps were the inevitable byproduct of an architecture in which identity flows through a central point.

The Centralization Trap

The concentration of identity into a few providers was not imposed. It was chosen, repeatedly, by users, developers, and businesses making individually rational decisions.

Users chose SSO because it eliminated the credential management burden. A person with accounts on fifty services faces a genuine cognitive load problem. Remembering fifty unique, strong passwords is not a realistic expectation. Password managers address this, but password managers are themselves a tool that must be installed, configured, and maintained – an overhead that the majority of internet users have not adopted. SSO reduces the problem to a single credential. The convenience is not trivial. It is the reason the architecture won.

Developers chose SSO because it eliminated the security liability of managing user credentials. Storing passwords correctly – using bcrypt or Argon2id, enforcing complexity requirements, implementing rate limiting, building account recovery flows – is expensive engineering work that generates no revenue and exposes the company to liability when (not if) it fails. Delegating authentication to Google or Facebook removes this liability entirely. The identity provider handles the security. The developer builds features. The economic logic is compelling.

Businesses chose SSO because it reduced friction in the conversion funnel. Every field in a registration form is a point where potential users abandon the signup process. "Sign in with Google" replaces a multi-field form with a single click. The improvement in conversion rates is measurable. For a business optimizing for growth, the calculus is straightforward.

Each of these decisions is rational. The collective outcome is an architecture where a few companies hold the authentication keys to the internet. This is the centralization trap: the individual incentives all point toward consolidation, and the consolidation enables surveillance at a scale that no individual decision-maker intended or desired.

The trap has a ratchet mechanism. Once a critical mass of websites accepts a given SSO provider, the provider's value to users increases (more places to use it), which increases adoption by users, which increases the provider's value to websites (more users who prefer it), which increases adoption by websites. This is a standard network effect. The result is that a small number of providers dominate, and switching costs escalate. A user who has connected forty services to their Google account faces a substantial migration cost to move to an alternative. The architecture is sticky by design.

The surveillance capability that centralization creates is not merely a privacy concern in the abstract. It has operational consequences. An identity provider can disable your access to every connected service by suspending your account. This has happened – to users who violated terms of service, to users caught in automated fraud detection sweeps, to users in jurisdictions where the provider faces government pressure. When your identity is centralized, your digital existence has a single point of failure, controlled by an entity whose interests may diverge from yours.

The centralization trap can be summarized concisely: consolidation solves the security problem and creates the surveillance problem. The two outcomes are not independent. They are the same architectural property viewed from different angles. The single point of authentication that eliminates password chaos is the same single point of authentication that enables behavioral profiling. You cannot have one without the other in a centralized architecture.

The Decentralization Trap

The centralization trap was recognized early. Cryptographers and privacy engineers proposed the obvious corrective: decentralize identity. Instead of relying on Google or Facebook to vouch for you, you would vouch for yourself. You would hold your own cryptographic keys, manage your own identifiers, present your own credentials. No central authority would mediate your authentication. No company would accumulate a map of your movements. The surveillance would end because the architecture would no longer permit it.

This is the self-sovereign identity (SSI) movement, and its theoretical foundations are sound. Public-key cryptography provides the primitives. A user generates a key pair, publishes the public key, and authenticates by proving possession of the private key. Verifiable credentials extend the model: a trusted issuer signs a statement about the user (this person is over 18, this person holds a valid driver's license, this person graduated from this university), and the user presents the signed statement to any verifier without the issuer's involvement in the transaction. The cryptography works. Zero-knowledge proofs can even allow the user to prove properties about credentials without revealing the credentials themselves – proving age without revealing birthdate, for instance.

The implementations were not usable.

Self-sovereign identity requires the user to manage cryptographic key material. This is a burden that the technical community consistently underestimates because the people designing these systems are not representative of the people who would need to use them. Key management involves generating keys with sufficient entropy, storing them in a secure location, backing them up against device loss, rotating them on a reasonable schedule, and revoking them if compromised. Each of these operations is technically straightforward and practically treacherous.

Key generation is handled by software and is generally invisible to the user. Key storage is where the problems begin. The private key must exist somewhere – on a device, in a file, in a hardware token. If it exists on a phone and the phone is lost, the key is gone. If the key is gone, the identity is gone, along with every credential, every account connection, and every piece of the digital life that was anchored to it. There is no "forgot my password" flow in self-sovereign identity. There is no customer support representative who can look up your account and reset your credentials. The key is the identity. Lose the key, lose everything.

The standard mitigation is backup. Write down a twelve-word seed phrase and store it in a safe place. This is the recovery mechanism used by cryptocurrency wallets, and the results are instructive. Chainalysis estimates that roughly 20% of all Bitcoin – hundreds of billions of dollars at various points in the currency's history – is in wallets whose owners have lost access to their keys. These are financially motivated users with strong incentive to maintain their key material. An identity system that relies on the same recovery mechanism can expect equal or higher loss rates, because the consequence of losing an identity key is less immediately tangible than losing money.

Hardware tokens (YubiKeys, smart cards) improve the security posture but add physical dependencies. The token must be present for authentication. If it breaks, authentication stops until a replacement is provisioned. If it is stolen, the attacker has the key. Multi-device synchronization – spreading key material across multiple devices so that no single device loss is catastrophic – adds complexity that compounds with each additional device.

The user experience of these systems has been, without exception, inadequate for general adoption. The W3C Decentralized Identifiers (DID) specification, the Sovrin network, the various blockchain-based identity proposals – all produced systems that worked reliably for users who understood public-key infrastructure and failed for users who did not. The failure was not in the cryptography. The failure was in the assumption that ordinary users would tolerate a level of operational responsibility that most IT professionals find burdensome.

This is the decentralization trap—a mirror of the centralization trap: self-sovereign identity eliminates the surveillance of centralized systems but imposes key management requirements that ordinary users cannot meet. The theoretical privacy properties are excellent. The practical usability properties are disqualifying. A system that works only for the technically sophisticated is not a solution to a problem that affects everyone. Neither position is acceptable, and moving between them does not resolve the underlying tension.

Why the Alternatives Fail

Between full centralization and full self-sovereignty, a range of alternative approaches have been proposed. Each addresses a visible symptom of the identity problem while leaving the structural cause intact. Examining why they fail clarifies the requirements that a working solution must satisfy.

Biometrics

Biometric authentication – fingerprints, facial recognition, iris scans, voice patterns – appears to eliminate the credential management problem entirely. The user does not need to remember anything or carry anything. The user is the credential. Apple's Face ID and Touch ID have demonstrated that biometric authentication can be fast, convenient, and widely adopted. The user experience is excellent.

The problem is that biometrics are not secrets. They are measurements of physical characteristics that the user cannot change. A password, if compromised, can be rotated. A cryptographic key, if compromised, can be revoked and replaced. A fingerprint, if compromised, is compromised permanently. The user has ten fingerprints, one face, and two irises. When these are exhausted, there are no more credentials to issue.

The permanence of biometric compromise is not a theoretical concern. The U.S.

Office of Personnel Management breach in 2015 exposed the fingerprint records of 5.6 million federal employees. Those fingerprints cannot be changed. The breach is permanent in a way that a password breach is not. Every system that those individuals authenticate to using fingerprints is now operating with compromised credentials, and this condition will persist for the remainder of their lives.

Biometric data must also be stored and compared somewhere, which reintroduces the centralization question. If the biometric template is stored on the user's device and never leaves it (as in Apple's Secure Enclave model), the architecture avoids centralized storage but limits the biometric to a single device. If the template is stored on a server for cross-device authentication, the server becomes a high-value target whose compromise yields irrevocable credentials. If the template is distributed across a decentralized network, the key management problems of self-sovereign identity reappear in a new form.

The fundamental issue is that biometrics are identifiers, not authenticators. They establish who you are, not that you are authorized. The distinction matters because identifiers should be public (or at least not secret) while authenticators must be secret. Using an identifier as an authenticator conflates two functions that have different security requirements, and the result is a system that fails when the identifier is exposed — which, given that your face is visible every time you leave your house, is a low bar for compromise.

Reputation Systems

Reputation systems attempt to replace institutional identity attestation with crowd-sourced trust. Instead of a central authority declaring "this person is trustworthy," the community's aggregate assessment determines trustworthiness. eBay's seller ratings, Reddit's karma, Stack Overflow's reputation points — these systems have demonstrated that crowd-sourced assessment can function at scale.

The failure mode is subtler than outright dysfunction. Reputation systems are subject to selection dynamics that cause them to measure something other than what they intend to measure. The mechanisms are well-characterized.

First, reputation accrues to visibility rather than quality. A user who posts frequently accumulates more reputation than a user who posts rarely, regardless of the quality of their contributions. The system measures engagement, not trustworthiness. Over time, high-reputation users are disproportionately those who optimize for the reputation metric rather than for the quality the metric was intended to proxy.

Second, reputation systems create incumbency advantages that resist correction. A high-reputation user who begins producing low-quality contributions retains their historical reputation. A new user who produces high-quality contributions starts from zero. The system's memory creates a structural bias toward established participants, which is conservative in the literal sense — it conserves the existing distribution of influence regardless of current performance.

Third, reputation is gameable. Any metric that confers advantage will be optimized against. Fake reviews, coordinated upvoting, sock-puppet accounts, purchased endorsements — these are not aberrations in reputation systems. They are the predictable response to attaching value to a metric. The cost of gaming a reputation system is finite. The benefit of a high reputation is ongoing. The economics favor gaming.

These dynamics are not implementation failures. They are structural properties of systems that attempt to derive trust from aggregated signals. The signals are corruptible because the incentive to corrupt them is proportional to their value. A reputation system that confers meaningful benefits will be meaningfully gamed. This is not a prediction. It is an observation of every reputation system that has achieved sufficient scale to matter.

The deeper problem is that reputation is not identity. Knowing that a user has a high reputation score does not tell you that the user is human, that the user is a single individual, or that the user can be held accountable for their actions. Reputation is a property of behavior within a system. Identity is a property of the entity that produces the behavior. Conflating them creates systems where trust is placed in behavioral patterns rather than accountable agents.

AI Watermarking and Content Authentication

The current wave of generative AI has produced a visible crisis: content that appears human-produced may be machine-generated, and distinguishing the two is increasingly difficult. The proposed technical response is watermarking – embedding detectable but imperceptible signals in AI-generated content that identify it as machine-produced.

Watermarking is technically tractable for certain content types. Statistical watermarks in text (biasing token selection toward detectable patterns), frequency-domain watermarks in images (embedding signals in spectral coefficients), metadata-based watermarks in video – all of these work in controlled conditions.

The problem is that watermarking is orthogonal to the identity question. A watermark tells you whether content was generated by an AI system. It does not tell you who directed the generation. It does not establish that a human was involved. It does not provide accountability for the content's claims or effects. Watermarking is a content-labeling mechanism, not an identity mechanism.

The orthogonality becomes clear when you consider the actual threat. The concern about AI-generated content is not that it exists but that it can be deployed at scale to deceive – fake news articles, synthetic social media personas, generated reviews, fabricated evidence. The watermark addresses the "is this AI-generated" question. It does not address the "who is responsible" question. An actor who generates a thousand fake reviews can evade watermark detection by using non-watermarked models, post-processing to remove watermarks, or paraphrasing generated text. The watermark is a filter that can be circumvented by anyone sufficiently motivated to circumvent it.

Content authentication schemes (such as the C2PA standard) go further by attaching provenance metadata to content – signing it with a certificate chain that traces back to a known origin. This is closer to the identity problem but still misses it. The provenance chain tells you which camera or which software produced the content. It does not tell you that the person who operated the camera or software is a specific accountable human. The chain of custody for the content is established. The identity of the responsible party is not.

The identity problem underlying the AI content crisis is not "which content is real" but "which actors are accountable." Watermarking and content authentication are answers to the first question. They leave the second question untouched.

The Structural Pattern

Biometrics, reputation systems, and watermarking all fail for the same reason: they tinker with the credential mechanism without questioning the assumption that authentication requires correlation. Each addresses a surface manifestation of the identity problem while leaving the architectural cause intact.

The architectural assumption is that authentication and correlation are inseparable. If a system vouches for your identity, the system knows your identity, and knowing your identity means being able to track your activity. This assumption is embedded so deeply in existing identity systems that it is rarely stated, let alone questioned. It appears in the SSO protocols, in the self-sovereign identity specifications, in the biometric authentication standards. It is treated as a given.

It is not a given. It is a design choice, and it can be made differently.

Requirements for a Solution

The analysis of existing systems and their failure modes produces a set of requirements that any working identity architecture must satisfy simultaneously. The word "simultaneously" is load-bearing. Satisfying any two of the three is straightforward and has been done. Satisfying all three has not.

Convenience. The system must work for users who will not manage cryptographic keys, remember seed phrases, maintain hardware tokens, or install specialized software beyond a standard browser or mobile app. The bar is "Sign in with Google" – a single click that completes authentication. Any system that requires more cognitive overhead than this will lose to SSO providers in the market, regardless of its privacy properties. Users have demonstrated, repeatedly and at scale, that they will trade privacy for convenience. A system that requires users to make that trade will see the same outcome. The system must not ask them to make it.

Privacy. The system must not enable the identity provider – or any single entity – to correlate a user's activity across services. The authentication event at one site must be unlinkable to the authentication event at another site, even by the entity that facilitated both. This is stronger than a privacy policy. Privacy policies are promises. Promises can be broken. The unlinkability must be structural – a property of the protocol, not a commitment of the operator. An adversarial provider, one that decides to violate its stated policies, must still be unable to build a cross-site behavioral profile.

Accountability. The system must be able to establish, when legally required, that a specific action was performed by a specific human. Anonymous identity without accountability enables abuse at scale – harassment, fraud, illegal commerce, coordinated disinformation. A system that provides perfect anonymity with no mechanism for accountability will be used for harm, and the harm will generate political pressure for surveillance that dismantles whatever privacy the system provided. Accountability is not the enemy of privacy. Accountability is the condition under which privacy is politically sustainable.

These three requirements produce a set of derived constraints.

The provider must facilitate authentication without learning which site the user is authenticating to. This seems contradictory – how can the provider participate in authentication without knowing what it is authenticating the user for? – but the contradiction is an artifact of existing protocol designs, not a mathematical necessity.

Each site must receive a token that proves the user is a legitimate, unique human without revealing which human. The token must be site-specific so that colluding sites cannot correlate their tokens to identify a shared user. The token must be unforgeable so that one user cannot impersonate another. The token must be deterministic for a given user-site pair so that the site can recognize returning users without the provider's involvement.

Accountability must require a legal process and the cooperation of the provider. The provider should be able to identify a specific user when presented with a valid legal demand, but should be unable to conduct mass surveillance. This is the "good police work" principle: targeted investigation of specific suspects is legitimate; dragnet surveillance of entire populations is not. The architecture must enforce this distinction structurally, making targeted queries cheap and mass queries computationally infeasible.

The system must degrade gracefully. If the provider goes offline, users should retain some level of access to connected services. If the provider is compromised, the breach should not retroactively expose users' browsing histories. If the provider changes ownership or policy, the architectural protections should persist independent of the operator's intentions.

These requirements are demanding. They are also non-negotiable, in the sense that relaxing any one of them produces a system that either fails for users (inconvenient), fails for privacy (surveilling), or fails for society (unaccountable). The identity systems that exist today each relax at least one, and each produces the corresponding failure. The requirements sound contradictory only if you assume the existing architectural paradigm, in which the identity provider must see everything in order to function. They are not contradictory. They require a different architecture – one that separates authentication from correlation at the protocol level, using cryptographic constructions that allow the provider to perform its function without accumulating the information that makes surveillance possible. The next chapter presents that architecture.

CHAPTER 3

Anonymous Identity Architecture

Single sign-on gave the internet convenient authentication and comprehensive surveillance as a structural byproduct. Chapter 2 showed why this is architectural, not incidental—the provider necessarily sees both the user's identity and the site's identity on every request, making correlation trivial.

The question is whether the convenience can be preserved without the surveillance. The answer is yes, but it requires rebuilding the identity layer so that the information necessary for cross-site correlation never exists in any single location. The mechanism is a hash construction that produces site-specific tokens—identifiers that are stable within a site, unlinkable across sites, and verifiable by the identity provider without the provider learning what they signify.

This chapter presents the construction in full. It covers the hash construction, the token routing protocol, the security properties that result, the cryptographic primitives recommended for implementation, and—because honest engineering requires it—the threats this architecture does not address.

What the Architecture Changes

In conventional SSO, the identity provider holds the user's identity, the requesting site's identifier, and a timestamp at the moment of token issuance—everything needed for a complete browsing profile. The structural problem is that the data exists, and data that exists can be accessed by operators, attackers, governments, or insiders. The only data that cannot be exploited is data that was never created.

The anonymous identity architecture prevents the data from being created. The provider still authenticates users and issues tokens, but the token derivation is structured so that the provider cannot trivially determine which sites a user visits from the tokens alone, and the sites cannot determine which other sites a user has authenticated to. The surveillance capability is not restricted by policy. It is eliminated by architecture.

The Hash Construction

> **Implementation note.** *The pseudocode in this section illustrates privacy properties and information flow—which values stay client-side, which cross trust boundaries, and what each party learns. For production password handling, use a standardized Password-Authenticated Key Exchange (PAKE) such as OPAQUE (RFC 9807) or SRP rather than transmitting password-derived hashes directly. The Design Decisions section at the end of this chapter discusses this tradeoff in detail.*

The construction operates in six steps. The first three happen during authentication. The last three handle token transmission and verification. Each step is designed so that no single party—not the client, not the identity provider, not the receiving site—holds enough information to compromise the system's privacy properties. Figure 3.1 traces the complete flow, annotating what each party learns at each step. Figure 3.2 maps which values cross trust boundaries and which remain client-side.

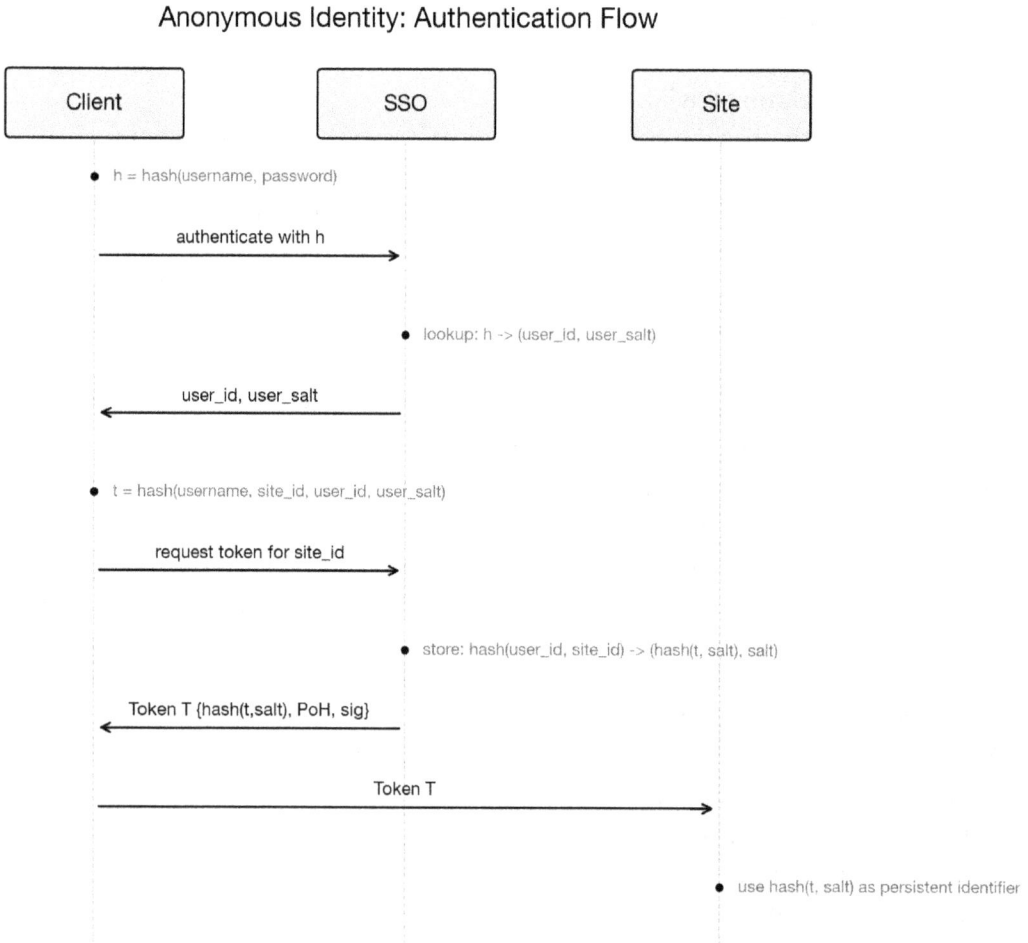

Figure 3.1: Anonymous Identity Authentication Flow. The following diagram shows the complete authentication protocol, including what each party learns at each step.

Token Derivation: Information Boundaries

Client Knows	SSO Knows	Site Knows
username	h -> (user_id,	hash(t, salt)
password	user_salt)	salt
h = hash(user, pass)	hash(user_id, site_id)	PoH_score
user_id	-> (hash(t,salt), salt)	site_id
user_salt		signature
t = hash(username,	Cannot derive t	
site_id, user_id,	Cannot link across sites	Cannot derive t
user_salt)	without brute-forcing	Cannot impersonate to SSO

Client -> SSO: h   SSO -> Client: user_id, user_salt   Client -> Site: Token T

Each party sees only its column. No single party holds enough to correlate users across sites.

Figure 3.2: Token Derivation Data Flow. This diagram shows which values flow between parties and which remain client-side. Values in the shaded client region never cross a trust boundary.

Step 1: Client-Side Credential Hashing

The user enters a username and password into their client application. Before anything leaves the client, the credentials are hashed:

```
h = hash(username || password)
```

The client sends h to the identity provider. The username and password are never transmitted in plaintext. The identity provider receives a fixed-length hash that it can use for lookup but cannot reverse to recover the original credentials.

This is the first structural decision. In conventional SSO, the provider receives the username directly and often participates in the password verification through a protocol that gives it access to credential material. Here, the provider receives an opaque hash. It knows that the hash maps to an account—it can verify this against its own stored records—but the hash itself reveals nothing about the username or password that produced it.

The concatenation operator || represents the combination of the two inputs into a single byte string before hashing. The specific method of combination matters for implementation—it must be unambiguous and deterministic—but the principle is straightforward: combine the credentials, hash the result, send the hash.

```
function client_authenticate(username, password):
    // Combine credentials into a single input
    credential_input = encode(username) || encode(password)

    // Hash locally—credentials never leave the client
    h = hash(credential_input)

    // Send only the hash to the identity provider
    return send_to_sso(h)
```

Step 2: SSO Lookup

The identity provider receives h and performs a lookup in its user database. The database maps credential hashes to internal records:

```
h -> (user_id, user_salt)
```

The provider returns user_id and user_salt to the client. These values are necessary for the next step—they are inputs to the token derivation function—but they are not sufficient, on their own, to derive any site-specific token. The derivation also requires the username, which the provider does not have.

The user_id is an internal identifier assigned by the provider. It is stable across sessions and unique per user. The user_salt is a cryptographically random value generated when the user's account was created. Its purpose is to ensure that even users with identical credentials (unlikely but possible) produce different tokens.

```
function sso_lookup(h):
    // Look up credential hash in the user database
    record = database.get(h)
    if record is null:
        return authentication_failed()

    // Return values needed for token derivation
    return (record.user_id, record.user_salt)
```

An important detail: the provider's database maps h to (user_id, user_salt). An attacker who breaches this database obtains credential hashes, not credentials. Reversing those hashes requires brute-forcing the username-password combination space. If users choose strong passwords, this is computationally infeasible. If they choose weak passwords, the hash construction does not save them—but that is a failure of credential hygiene, not of the architecture.

Step 3: Site-Specific Token Derivation

The client now holds four values: the username (which it always had), the site identifier (which it knows from the authentication request), and the user_id and user_salt (which the provider just returned). The client combines all four and hashes the result:

```
t = hash(username || site_id || user_id || user_salt)
```

This is the critical computation. It happens entirely on the client. The identity provider does not see this hash. The site does not see this hash (it will receive a further transformation, described in Step 5). Only the client computes it, and only the client knows all four inputs.

The token t is site-specific because site_id is an input. For the same user, different sites produce different tokens. The tokens are unlinkable because recovering the relationship between two tokens requires knowing the username—and the username is a client-side secret that never leaves the client device.

```
function derive_site_token(username, site_id, user_id, user_salt):
    // Combine all four inputs
    token_input = encode(username) || encode(site_id)
                  || encode(user_id) || encode(user_salt)

    // Derive site-specific token—client-side only
    t = hash(token_input)

    return t
```

Consider what each party knows at this point. The client knows everything: username, site_id, user_id, user_salt, and the derived token t. The identity provider knows h (the credential hash), user_id, and user_salt, but it does not yet know the username or site_id (it received h, not its components). At this step, the provider has not learned which site the user is authenticating to. That changes in Step 4, when the provider stores a record indexed by hash(user_id || site_id)—at which point the provider does learn site_id. The security analysis in the "Cross-Site Unlinkability" section addresses this. The receiving site knows nothing yet.

This asymmetry is the foundation of the privacy guarantee. The computation that matters—the derivation of t—requires inputs that no single server-side entity possesses.

Step 4: Token Storage at the SSO

The client sends t back to the identity provider. The provider does not store t directly. It creates a salted hash for verification:

```
storage_key = hash(user_id || site_id)
storage_value = (hash(t || salt), salt)
```

The provider stores the mapping: storage_key -> storage_value. The salt is a fresh random value, distinct from user_salt, generated specifically for this storage record. The provider can later verify that a presented token matches by recomputing hash(t || salt) and comparing.

```
function sso_store_token(user_id, site_id, t):
    // Generate a fresh salt for storage
    salt = random_bytes(16)    // 128 bits
```

```
// Compute verification hash
verification_hash = hash(encode(t) || salt)

// Compute storage key
storage_key = hash(encode(user_id) || encode(site_id))

// Store the mapping
database.put(storage_key, (verification_hash, salt))
```

Note what the provider's database now contains. It has a mapping from hash(user_id || site_id) to (hash(t || salt), salt). The storage key is itself a hash—an attacker who breaches the database cannot directly enumerate which users have accounts on which sites without brute-forcing the user_id/site_id combinations. The storage value is a salted hash of the token, not the token itself. The database is a collection of hashes of hashes.

This is defense in depth. Even a complete database breach yields material that requires substantial computational effort to exploit. The attacker must first reverse the storage keys to learn user-site associations, then reverse the storage values to recover tokens. Both operations require brute-force search over their respective input spaces.

Step 5: Token Construction

The identity provider constructs a signed token for transmission to the receiving site:

```
Token T = {
    hash(t || salt),      // verification hash
    salt,                 // salt used in verification hash
    PoH_score,            // Proof of Human score (Chapter 7)
    site_id,              // the requesting site
    signature             // SSO's Ed25519 signature over T
}
```

The token carries the verification hash—not the token t itself. It also carries metadata: the salt (so the site can verify returning users by recomputing the hash), a humanness score (the subject of a later chapter, but relevant here because it travels with the identity token), and the site identifier. The entire structure is signed by the identity provider.

```
function sso_construct_token(t, salt, poh_score, site_id, sso_private_key):
    // Build the verification hash
    verification_hash = hash(encode(t) || salt)

    // Assemble token payload
    payload = {
        "verification_hash": verification_hash,
        "salt": salt,
        "poh_score": poh_score,
```

```
        "site_id": site_id,
        "issued_at": current_timestamp()
    }

    // Sign the entire payload
    signature = ed25519_sign(sso_private_key, serialize(payload))

    // Return the complete token
    return {
        "payload": payload,
        "signature": signature
    }
```

The signature is essential. Without it, anyone could fabricate tokens. With it, the receiving site can verify that the token was issued by the identity provider without contacting the provider. The site needs only the provider's public key, which can be distributed through standard mechanisms (HTTPS well-known endpoints, DNS records, certificate pinning).

Step 6: Site Verification

The receiving site gets token T. It verifies the signature against the identity provider's known public key. If the signature is valid, the site extracts hash(t || salt) and uses it as a persistent user identifier.

```
function site_verify_token(T, sso_public_key):
    // Verify the SSO's signature
    if not ed25519_verify(sso_public_key, serialize(T.payload),
T.signature):
        return reject("invalid signature")

    // Verify this token is intended for this site
    if T.payload.site_id != this_site.id:
        return reject("token not issued for this site")

    // Check token freshness
    if current_timestamp() - T.payload.issued_at > MAX_TOKEN_AGE:
        return reject("token expired")

    // Use verification hash as the user's persistent identifier
    user_identifier = T.payload.verification_hash

    // Optionally check humanness score
    if T.payload.poh_score < this_site.minimum_poh:
        return reject("insufficient humanness score")

    return accept(user_identifier, T.payload.poh_score)
```

The site cannot derive t from hash(t || salt). It cannot impersonate the user to the identity provider. It cannot determine what other sites this user has authenticated to. The verification hash is a dead end—it proves that the user authenticated, identifies them stably on this site, and reveals nothing else.

From the site's perspective, this identifier functions exactly like a traditional OAuth user ID. It is stable across sessions. It is unique per user (with the collision resistance of the underlying hash function). It allows the site to maintain user accounts, store preferences, and recognize returning visitors. The only capability it lacks is cross-site linkability, and that capability was never necessary for any legitimate site function.

The Routing Layer

Authentication is only half the problem. Sites need to reach users. Password resets, purchase confirmations, security alerts—these require a communication channel. In conventional SSO, the identity provider holds the user's email address and can relay or disclose it as needed. In the anonymous identity architecture, the provider does not know who the user is. How does Reddit send a notification to someone identified only by an opaque hash?

The routing layer solves this by separating the capability to reach a user from the knowledge of how to reach them. The identity provider becomes a message relay: it accepts messages addressed to tokens and delivers them through channels that only the user has configured.

Routing Key Derivation

When a user opts into contact for a particular site, the client computes a routing key:

```
function derive_routing_key(username, site_id, user_id, user_
salt):
    routing_input = encode(username) || encode("routing")
                    || encode(site_id) || encode(user_id)
                    || encode(user_salt)
    routing_key = hash(routing_input)
    return routing_key
```

The routing key is a one-way derivation from the site-specific token inputs, with a domain separator ("routing") to ensure it is distinct from the token itself. The client then encrypts the user's contact information and registers it with the identity provider, indexed by this routing key.

```
function register_routing(routing_key, contact_info, sso_public_
key):
    // Encrypt contact information for the SSO
    encrypted_contact = encrypt(sso_public_key, encode(contact_
info))

    // Register the mapping
    send_to_sso("register_route", routing_key, encrypted_contact)
```

The identity provider stores the mapping routing_key -> encrypted_contact. It cannot correlate routing keys to user accounts without brute-forcing the input space, because the routing key derivation includes the username, which the provider does not possess.

Message Delivery

When a site needs to reach a user, it sends a message to the identity provider along with the routing key:

```
function site_send_notification(routing_key, message, site_
credentials):
    request = {
        "routing_key": routing_key,
        "message": message,
        "site_id": site_credentials.id,
        "signature": sign(site_credentials.key, message ||
routing_key)
    }
    send_to_sso("deliver", request)
```

The identity provider looks up the routing key, decrypts the contact information, delivers the message, and discards the plaintext contact information. The site never learns the user's email address or phone number. The identity provider handles contact information transiently—decrypting only for the moment of delivery.

```
function sso_deliver(request, sso_private_key):
    // Verify the site's signature
    if not verify_site_signature(request):
        return reject()

    // Look up routing
    encrypted_contact = routing_database.get(request.routing_key)
    if encrypted_contact is null:
        return reject("no routing registered")

    // Decrypt contact information
    contact_info = decrypt(sso_private_key, encrypted_contact)

    // Deliver through appropriate channel
    deliver_message(contact_info, request.message)

    // Discard plaintext contact information
    clear_memory(contact_info)
```

The trust model is explicit. The identity provider sees the user's contact information at the moment of delivery. This is operational trust—the same trust already placed in email providers, cellular carriers, and postal services. The entity that delivers a message necessarily knows where to deliver it. The difference is scope: the identity provider sees delivery information, not browsing history. The surveillance capability has been narrowed from comprehensive observation to a single operational function.

Preference Abstraction

The routing layer abstracts the communication medium. A site does not specify "send an email." It specifies "send a message." The identity provider checks the user's configured preferences and routes accordingly—email, SMS, push notification, or any future channel. If the user changes their email address, they update the routing configuration once. Every site that has ever sent them a message continues to work without modification. The routing keys remain valid. The mappings update transparently.

This is centralization without surveillance. The contact information is managed in one place—which is operationally convenient—but the identity provider cannot correlate that contact information with browsing activity, because the architecture does not give it the inputs needed for correlation.

Security Properties

The construction produces three security properties. Each follows from the structure of the hash construction and the distribution of information across parties.

Cross-Site Unlinkability

Two tokens issued for the same user on different sites cannot be correlated without the username.

The argument is straightforward. Token for site A:

```
t_A = hash(username || site_A || user_id || user_salt)
```

Token for site B:

```
t_B = hash(username || site_B || user_id || user_salt)
```

The inputs differ in one component: the site identifier. The outputs—assuming a cryptographic hash function modeled as a random oracle[1]—are unlinkable: given t_A and t_B, no efficient algorithm can determine whether they share a common input without testing candidate usernames against the hash function. For a hash with adequate preimage resistance (256-bit for SHA-256)[2] and a username with sufficient entropy, this search is computationally infeasible.

---

1   The random oracle model (ROM) assumes the hash function behaves as a truly random function. SHA-256 is not a random oracle, but the ROM provides a useful analytical framework. See Mihir Bellare and Phillip Rogaway, "Random Oracles are Practical: A Paradigm for Designing Efficient Protocols," *Proceedings of the 1st ACM Conference on Computer and Communications Security (CCS '93)*, pp. 62–73, 1993.

2   SHA-256 provides 256-bit preimage resistance: finding an input that produces a given output requires on average 2255 hash evaluations. This is a standard result from the hash function's design. See NIST FIPS 180-4, "Secure Hash Standard (SHS)," August 2015.

The sites receive `hash(t || salt)`, not t directly. This adds a second layer: even if two sites collude and share their verification hashes, they cannot correlate users without first reversing the salted hash to recover t, then reversing the token derivation to recover the username, then recomputing tokens for the other site. Each step requires brute-force search. The combined effort is multiplicative.

The identity provider is in a slightly different position. It holds `user_id` and `user_salt` for every user, and it stores `hash(user_id || site_id)` as the storage key. If the provider wanted to determine which sites a given user visits, it could compute `hash(user_id || site_id)` for all known site identifiers and check which keys exist in its database. This is a known-plaintext search—feasible if the number of sites is manageable.

This is the one correlation capability the architecture does not fully eliminate at the SSO level. The provider knows `user_id` (it assigned it) and can enumerate `site_id` values (they are public). The mitigation is twofold. First, the storage keys can be computed using a keyed hash where the key is held in a separate security domain (an HSM, for example), limiting the ability to perform bulk enumeration. Second, and more fundamentally, the composition with the Blind Database (Chapter 5) eliminates this leakage entirely by making the identity mappings themselves encrypted with keys the operator does not hold.

Breach Resistance

An attacker who compromises the identity provider's database obtains:

- Credential hashes: `h = hash(username || password)`
- Storage keys: `hash(user_id || site_id)`
- Storage values: `(hash(t || salt), salt)`

From the credential hashes, the attacker can attempt offline dictionary attacks against usernames and passwords. This is the standard risk of any password-based system and is mitigated by the same standard mechanisms: strong passwords, rate-limited authentication, and the use of slow hash functions (`bcrypt`, `scrypt`, `Argon2`) for the credential hash. The construction does not make this better or worse than conventional password storage.

From the storage keys, the attacker can attempt to enumerate user-site associations by computing `hash(user_id || site_id)` for candidate pairs. This requires knowing or guessing both user_id values and site_id values. If user IDs are sequential integers and site IDs are known domain names, the search space is the product of the two—potentially large, but not cryptographically hard. Mitigation: use UUIDs for user IDs (128-bit random, effectively unguessable) and keyed hashing for storage keys.

From the storage values, the attacker obtains salted hashes of tokens. Reversing these to tokens requires brute-forcing the token space—which is the output space of a cryptographic hash function (2^{256} for SHA-256), computationally infeasible under standard assumptions.[3]

---

3   SHA-256 provides 256-bit preimage resistance: finding an input that produces a given output

The net result: a database breach does not yield plaintext credentials, does not reveal which sites users visit (assuming reasonable user ID entropy), and does not produce tokens that could be used for impersonation. Compare this to a conventional SSO breach, which yields email addresses, password hashes, and a complete record of which users authenticated to which sites.

Impersonation Resistance

The receiving site gets hash(t || salt)—not t. It cannot present t to the identity provider because it does not have it. Even if the site wanted to impersonate the user to the identity provider (to, say, access the user's account on another site), it lacks the necessary material.

The identity provider verifies users by checking hash(t || salt) against its stored value. This verification requires t. The site has hash(t || salt), which is the output of the verification, not the input. The hash function's preimage resistance ensures that the site cannot work backward from the output to the input.

```
// What the site has:
verification_hash = hash(t || salt)      // cannot recover t

// What verification requires:
check = hash(candidate_t || salt)        // requires t to compute

// The site cannot produce a valid candidate_t
// without brute-forcing the hash function
```

Similarly, the identity provider cannot impersonate a user to a site. The provider does not know t—it stores only hash(t || salt). Even if the provider wanted to generate a valid token for a site, it would need to reverse its own salted hash—computationally infeasible under the preimage resistance of the hash function.[4]

The construction achieves mutual impersonation resistance: neither the provider nor the site can impersonate the user to the other, assuming the hash function's preimage resistance holds. This is a stronger property than conventional SSO provides. In conventional SSO, the provider can trivially impersonate any user to any site, because it issues the tokens and controls the verification.

Recommended Cryptographic Primitives

The construction is described in terms of generic operations—hash(), sign(), encrypt(). Production implementations must choose specific algorithms. The following recommendations prioritize well-studied, widely-deployed primitives with conservative

---

requires on average 2255 hash evaluations. This is a standard result from the hash function's design. See NIST FIPS 180-4, "Secure Hash Standard (SHS)," August 2015.

4   SHA-256 provides 256-bit preimage resistance: finding an input that produces a given output requires on average 2255 hash evaluations. This is a standard result from the hash function's design. See NIST FIPS 180-4, "Secure Hash Standard (SHS)," August 2015.

security margins.

Hash Function: SHA-256 or SHA-3-256

Both provide 256-bit output with 128-bit collision resistance and 256-bit preimage resistance. SHA-256 is the more widely deployed choice. SHA-3-256, based on the Keccak sponge construction, offers structural diversity—it is not vulnerable to length-extension attacks that affect raw SHA-256 (though HMAC-SHA-256 is immune to these).

For the credential hash in Step 1, a slow hash function is preferable: Argon2id, bcrypt, or scrypt. These are deliberately expensive to compute, making offline brute-force attacks against credential hashes costly. The remaining hash operations (token derivation, storage keys, verification hashes) use fast hashes because they operate on inputs with sufficient entropy that brute-force is already infeasible.

Signature Scheme: Ed25519

Ed25519 is an Edwards-curve Digital Signature Algorithm providing 128-bit security. It produces 64-byte signatures, uses 32-byte public keys, and is deterministic—the same message and key always produce the same signature, eliminating the class of implementation errors caused by bad random number generation during signing.

The identity provider signs tokens with its Ed25519 private key. Sites verify with the corresponding public key. Key distribution can follow existing patterns: publish the public key at a well-known HTTPS endpoint, pin it in site configurations, or distribute it through DNS (DNSKEY records or TXT records).

Salt Generation: 128-Bit Cryptographically Secure Random

All salts—user_salt in Step 2, the verification salt in Step 4—must be generated from a cryptographically secure random number generator (CSPRNG). The minimum length is 128 bits (16 bytes). This ensures that the probability of salt collision is negligible (birthday bound at 2^{64}—far beyond any practical user base).

Using the operating system's CSPRNG is the correct approach: /dev/urandom on Linux/macOS, BCryptGenRandom on Windows, or the equivalent in your language's standard library. Do not use general-purpose random number generators (the rand() family, Mersenne Twister, or similar). These are not cryptographically secure and produce predictable output given sufficient observation.

Summary of Primitives

Operation	Recommended Primitive
Credential hash (Step 1)	Argon2id (or bcrypt/scrypt)
Token derivation (Step 3)	SHA-256 or SHA-3-256
Storage key (Step 4)	SHA-256 or SHA-3-256
Verification hash (Step 4)	SHA-256 or SHA-3-256

Token signature (Step 5)	Ed25519
Salt generation	CSPRNG, minimum 128 bits
Routing encryption	X25519 + ChaCha20-Poly1305

These choices are deliberately conservative. They are not the newest or the most theoretically interesting algorithms. They are the most extensively studied, most widely implemented, and most likely to have correct implementations available in your language's cryptographic library. In cryptography, boring is a feature.

Composition with Blind Database

The anonymous identity architecture stands on its own. It provides unlinkable authentication without requiring changes to the underlying storage infrastructure. But one limitation was noted in the security analysis: the identity provider's storage keys are computed from hash(user_id || site_id), and the provider—which knows all user_id values and can enumerate public site_id values—can perform a brute-force search to determine user-site associations.

This leakage disappears if the identity mappings are stored in a Blind Database (Chapter 5). In that composition, the client derives record identifiers and encryption keys from a master secret the server never possesses:

```
record_id = hash(master_secret || "identity_mapping" || site_id)
key = HKDF(master_secret, record_id, "encrypt")
ciphertext = encrypt(key, (user_id, user_salt, site_token_hash))
```

The server stores record_id -> ciphertext. It cannot read which users have accounts on which sites. It cannot enumerate associations. It cannot perform the known-plaintext search described above. The identity mappings become opaque data that the operator stores but cannot interpret.

This is worth mentioning here because it illustrates a general principle of the architecture: components compose to eliminate each other's residual weaknesses. The anonymous identity layer on its own is significantly better than conventional SSO. Combined with the blind database layer, it closes the remaining gap. Neither component was designed with the other in mind in the sense of tight coupling—they compose cleanly because they follow the same structural principle of keeping secrets on the client side.

The Full Flow

To consolidate the steps into a single picture, here is the complete authentication flow from the user's initial action to the site's final verification.

```
function full_authentication_flow(username, password, site_id):
    // === CLIENT SIDE ===

    // Step 1: Hash credentials
    h = hash(username || password)

    // Step 2: Send to SSO, receive lookup values
```

```
(user_id, user_salt) = sso.lookup(h)

// Step 3: Derive site-specific token
t = hash(username || site_id || user_id || user_salt)

// Step 4: Send token to SSO for storage/verification
sso.store_or_verify(user_id, site_id, t)

// === SSO SIDE ===

// Step 5: Construct signed token
// PoH score is computed client-side and verified via
// identity service attestation (see Chapter 7)
assert verify_poh_attestation(client_poh_attestation)
salt = random_bytes(16)
T = {
    verification_hash: hash(t || salt),
    salt: salt,
    poh_score: client_poh_attestation.score,
    site_id: site_id,
    signature: ed25519_sign(sso_private_key, payload)
}

// === SITE SIDE ===

// Step 6: Verify and accept
assert ed25519_verify(sso_public_key, T.payload, T.signature)
assert T.site_id == expected_site_id
user_identifier = T.verification_hash
// User is authenticated. user_identifier is their stable,
// site-specific, unlinkable identity.
```

From the user's perspective, none of this is visible. They click a button, enter credentials, and arrive at the site. The client software handles Steps 1 through 3 automatically. The token exchange in Steps 4 and 5 happens in the background, in the same time it takes a conventional OAuth redirect to complete. Step 6 is identical to how sites already process OAuth tokens. The user experience is indistinguishable from conventional SSO.

From the site's perspective, the integration is minimal. The site receives a signed token containing a user identifier, a humanness score, and a signature it can verify against a known public key. This is the same data shape as a conventional SSO token. The site does not need to understand the hash construction or the privacy properties. It needs to verify a signature and extract an identifier. Standard OAuth libraries can be adapted to handle this with minor modifications.

From the identity provider's perspective, the architecture requires maintaining a database of credential hashes and storage records, signing tokens, and optionally operating the routing layer. The provider's operational complexity is comparable to running a conventional SSO service. The difference is in what the provider's data reveals—which, by construction, is far less than what a conventional provider's data reveals.

Prior Art and Design Rationale

The anonymous identity construction is not the first attempt to decouple authentication from surveillance. Several systems have addressed parts of this problem, and understanding where they succeeded, where they stalled, and what tradeoffs they accepted clarifies why this architecture makes the choices it does.

Attribute-based credentials—particularly IBM's Idemix5 and the Netherlands' IRMA/Yivi system6—allow users to prove properties about themselves (age, citizenship, membership) without revealing their full identity. IRMA has seen real deployment in Dutch municipalities. The cryptographic foundations are sound: zero-knowledge proofs, Camenisch-Lysyanskaya signatures, selective disclosure. But attribute-based credentials solve a different problem. They answer "can you prove you're over 18?" rather than "can you authenticate to this site without the authenticator learning which site?" The complexity of the credential issuance and verification protocols has limited adoption outside institutional contexts where the proving party has strong motivation to comply.

Microsoft's U-Prove7 offered unlinkable tokens—a user could obtain a credential and present it to multiple verifiers without those presentations being linkable. The cryptography worked. Microsoft published the specification and released an SDK. Then the project went dormant. The lesson is not about the protocol's security properties but about the adoption dynamics of systems that require all parties (issuers, holders, verifiers) to upgrade simultaneously. U-Prove failed the same test that this architecture is designed to pass: it required coordinated adoption rather than incremental deployment.

W3C Decentralized Identifiers (DIDs) and Verifiable Credentials8 represent the standards-body approach. DIDs decouple identifiers from centralized registries; Verifiable Credentials provide a data model for tamper-evident claims. The specifications are comprehensive. Adoption has been slow, partly because the ecosystem requires resolver infrastructure, wallet software, and issuer participation before any single user benefits. The architecture described here requires only a client library and a cooperating identity provider—a lower coordination bar.

The OPAQUE protocol9 (now RFC 9807) and the broader PAKE family address

5   Jan Camenisch and Anna Lysyanskaya, "An Efficient System for Non-transferable Anonymous Credentials with Optional Anonymity Revocation," *Advances in Cryptology—EUROCRYPT 2001,* Lecture Notes in Computer Science, vol. 2045, pp. 93–118, Springer, 2001. IBM's Identity Mixer (Idemix) implemented these protocols for enterprise identity management.

6   IRMA (I Reveal My Attributes), now Yivi, is an open-source attribute-based credential system deployed in the Netherlands. Originated from Gergely Alpár and Bart Jacobs, "Credential Design in Attribute-Based Identity Management," *Bridging Distances in Technology and Regulation: Proceedings of the 3rd TILTing Perspectives Conference,* pp. 189–204, 2013. Maintained by the Privacy by Design Foundation (established 2016). Production deployments include Dutch municipal services and healthcare applications.

7   Christian Paquin and Greg Zaverucha, "U-Prove Cryptographic Specification V1.1," Microsoft Corporation, 2013. The specification was published under an Open Specification Promise, and an open-source SDK was released. Development ceased around 2014.

8   W3C Recommendation, "Decentralized Identifiers (DIDs) v1.0," July 2022; W3C Recommendation, "Verifiable Credentials Data Model v1.1," March 2022.

9   Stanislaw Jarecki, Hugo Krawczyk, and Jiayu Xu, "OPAQUE: An Asymmetric PAKE Protocol Secure Against Pre-Computation Attacks," *Advances in Cryptology—EUROCRYPT 2018,* Lecture

the authentication exchange specifically. OPAQUE ensures the server never learns the password, even transiently—a stronger guarantee than this chapter's hash construction provides during the initial authentication. As noted in the Design Decisions section, replacing Step 1 with OPAQUE is possible and recommended for high-security deployments. The hash construction was chosen for this presentation because it makes the information flow transparent and because the privacy properties of the *architecture*— cross-site unlinkability, breach resistance, mutual impersonation resistance—do not depend on OPAQUE-level password protection during the exchange. They depend on the token derivation in Step 3, which is orthogonal to the authentication protocol.

The construction described in this chapter trades the formal sophistication of these prior systems for something they lacked: simplicity sufficient for unilateral adoption. A single identity provider can deploy this architecture without waiting for a standards body, a credential ecosystem, or coordinated multi-party upgrade. The cost of that simplicity is real—the construction does not provide zero-knowledge attribute proofs, does not eliminate trust in the identity provider for availability, and relies on the username as a client-side secret rather than on a formally verified key exchange. These limitations are documented in the sections that follow. The claim is not that this approach is cryptographically superior to Idemix or U-Prove. The claim is that it is deployable in contexts where those systems are not, and that deployable-but-simpler beats elegant-but-unadopted.

What This Does Not Protect Against

No security architecture protects against everything. Honest engineering requires identifying the threats that remain. The anonymous identity construction has clear boundaries, and those boundaries should be stated plainly.

Endpoint Compromise

If the user's device is compromised—malware on the laptop, a keylogger recording keystrokes, a compromised browser extension—the attacker captures the username and password at the point of entry, before any hashing occurs. The hash construction operates on the assumption that the client is trustworthy. If the client is not trustworthy, the attacker obtains the raw credentials and can derive any site-specific token, impersonate the user everywhere, and reconstruct the complete browsing profile from the inputs.

This is not a flaw unique to this architecture. Every authentication system fails when the client is compromised. The anonymous identity layer does not create new defenses at the endpoint. It operates above the endpoint, in the protocol layer. Endpoint security—disk encryption, secure boot, malware detection, hardware security keys—remains necessary and is orthogonal to the identity architecture.

Compromised SSO Operator

The architecture limits what the identity provider can learn, but it does not eliminate

Notes in Computer Science, vol. 10822, pp. 456–486, Springer, 2018. Standardized as RFC 9807, "The OPAQUE Augmented PAKE Protocol," July 2025.

trust in the provider entirely. The provider must be available for authentication to work. If the provider goes offline, users cannot authenticate to any site. If the provider is malicious, it can deny service selectively—refusing to authenticate specific users to specific sites. This is an availability attack, not a privacy attack, but it is real.

The provider could also serve modified client-side code. If users run the provider's JavaScript in a browser (as opposed to a native application they install and inspect), the provider could ship a modified version that exfiltrates the username before hashing. This is the fundamental limitation of browser-based clients: the server that delivers the code can modify the code. The mitigation is client-side verification—published, open-source client implementations that can be audited, with reproducible builds and hash-verified distributions.

The provider is trusted for availability and for the integrity of the client code it serves. It is not trusted for privacy—the architecture ensures that the provider's database does not contain plaintext browsing profiles—though as noted in the security analysis, the provider can enumerate user-site associations through its storage keys, a residual leakage that the Blind Database composition (Chapter 5) eliminates.

Traffic Analysis at the Network Level

The hash construction prevents the identity provider from learning which sites a user visits through the content of the authentication tokens. But the authentication protocol itself involves network communication. A network-level observer—an ISP, a government surveillance program, an attacker with access to network infrastructure—can observe that the user's device communicated with the identity provider and then communicated with a specific site. The timing and sequence of these communications reveals the user-site association even if the content is encrypted.

This is a traffic analysis attack. It operates below the application layer, at the level of IP addresses and TCP connections. The anonymous identity architecture does not address it because it operates at the application layer. Defenses against traffic analysis exist—Tor, VPNs, mix networks—but they are separate infrastructure with separate tradeoffs.

The architecture is transparent about its layer of operation. It protects identity at the application layer. It does not protect network metadata. Users who face network-level adversaries need network-level protections in addition to the identity layer.

Social Engineering

The strongest cryptographic architecture is irrelevant if the user can be persuaded to hand over their credentials to a phishing site. Social engineering attacks target human judgment, not protocol design. A convincing fake login page that captures the username and password before the client-side hashing occurs defeats the system entirely.

Standard anti-phishing measures apply: hardware security keys (FIDO2/WebAuthn) that bind authentication to specific origins, client-side indicators that verify the identity provider's authenticity, user education. The anonymous identity architecture is compatible with these measures but does not replace them.

Credential Loss and Account Recovery

If a user loses their credentials—forgets their password, loses the device that stored it—the tokens derived from those credentials become inaccessible through the normal derivation path. The user cannot re-derive their site-specific tokens because they cannot reproduce the hash inputs.

Account recovery is solvable but adds complexity. Recovery mechanisms must be designed to preserve the privacy properties that make the architecture valuable. A recovery process that requires the identity provider to associate a user's real-world identity with their account undermines the unlinkability guarantee. The design of secure, privacy-preserving recovery is a genuine engineering challenge, not a trivial implementation detail.

Collusion Between Provider and Site

If the identity provider and a specific site collude—actively sharing data and cooperating to deanonymize users—the combined information may be sufficient to narrow the set of possible users. The provider knows user_id and can enumerate possible tokens for a site. The site knows the verification hash. If the provider computes candidate tokens for all its users and the site confirms which verification hash matches, the user is identified.

This is a targeted attack requiring active cooperation between two parties. It does not scale to passive surveillance—the provider cannot deanonymize all users across all sites without the cooperation of each individual site. The composition with Blind Database eliminates this vector entirely by making the provider's identity mappings unreadable even to the provider.

Design Decisions and Their Rationale
Several design choices involve tradeoffs that implementers will encounter.

Why hash the credentials client-side rather than using a standard password protocol like OPAQUE?

OPAQUE and similar protocols (SRP, PAKE variants) provide stronger guarantees against server compromise during the authentication exchange—the server never learns the password, even transiently. The hash construction in Step 1 is simpler and provides weaker guarantees during the exchange but stronger guarantees for the overall privacy architecture, because the credential hash serves double duty as both an authentication credential and an input to the token derivation. Replacing Step 1 with OPAQUE is possible and may be desirable for high-security deployments, but it complicates the token derivation step because the client and server must agree on the values used as inputs to Step 3 without the server learning those values.

Why include user_id and user_salt in the token derivation?

Without user_id, two users with the same username on different accounts would derive identical tokens. Without user_salt, the token derivation is deterministic given the username and site_id alone—an attacker who guesses a username can compute what their token should be for any site and verify the guess against a stolen database. The salt adds entropy that the attacker cannot predict.

Why does the SSO store hash(user_id || site_id) as the storage key rather than the pair directly?

Storing the pair directly would allow a database breach to trivially enumerate all user-site associations. Storing the hash of the pair forces the attacker to enumerate candidate pairs and check whether any hash matches a stored key. This is a speed bump, not a wall—but combined with high-entropy user IDs (UUIDs rather than sequential integers), it raises the cost of enumeration significantly.

Why Ed25519 for signatures rather than RSA or ECDSA?

Ed25519 signatures are deterministic (eliminating the class of catastrophic failures caused by bad randomness in signing, which has historically affected ECDSA), fast (verification is roughly 3x faster than ECDSA on curve P-256), and compact (64-byte signatures versus 72+ bytes for ECDSA, several hundred bytes for RSA). There is no technical advantage to RSA or ECDSA for this use case.

Implementation Considerations

A few practical notes for implementers.

Token expiration. The signed token in Step 5 should include a timestamp and a short validity window. Sites should reject tokens that are too old. This limits the utility of stolen tokens and prevents replay attacks where an attacker captures a token and presents it later.

Token refresh. For long-lived sessions, the client should periodically re-derive and re-present tokens rather than relying on a single token for the duration. This is analogous to OAuth token refresh and can use the same session management patterns.

Rate limiting. The identity provider should rate-limit authentication attempts per credential hash to mitigate online brute-force attacks. Standard rate-limiting techniques apply: exponential backoff, account lockout after repeated failures, CAPTCHA challenges.

Constant-time comparison. All hash comparisons—credential verification, token verification, signature verification—must use constant-time comparison functions. Variable-time string comparison leaks information about which bytes matched, enabling timing attacks. Every modern cryptographic library provides constant-time comparison; use it.

Client-side storage. The client must store user_id and user_salt somewhere between sessions (otherwise the user would need to contact the SSO before every authentication, which is the normal flow but adds latency). If stored, these values should be encrypted at rest using the device's secure storage (Keychain on macOS/iOS, Keystore on Android, Credential Manager on Windows). These values are not sufficient to derive tokens without the username and password, but they reduce the brute-force search space for an attacker who steals them.

Auditability. The identity provider should maintain minimal logs—enough to detect abuse and satisfy operational requirements, not enough to reconstruct user behavior. This is a judgment call that depends on the threat model and regulatory environment, but the default should be to log less rather than more. Every log entry is a data point that a breach or subpoena can expose.

Summary

The anonymous identity architecture replaces the core computation of single sign-on. Instead of the identity provider issuing a token that it can correlate across sites, the client derives a token that no single party can correlate. The hash construction ensures that different sites receive different tokens for the same user, that the tokens cannot be linked without the username (a client-side secret), and that neither the provider nor the sites can impersonate the user to each other.

The routing layer extends the architecture to cover contact—sites can reach users through the identity provider without learning the user's contact information, and the identity provider relays messages without learning the user's browsing history.

The construction uses well-studied cryptographic primitives. SHA-256 or SHA-3 for hashing. Ed25519 for signatures. 128-bit cryptographically secure random salts. Argon2id for credential hashing. These are not novel. That is the point. The innovation is in the protocol structure—how information is distributed across parties—not in the cryptographic building blocks.

The architecture has honest limitations. It does not protect against endpoint compromise, network-level traffic analysis, social engineering, or a collusive attack between the provider and a site. It requires trust in the provider for availability and client code integrity, though not for privacy. These limitations are inherent in operating at the application layer with a centralized authentication service, and no amount of clever hashing eliminates them.

What the architecture does eliminate is the structural surveillance that existing SSO systems make inevitable. The identity provider cannot build browsing profiles because the architecture does not give it the information required to build them. The protection is mathematical, not contractual. Cross-site linkability by sites and third parties depends on the computational intractability of reversing cryptographic hash functions—not on the provider's good intentions, its privacy policy, or its resistance to subpoenas. The provider retains a limited enumeration capability over user-site associations, which the Blind Database composition (Chapter 5) closes. That combined foundation is worth building on.

The identity layer is now private. The next problem is the storage layer. When a user authenticates and stores data, the server that holds the data can read it. The next chapter examines why this is harder to solve than it appears, and the chapter after that presents the Blind Database architecture that solves it.

CHAPTER 4

The Storage Problem

Every major database breach in the last decade has produced the same reassurance: "The data was encrypted at rest." The implication is that encryption solved the problem—that the stolen data is unreadable, and therefore the breach is a non-event. This reassurance is, in the general case, wrong. Not because the encryption failed, but because the encryption worked exactly as designed, and its design leaks information.

The privacy problem in data storage is not that we lack encryption. We have excellent encryption. The problem is that the way we deploy encryption in database systems preserves exactly the structural properties that attackers exploit. The result is a protection mechanism that defends against threats that rarely materialize while failing against threats that routinely do.

This chapter examines why encryption at rest does not protect stored data against the threats that actually materialize in practice, why the industry's attempts to fix this have made the problem worse, and what constraints a real solution must satisfy.

Encryption at Rest: What It Actually Guarantees

Encryption transforms readable data into unreadable data. The transformation is reversible for anyone who holds the key. For properly designed schemes—AES-256 in authenticated modes, for instance—reversing the transformation without the key requires computational resources that exceed what any attacker can practically deploy. The mathematics is sound. The mathematics has never been the problem.

The problem is operational. Encrypted data must be decrypted to be used, and the entity that decrypts it is the entity that stores it. If the database server holds both the encrypted data and the key material necessary to decrypt it, then compromising the server yields both. The encryption becomes a locked door with the key hanging on a hook beside it.

The standard mitigation is key separation: store keys in a hardware security module (HSM) or a separate key management service (KMS). This raises the cost of attack. An attacker who compromises only the database server gets ciphertext. An attacker who also compromises the KMS gets plaintext. In practice, these systems share authentication boundaries. An application server that can request decryption from the KMS is an application server whose compromise yields decryption capability. The separation is real but thinner than it appears.

Consider what happens during a breach of a medical database. The breach notification states that all records were encrypted and that no evidence exists of key compromise. Regulators accept this. Patients file the letter and move on. But the encrypted database circulates through markets where stolen data is traded, and the encryption scheme used—one that preserves enough structure for the database to perform queries—turns out to leak sufficient information for statistical reconstruction of sensitive fields. Mortality risk, diagnostic categories, patient demographics: all recoverable without any key, using techniques that exploit the structure the encryption preserved.

The patient's diagnosis is inferred, not decrypted. The inference is probabilistic—a statistical likelihood rather than a certainty. But insurance underwriting operates on probability. The aggregator who assembles a patient's risk profile does not need to prove a diagnosis. The aggregator needs only to establish a likelihood sufficient to justify a coverage exclusion. The mathematics of encryption was satisfied. The mathematics of discrimination was satisfied as well.

Even with perfect key separation, encryption at rest protects against exactly one threat: offline theft of storage media. If someone steals a hard drive from a data center, the data on it is unreadable. This is a genuine protection against a genuine threat. It is also an increasingly irrelevant threat. Modern breaches occur through application-layer compromise, credential theft, insider access, and supply-chain attacks—all of which operate through the same authentication channels that the application uses to access plaintext.

Encryption at rest does not protect against a compromised administrator. It does not protect against a valid subpoena served on the operator. It does not protect against an insider who has legitimate query access. It does not protect against an application vulnerability that exposes query results. It protects the data from people who are not authorized to access it through the system's own interfaces. It does nothing when the attacker is already inside, or when the legal system compels the operator to hand over the keys.

The regulatory framework reinforces the illusion. HIPAA, GDPR, PCI-DSS—all treat encryption at rest as a sufficient technical safeguard. An organization that encrypts its database has satisfied its compliance obligations even if the encryption scheme leaks enough structure to reconstruct the data. The regulations treat encryption as a binary property: data is either encrypted or it is not. The meaningful question—what does the encryption actually hide?—is not one the regulatory frameworks ask.

The gap between regulatory compliance and actual protection is not a detail. It is the central problem. Organizations that have done everything the law requires have nonetheless failed to protect their users' data. The failure is structural, not negligent. The tools the industry provides—and the regulations endorse—are inadequate to the threat.

The Database Functionality Problem

A database is not a storage system. A storage system holds data and returns it on request. A database searches, sorts, filters, aggregates, joins, and indexes. These operations are the reason databases exist. A system that can only store and retrieve opaque blobs is a file system, not a database.

This creates a structural conflict with encryption. If data is encrypted and the server does not hold the key, the server cannot perform database operations. It cannot search encrypted fields because it cannot read them. It cannot sort encrypted values because it cannot compare them. It cannot compute aggregates because it cannot perform arithmetic on ciphertexts. The database becomes a key-value store—functional, but stripped of everything that makes it useful for application development.

The alternative is equally bad. If the server holds the key and can decrypt on demand, then it can perform operations—but the encryption provides no protection against server compromise. The data is encrypted on disk but decrypted in memory for every query. Any attacker who gains access to the running server process has access to plaintext. The protection is temporal—data is safe at rest but exposed during use—and the database is in use most of the time.

Consider the operations a typical application requires from its database. A health-care application searches by patient identifier. A financial application retrieves transactions within a date range. An HR system filters employees by department. Each of these operations requires the server to compare values: does this record match the query? Is this date within the range? Does this field equal the filter value? Comparison requires reading, and reading requires the key.

This is the encryption paradox: encryption that preserves database functionality leaks information; encryption that preserves security destroys functionality. The tradeoff appears fundamental. The database industry has spent two decades trying to thread this needle, and the results are instructive.

Property-Preserving Encryption: The Industry's Answer

The database industry's response to the encryption paradox has been property-preserving encryption (PPE). These schemes encrypt data while preserving specific mathematical properties that permit server-side operations without decryption.

Deterministic encryption preserves equality. The same plaintext always produces the same ciphertext. This allows the database to match records—an equality comparison on ciphertext produces the same result as an equality comparison on plaintext. The server cannot read the values, but it can determine which records have the same value. This is a substitution cipher. It has been two centuries since substitution ciphers provided meaningful security.

Order-preserving encryption (OPE) preserves ordering. If plaintext value A is less than plaintext value B, then ciphertext A is less than ciphertext B. This allows range queries: "find all records where age is between 30 and 50" works on encrypted data because the ordering is preserved. Boldyreva, Chenette, Lee, and O'Neill introduced OPE in 2009 and proved that standard indistinguishability-based security is impossible for any order-preserving scheme.[1] Their follow-up work showed that any OPE scheme achieving

---

1   Alexandra Boldyreva, Nathan Chenette, Younho Lee, and Adam O'Neill, "Order-Preserving Symmetric Encryption," *Advances in Cryptology—EUROCRYPT 2009*, LNCS vol. 5479, pp. 224–241, Springer, 2009. This paper introduced OPE and proved IND-CPA security is impossible for order-preserv-

the best possible security notion leaks approximately half the plaintext bits—not as a flaw in any particular construction, but as a mathematical consequence of preserving order.

Order-revealing encryption (ORE) is a weaker variant that reveals ordering through a comparison function rather than through the ciphertext values themselves, but the information leakage is similar in practice.

These are not the only variants. Searchable symmetric encryption (SSE) builds encrypted indexes that allow keyword searches without revealing the search terms (in theory). Format-preserving encryption (FPE) produces ciphertexts that match the format of the plaintext—an encrypted Social Security number looks like a Social Security number—which simplifies integration with existing systems that validate input formats.

These schemes are deployed in commercial products and marketed under various names: "always encrypted," "transparent data encryption with queryable columns," "encryption-in-use." The marketing is accurate about the capability and consistently silent about the cost.

What Property Preservation Leaks

The previous section described what property-preserving encryption does. This section describes what it leaks—and the leakage is worse than the industry acknowledges.

Every property preserved is information leaked. This is not a flaw in any particular scheme. It is a mathematical consequence of what "preserving a property" means. If an encryption scheme preserves a property, then that property is visible to anyone who observes the ciphertext—including an attacker who steals the encrypted database.

Deterministic encryption leaks frequency. Because the same plaintext always produces the same ciphertext, the frequency distribution of ciphertexts matches the frequency distribution of plaintexts. An attacker who knows the approximate frequency distribution of values in the population can map ciphertexts to plaintexts by matching frequencies. The most common ciphertext corresponds to the most common value. This is a frequency analysis attack, the same technique that has broken substitution ciphers for centuries.

Order-preserving encryption leaks ordering and distribution. The attacker gains not just frequency information but the complete rank ordering of all values. Combined with knowledge of the value domain (ages range from 0 to 120, zip codes follow known geographic distributions), the ordering maps directly onto plaintext values. Each ciphertext's position in the sorted order corresponds to its position in the plaintext distribution.

The following pseudocode demonstrates the frequency analysis attack on deterministic encryption:

```
function frequency_attack(encrypted_column, known_distribution):
    // Count frequency of each ciphertext value
```

---

ing schemes. The "approximately half the plaintext bits" leakage result was established in the follow-up: Boldyreva, Chenette, and O'Neill, "Order-Preserving Encryption Revisited: Improved Security Analysis and Alternative Solutions," *CRYPTO 2011*, LNCS vol. 6841, pp. 578–595, Springer, 2011.

```
cipher_frequencies = count_occurrences(encrypted_column)

// Sort ciphertexts by frequency (most common first)
sorted_ciphers = sort_by_frequency(cipher_frequencies,
descending)

// Sort known plaintext values by expected frequency
sorted_plains = sort_by_frequency(known_distribution,
descending)

// Map: most common ciphertext → most common plaintext
mapping = {}
for i in range(length(sorted_ciphers)):
    mapping[sorted_ciphers[i]] = sorted_plains[i]

return mapping
```

This is not a sophisticated attack. An undergraduate with a statistics textbook can implement it in an afternoon. The attack works because deterministic encryption is, by design, a substitution cipher—and substitution ciphers are broken by frequency analysis.

For order-preserving encryption, the attack is even simpler:

```
function ope_attack(encrypted_column, domain_min, domain_max):
    // Sort all unique ciphertexts
    sorted_ciphers = sorted(unique(encrypted_column))
    n = length(sorted_ciphers)

    // Map each ciphertext to its position in the domain
    mapping = {}
    for i in range(n):
        // Linear interpolation across the known domain
        plaintext = domain_min + (i / (n - 1)) * (domain_max -
domain_min)
        mapping[sorted_ciphers[i]] = round(plaintext)

    return mapping
```

These are not theoretical concerns. Naveed, Kamara, and Wright demonstrated inference attacks against PPE-encrypted medical databases.[2] From encrypted hospital records, they recovered:

- **Mortality risk, sex, and race** (DTE-encrypted): correctly recovered for more than 60% of patient records across more than 60% of hospitals

- **Patient age and disease severity** (OPE-encrypted): correctly recovered for more

---

2   Muhammad Naveed, Seny Kamara, and Charles V. Wright, "Inference Attacks on Property-Preserving Encrypted Databases," *Proceedings of the 22nd ACM SIGSAC Conference on Computer and Communications Security (CCS '15)*, pp. 644–655, ACM, 2015. The attacks recovered sensitive fields from real encrypted medical databases using only the structural properties preserved by the encryption, without any decryption key.

than 80% of patient records across 95% of hospitals

All of this was recovered without any decryption key, using only the structural properties that the encryption scheme preserved.

Grubbs, Sekniqi, Bindschaedler, Naveed, and Ristenpart extended the result.[3] Even leakage-minimizing variants of OPE and ORE—schemes explicitly designed to reduce structural leakage—still leak enough for practical attacks when combined with auxiliary information. The attacker does not need the exact distribution; an approximate distribution drawn from public data is sufficient.

The fundamental issue is the auxiliary information assumption. An attacker with access to an encrypted medical database and a public health statistics dataset has everything needed for inference. The encrypted database provides the structural signal. The public dataset provides the reference distribution. The attack is the mapping between them. No additional access, no key compromise, no insider knowledge required.

Searchable symmetric encryption schemes have their own leakage profiles. Most SSE schemes leak *access patterns*—the server learns which encrypted records match a given encrypted query, even though it cannot read the query or the records. Over time, access patterns leak significant information. If the server observes that the same encrypted query consistently retrieves the same set of encrypted records, and the server knows approximate query frequencies from public data, the same frequency-matching attack applies to queries rather than values.

The pattern repeats across every variant. Each scheme trades a specific form of leakage for a specific operational capability. The leakage is inherent in the capability. Reducing leakage reduces capability. Eliminating leakage eliminates capability. There is no free lunch.

Why does this matter beyond academic interest? Encrypted databases that leak structure are not failing in obscure theoretical ways. They are failing in ways that translate directly to real harm: insurance denials based on inferred medical conditions, employment discrimination based on inferred demographics, targeted advertising based on inferred behaviors. The inference is probabilistic, but the systems that consume the inferred data operate on probability. An insurer does not need certainty. An insurer needs a risk score, and a risk score computed from inferred data functions identically to one computed from known data.

The Inference Gap

The distinction between decryption and inference is critical and underappreciated.

Decryption means recovering plaintext from ciphertext using mathematical inversion. It is what encryption is designed to prevent, and modern encryption prevents it effectively. No one is brute-forcing AES-256.

---

3   Paul Grubbs, Kevin Sekniqi, Vincent Bindschaedler, Muhammad Naveed, and Thomas Ristenpart, "Leakage-Abuse Attacks against Order-Revealing Encryption," *2017 IEEE Symposium on Security and Privacy (SP)*, pp. 655–672, IEEE, 2017. Extended the inference attack results to leakage-minimizing variants of OPE and ORE, demonstrating practical attacks using approximate auxiliary distributions.

Inference means deducing information about the plaintext from observable properties of the ciphertext—frequency, ordering, length, timing, co-occurrence patterns. Inference does not require breaking the encryption. Inference exploits the information that the encryption was designed to preserve.

PPE schemes are designed to enable inference. That is their purpose: to allow the database server to infer enough about the plaintext to perform operations. The problem is that the server's inference capability is also the attacker's inference capability. There is no way to give the server the ability to compare encrypted values while denying that ability to an attacker who steals the same encrypted values.

The following pseudocode demonstrates the general structure of an inference attack that combines frequency analysis with auxiliary data:

```
function inference_attack(encrypted_db, auxiliary_data):
    // Phase 1: Extract structural information from encrypted
columns
    for each column in encrypted_db:
        frequencies[column] = count_unique_values(column)
        if is_order_preserving(column):
            ordering[column] = extract_sort_order(column)
        co_occurrence[column] = correlate_with(other_columns)

    // Phase 2: Match against known distributions
    for each column in encrypted_db:
        candidates = auxiliary_data.distributions_matching(
            frequencies[column],
            ordering[column]    // if available
        )
        if length(candidates) == 1:
            mapping[column] = candidates[0]   // unique match
        else:
            // Phase 3: Use co-occurrence to disambiguate
            mapping[column] = disambiguate(candidates, co_
occurrence[column])

    // Phase 4: Reconstruct records
    for each row in encrypted_db:
        plaintext_row = apply_mapping(row, mapping)
        confidence = compute_confidence(row, mapping, auxiliary_
data)
        emit(plaintext_row, confidence)
```

The auxiliary data need not be secret. Census distributions, actuarial tables, publicly available health statistics—any reference dataset that describes the distribution of values in the population can serve as the basis for frequency matching. The attack succeeds not because the attacker knows anything about the specific database, but because the encrypted database's structure matches the structure of the population it was drawn from.

This is not a problem that better PPE schemes can solve. It is inherent in the approach.

Any scheme that permits server-side operations permits those operations because it preserves the properties they require. Those properties are information. That information is available to anyone who has the ciphertext. Improving the encryption scheme within the PPE framework is like building a better lock for a glass door—the issue is the transparency, not the lock.

Fully Homomorphic Encryption: The Theoretical Fix

Fully homomorphic encryption (FHE) offers a theoretically different approach. FHE allows arbitrary computation on encrypted data, producing encrypted results that, when decrypted, match the results of computing on plaintext. The server can search, sort, aggregate, and compute without learning anything about the data.

FHE does not preserve properties in the way PPE does. It does not leak frequency or ordering. It provides genuine computational confidentiality.

FHE is also impractically slow. A query that takes milliseconds on plaintext data takes minutes to hours on FHE-encrypted data, depending on the complexity of the computation. Bootstrapping operations (necessary to manage noise growth in FHE ciphertexts) dominate runtime. Despite significant progress—the performance gap has narrowed from a factor of 10^9 to roughly 10^4-10^6 over the past decade—FHE remains unusable for general-purpose database operations at production scale.

Partial solutions exist. Somewhat homomorphic encryption (SHE) supports limited operations efficiently but restricts the computations available. Trusted execution environments (TEEs) like Intel SGX attempt a hardware-based escape: encrypt data, decrypt it inside a hardware enclave that the operating system cannot inspect, perform computation in the enclave, encrypt the results. TEEs have suffered repeated side-channel attacks—Spectre, Meltdown, Foreshadow, Plundervolt—that undermine the isolation guarantees they depend on. Hardware is not software; when hardware security assumptions fail, they fail in ways that cannot be patched.

Hybrid approaches perform some operations homomorphically and others on plaintext, trading security for performance. These are active areas of research. They are not deployed solutions for general-purpose database workloads.

The Compliance Trap

The inadequacy of existing encryption approaches would be less damaging if the regulatory environment recognized it. It does not.

Major data protection regulations—HIPAA in healthcare, PCI-DSS in payment processing, GDPR in the European Union—treat encryption as a binary safeguard. Data is encrypted or it is not. If it is encrypted, certain requirements are relaxed. HIPAA's breach notification rule, for example, provides a safe harbor for encrypted data: if a breach involves data encrypted according to NIST guidelines and the keys were not compromised, the organization need not notify affected individuals. The regulation does not ask whether the encryption preserves structure that enables inference. It asks whether the keys were stolen.

This creates a perverse incentive. Organizations adopt property-preserving encryption because it satisfies the regulatory checkbox while preserving the database functionality they depend on. The encryption is real. The compliance is real. The protection is illusory. The organization has optimized for the regulatory framework rather than for the threat model. When the threat materializes through inference rather than decryption, the organization is compliant and the patient is harmed.

The situation is worse than mere regulatory lag. The compliance framework actively discourages better solutions. An organization that adopts a genuinely protective architecture—one where the server cannot perform queries because it cannot read the data—may find itself unable to satisfy audit requirements that assume server-side access to records. An auditor who asks "show me all records matching criteria X" expects a database query, not a cryptographic proof that the data exists but cannot be read by the operator. The architecture that protects users best may be the architecture that satisfies auditors least.

This is not an argument against regulation. It is an observation that regulation designed around one threat model does not automatically protect against another. The threat model has shifted from "unauthorized access to plaintext" to "statistical inference from ciphertext structure." The regulations have not followed.

The Wrong Question

The encryption paradox—that security and functionality cannot coexist in encrypted databases—rests on an assumption that deserves examination. The assumption is that the server must operate on the data. The paradox takes this as given and then asks how to encrypt data while preserving enough functionality for the server to do its job.

But the server's job is a design choice, not a law of nature. The server searches, sorts, and aggregates because databases are traditionally designed with the server performing computation and the client consuming results. This architecture made sense when servers were powerful and clients were thin terminals. It makes less sense when every client is a general-purpose computer capable of performing the operations locally.

What if the architecture changed? What if the server stored encrypted data it could not read, and the client performed all meaningful computation? The server would hold opaque blobs, indexed by opaque keys derived from user-held secrets. The client would download the blobs it needed, decrypt locally, and perform any necessary operations on plaintext in its own memory.

This eliminates the need for property-preserving encryption entirely. The encryption can be semantically secure—the strongest standard available—because the server never needs to compare, sort, or search ciphertexts. The server is a storage service, not a computation service. Its compromise yields encrypted data with no structural leakage, no frequency information, no ordering, nothing an attacker can use for inference.

This is not a novel observation in cryptography. End-to-end encrypted messaging systems already work this way—the server stores ciphertext it cannot read and routes it based on opaque identifiers. Password managers work this way: the server stores an encrypted vault it cannot open. The question is whether the same principle can extend from these specific cases to general structured data storage. The answer is yes, but it requires rethinking what the server does and what the client does. The application cannot issue SQL queries to the server. The application must know how to request the specific encrypted blobs it needs and how to process them locally.

This restructuring is possible but constrained. Client-side computation increases resource requirements. Some operations—full-table scans, multi-table joins, ad-hoc analytical queries—become expensive or impractical. But for privacy-sensitive applications—which are predominantly store-and-retrieve—the constraints are manageable. For applications that require server-side analytics across all users' data simultaneously, the constraint may be disqualifying. The architecture has a scope of applicability, and honesty about that scope is part of getting the engineering right.

The question of whether this restructuring is possible for a given application is a different question from whether the encryption paradox is fundamental. The paradox is fundamental only if server-side computation is mandatory. For applications where it is not—and many privacy-sensitive applications fall into this category—the paradox dissolves. The question changes from "how do we encrypt data while preserving server-side operations?" to "how do we design applications that do not require server-side operations on sensitive data?"

Requirements for a Solution

The analysis produces a set of requirements for any database architecture that genuinely protects stored data:

Operational blindness. The server operator must be unable to read the data, not merely unauthorized to read it. The protection must be mathematical, not policy-based. A compromised server, a subpoenaed operator, a malicious insider—none of these should yield usable data.

No structural leakage. The encrypted data must not reveal frequency distributions, ordering relationships, value lengths, co-occurrence patterns, or any other property that enables inference. This rules out all forms of property-preserving encryption as the primary protection mechanism.

Functional sufficiency. The system must support the operations that applications actually require: storing records, retrieving records by known identifiers, updating records, deleting records. It need not support arbitrary SQL. Most applications do not require their storage layer to perform complex joins or full-text search—they require reliable storage and retrieval by key. The assumption that every application needs the full power of a relational database engine operating on plaintext is widespread and, for privacy-sensitive applications, frequently wrong.

Crypto-erasure. Deleting a user's data should be as simple as deleting their encryption keys. If the keys are gone, the encrypted data is computationally indistinguishable from random noise. This transforms "delete my data" from an operational nightmare—

find every copy, every backup, every replica, every log entry, every analytics pipeline that ingested the data, every downstream system that cached it—into a key management operation. Delete the key. The data remains on disk but is now meaningless noise. Backups contain noise. Replicas contain noise. The data is destroyed without being located.

No god mode. No administrator, no DBA, no root account should be able to access plaintext data in bulk. The system should have no single point of compromise that yields the entire database in readable form. This is distinct from access control. Access control restricts who is authorized to read data. Operational blindness ensures that no one—authorized or not—can read it without the user's key material.

Key-holder sovereignty. The user must be the root of trust. The user holds the keys, derives the access tokens, and controls what is readable. The server is a custodian of ciphertext, not a gatekeeper of access.

These requirements are demanding. They rule out the vast majority of existing database architectures. They rule out every deployment where the server holds encryption keys, every deployment that uses property-preserving encryption, every deployment where administrators can run arbitrary queries against plaintext data. They rule out the standard model of "encrypt at rest, decrypt in the application tier" that has become the industry default.

They also describe something that is architecturally achievable. The next chapter presents a database architecture—a cryptographically blind database—that satisfies all of them. The server stores data it cannot read, indexed by keys it cannot derive, encrypted with schemes it cannot invert. The operator's blindness is not a limitation to be worked around. It is the security property.

CHAPTER 5

Blind Database Architecture

Every database breach in history shares a structural prerequisite: the server could read what it stored.

The previous chapter established six requirements for a database that genuinely protects stored data: operational blindness, no structural leakage, functional sufficiency, crypto-erasure, no god mode, and key-holder sovereignty. These requirements rule out the industry's standard approaches—encryption at rest with server-held keys, property-preserving encryption, transparent data encryption with queryable columns—because all of them give the server enough information to read, infer, or structurally reconstruct the data it stores.

This chapter presents an architecture that satisfies all six. The construction is not complex. The cryptographic primitives are standard, well-studied, and available in production-quality libraries. What makes the architecture unusual is not the sophistication of its components but the simplicity of its organizing principle: the server never holds key material. Everything follows from that.

The client derives identifiers. The client derives encryption keys. The client encrypts before upload and decrypts after download. The server stores opaque blobs indexed by opaque identifiers. The server participates in storage and retrieval. The server participates in nothing else.

This is the blind database. The name describes what it is. The database is blind to what it holds.

Key Derivation

The foundation of the architecture is a key derivation scheme that produces two things from client-held secrets: a record identifier that tells the server *where* to store the data, and an encryption key that protects *what* is stored. The server sees the identifier. The server never sees the key.

The derivation begins with a master secret. This is a value the client holds and never transmits. It might be derived from a password. It might be generated randomly and stored in a device's secure enclave. It might be a combination of both. The specific origin matters for recovery—a topic addressed later in this chapter—but not for the derivation itself. What matters is that the server does not have it.

From the master secret, the client derives a record identifier:

```
record_id = HASH(master_secret || record_type || record_
discriminator)
```

The `record_type` is a label that categorizes the record—"medical_record", "preference", "message", whatever the application domain requires. The `record_discriminator` distinguishes individual records within that type—a date, a sequence number, a site identifier. The concatenation of these three values, passed through a cryptographic hash function, produces a fixed-length identifier that is unique to this record, deterministic given the same inputs, and meaningless to anyone who does not hold the master secret.

The hash function is a one-way function. Given the output, computing the inputs is computationally infeasible.[1] The server that stores `record_id` cannot work backwards to discover the master secret, the record type, or the discriminator. The identifier is an opaque string. It could be a medical record. It could be a grocery list. The server cannot distinguish the two.

From the master secret and the record identifier, the client derives an encryption key:

```
encryption_key = KDF(master_secret, record_id, "encrypt")
```

The KDF—key derivation function—is a distinct primitive from the hash function, though they are related. HKDF, the HMAC-based key derivation function standardized in RFC 5869, is the standard choice. It takes input keying material (the master secret), a salt (the record identifier), and an info string (the context label "encrypt") and produces a key of the desired length suitable for use with a symmetric cipher.

The context label matters. The same master secret and record identifier, combined with a different context string—"authenticate" instead of "encrypt", for instance—would produce a different key. This allows the derivation scheme to generate multiple keys per record without any single key compromising any other. The encryption key and an authentication key for the same record are cryptographically independent.[2]

The complete derivation, expressed as pseudocode:

```
function derive_record_id(master_secret, record_type,
discriminator):
    return SHA256(master_secret || record_type || discriminator)

function derive_encryption_key(master_secret, record_id):
    return HKDF(
```

---

1   Preimage resistance is a standard security property of cryptographic hash functions. For SHA-256, the best known preimage attack has complexity 2256, far beyond any foreseeable computational capability. See NIST FIPS 180-4, "Secure Hash Standard," August 2015.

2   HKDF's security proof, given in the random oracle model, guarantees that outputs derived with distinct `info` parameters are computationally independent—that is, knowledge of one output provides no advantage in predicting another. See H. Krawczyk, "Cryptographic Extraction and Key Derivation: The HKDF Scheme," IACR Cryptology ePrint Archive, Report 2010/264, 2010. Standardized as RFC 5869.

```
        input_key_material = master_secret,
        salt                = record_id,
        info                = "encrypt",
        length              = 32          // 256 bits for AES-256
    )
```

Two properties matter. First, the derivation is deterministic. The same inputs always produce the same outputs. This means the client can reconstruct the record identifier and encryption key at any time, from any device, given the master secret and the knowledge of what record type and discriminator were used. There is no state to synchronize. There is no key database to maintain. The keys are derived, not stored.

Second, the derivation is one-way. The server, which holds the record identifier, cannot derive the encryption key from it—that requires the master secret, which the server does not possess. An attacker who obtains the entire server-side database gets a collection of record identifiers mapped to ciphertexts. Neither the identifiers nor the ciphertexts yield anything without the master secrets of the individual users who created them.

The Write Protocol

Writing a record to a blind database is a four-step process, all performed client-side except for the final storage operation. In both directions, the server handles opaque bytes and learns nothing about what they mean.

The pseudocode for the write operation:

```
function write_record(master_secret, record_type, discriminator,
plaintext):
    // Step 1: Derive the record identifier
    record_id = derive_record_id(master_secret, record_type,
discriminator)

    // Step 2: Derive the encryption key
    key = derive_encryption_key(master_secret, record_id)

    // Step 3: Encrypt the plaintext
    nonce = random_bytes(24)
    ciphertext = AEAD_encrypt(key, nonce, plaintext, associated_
data = record_id)
    stored_value = nonce || ciphertext

    // Step 4: Send to server
    server.store(record_id, stored_value)
```

Blind Database: Write and Read Protocols

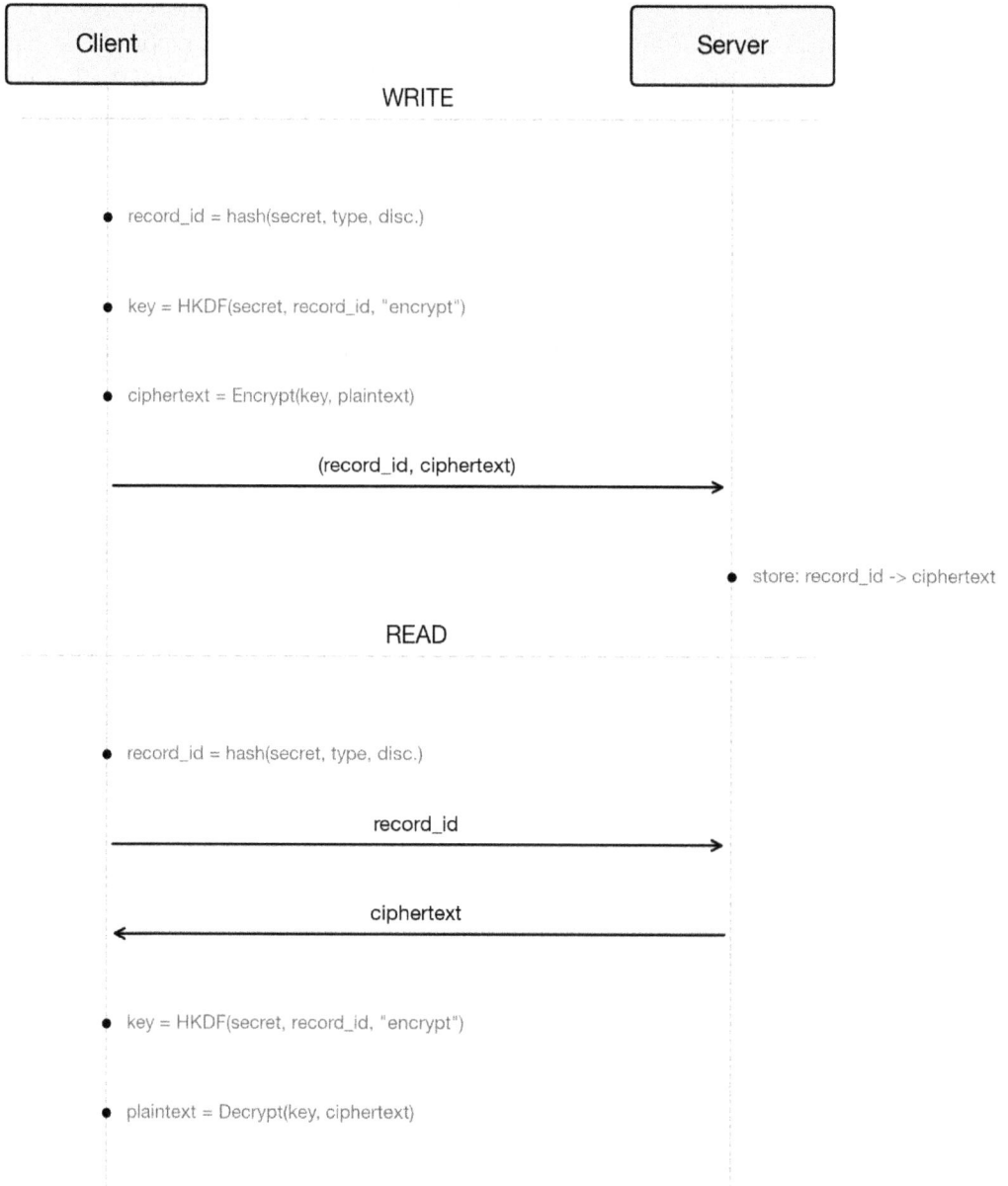

```
┌─────────────┐                              ┌─────────────┐
│   Client    │                              │   Server    │
└─────────────┘                              └─────────────┘
                      WRITE

  ● record_id = hash(secret, type, disc.)

  ● key = HKDF(secret, record_id, "encrypt")

  ● ciphertext = Encrypt(key, plaintext)

                (record_id, ciphertext)
  ──────────────────────────────────────────────►

                                    ● store: record_id -> ciphertext

                      READ

  ● record_id = hash(secret, type, disc.)

                      record_id
  ──────────────────────────────────────────────►

                      ciphertext
  ◄──────────────────────────────────────────────

  ● key = HKDF(secret, record_id, "encrypt")

  ● plaintext = Decrypt(key, ciphertext)
```

Figure 5.1: Blind Database Write and Read Protocols. The following diagram shows the complete write and read cycle, annotating what each party learns at each step.

Step 1 and Step 2 are the derivations described above. Step 3 encrypts the plaintext using an authenticated encryption scheme—AES-256-GCM or ChaCha20-Poly1305, both of which are AEAD (Authenticated Encryption with Associated Data) constructions. The nonce is a random value that ensures the same plaintext encrypted twice produces different ciphertexts. The associated data binds the ciphertext to the record identifier, preventing an attacker from moving a ciphertext from one record to another.

Step 4 is the only network operation. The client sends a pair—(record_id, stored_value)—to the server. The server stores the pair. The server does not parse the stored value. The server does not validate its contents. The server receives opaque bytes and writes them to storage indexed by an opaque key. That is the extent of the server's involvement.

The server's API for a blind database is minimal:

```
store(record_id, value)    → success | error
retrieve(record_id)        → value | not_found
delete(record_id)          → success | error
```

Three operations. No query language. No filtering. No search. No aggregation. The server is a key-value store with no knowledge of what the keys mean or what the values contain.

This simplicity is a feature, not a limitation. Every operation the server can perform on the data is an operation that a compromised server can perform on the data. A server that can search can be compelled to search. A server that can aggregate can be compelled to aggregate. A server that can only store and retrieve can only store and retrieve—and that constraint applies equally to legitimate operators, malicious insiders, and anyone who compromises the server.

The Read Protocol

Reading is the write protocol in reverse. The client reconstructs the record identifier, requests the ciphertext from the server, derives the encryption key, and decrypts locally.

```
function read_record(master_secret, record_type, discriminator):
    // Step 1: Derive the record identifier
    record_id = derive_record_id(master_secret, record_type,
discriminator)

    // Step 2: Request from server
    stored_value = server.retrieve(record_id)
    if stored_value is not_found:
        return not_found

    // Step 3: Derive the encryption key
    key = derive_encryption_key(master_secret, record_id)

    // Step 4: Decrypt locally
    nonce = stored_value[0:24]
```

```
    ciphertext = stored_value[24:]
    plaintext = AEAD_decrypt(key, nonce, ciphertext, associated_
data = record_id)

    return plaintext
```

The server's contribution to the read operation is a single lookup: given a record identifier, return the corresponding value. The server does not know what was requested. The server does not know what was returned.

Notice that the client must know the `record_type` and `discriminator` to request a record. The client cannot browse. The client cannot ask the server "what records do I have?" because the server does not know which records belong to which client. All record identifiers look the same to the server—random strings with no visible ownership structure. The client must maintain its own knowledge of what it has stored: which record types exist, which discriminators were used, what the records contain.

This is a genuine constraint. In a traditional database, the server maintains indexes, catalogs, and metadata that let clients discover what exists. In a blind database, that knowledge lives exclusively on the client side. Applications must be designed accordingly. A medical records application, for instance, might maintain a local index of record discriminators—dates of visits, types of records—encrypted with the master secret and itself stored in the blind database as a single "index" record. The client downloads and decrypts this index to discover what other records exist, then requests them individually.

The pattern is recursive: the index of records is itself a record in the blind database, stored at a well-known derivation path (e.g., `record_type` = "index", `discriminator` = "master"). The client always knows how to find the index because the derivation inputs are fixed by convention. The index, once decrypted, tells the client how to find everything else.

Operational Blindness vs. Zero-Knowledge

The term "zero-knowledge" has a specific meaning in cryptography. A zero-knowledge proof is a protocol in which one party (the prover) convinces another party (the verifier) that a statement is true without revealing any information beyond the truth of the statement itself. The definition is formal. It involves simulation arguments—the verifier could have generated the transcript of the interaction without the prover's participation, which proves that the verifier learned nothing from the interaction.

The blind database is not a zero-knowledge system. It does not produce proofs. It does not involve interactive protocols between prover and verifier. It does not satisfy the formal definition of zero-knowledge in the cryptographic literature.

What the blind database provides is operational blindness. The server cannot read the data it stores. This is not because a mathematical proof demonstrates that the server learns nothing. It is because the server lacks the key material required for decryption. The server holds ciphertexts encrypted with keys it does not possess. Decrypting those ciphertexts requires the master secret, which the client never transmits. The server's inability to read the data is a consequence of key distribution, not a consequence of proof systems.

The distinction matters for two reasons.

First, the blind database leaks information that a zero-knowledge system would not. The server learns that a record exists. The server learns when a record is written, read, updated, or deleted. The server learns the size of each record. The server learns which record identifiers are accessed together. These are real information leakages. A zero-knowledge system, if one could be built for this purpose at acceptable performance cost, would not leak them. The blind database does, and honesty about what the architecture does and does not protect is a precondition for trusting it.

Second, describing the system as "zero-knowledge" when it does not meet the formal definition would be misleading in a way that undermines trust. Security claims must be precise. If a system claims zero-knowledge and later turns out to leak access patterns, the revelation damages confidence not only in the system but in the class of privacy-preserving architectures. Calling the property what it is—operational blindness, meaning the server cannot read record contents—is both more accurate and more useful. Users and developers know exactly what is protected (content) and what is not (metadata).

The operational blindness guarantee is strong within its scope. An attacker who compromises the server gets ciphertexts encrypted under AES-256-GCM or ChaCha20-Poly1305 with keys derived through HKDF from secrets that never existed on the server. Breaking this without the keys requires breaking the underlying cipher—this is beyond current computational reach—the entire cryptographic community operates on that assumption.[3] The data is safe against content disclosure. It is not safe against traffic analysis. Both facts matter, and conflating them by using imprecise terminology helps no one.

Security Levels

Not all data has the same recovery requirements. A user's display name preferences might reasonably survive a password change. A session encryption key should not. A record containing secrets that must remain bound to a specific physical device should be irrecoverable if that device is lost.

The blind database supports three security levels, distinguished by what inputs contribute to the master secret derivation:

Security Level	Key Derivation Inputs	Survives Password Change	Survives Device Loss	Recovery Possible

---

3   AES-256-GCM provides IND-CPA (indistinguishability under chosen-plaintext attack) and INT-CTXT (integrity of ciphertext) security under standard assumptions. The best known attack on AES-256 is a biclique attack with complexity 2254.4, which is a negligible improvement over brute force. See A. Bogdanov, D. Khovratovich, and C. Rechberger, "Biclique Cryptanalysis of the Full AES," ASIACRYPT 2011. ChaCha20-Poly1305 has comparable security margins; see D. J. Bernstein, "ChaCha, a variant of Salsa20," 2008, and Y. Nir and A. Langley, RFC 8439, "ChaCha20 and Poly1305 for IETF Protocols," 2018.

Recoverable	HASH(pur- pose, user- name, serv- er_salt)	Yes	Yes	Yes, via account recovery
Session-bound	Includes pass- word-derived value	No	Yes (if password known)	Only with cur- rent password
Unrecoverable	Includes de- vice-specific secret	No	No	Never

Recoverable records derive their master secret from values that persist across password changes. The username does not change. The server_salt is a value the server stores and returns during authentication—it changes only if the account itself is reset. The purpose is a fixed string. Because none of these inputs depend on the password, a password change does not alter the derived keys. The records remain accessible.

This is the appropriate level for data that must survive account recovery: contact preferences, application settings, long-term identity mappings. The tradeoff is that the derivation inputs include the username, which the server knows (in hashed form) through the authentication process. An attacker who compromises both the server and the authentication system could, in principle, reconstruct the derivation inputs for recoverable records. The security of recoverable records is real but weaker than the other levels.

Session-bound records include a password-derived component in the master secret derivation. This means the keys change when the password changes. Old records encrypted under the old keys become inaccessible unless the application explicitly re-encrypts them during the password change process. The password-derived component ensures that an attacker who compromises the server but does not know the password cannot derive the keys, even if the attacker has the username and server salt.

This is the appropriate level for data tied to an active session: cached credentials, session-specific encryption keys, temporary authentication tokens stored for convenience. The data matters only while the session is active. When the password changes, the old session data should become inaccessible.

Unrecoverable records include a device-specific secret—a value generated randomly and stored only on the device, never transmitted, never backed up. If the device is lost or destroyed, the secret is gone. If the secret is gone, the records encrypted under keys derived from it are permanently inaccessible.

This is the appropriate level for data that must never be recoverable by anyone other than the current holder of the physical device: private keys for end-to-end encryption, local authentication credentials, device-specific signing keys. The unrecoverability is the security property. It ensures that even the user cannot be compelled to recover the data from a different device, because the recovery is computationally infeasible—there is no backdoor, no recovery key, and no known method to derive the encryption keys without the device secret.

The three levels are not three different systems. They are three different inputs to the same derivation functions. The write protocol, read protocol, encryption scheme, and server API are identical across all three. The only difference is what the client feeds into `derive_record_id` and `derive_encryption_key` as the master secret. The architecture does not change. The trust assumptions narrow.

Crypto-Erasure

In a traditional database, deleting data means finding every copy and destroying it. The active database. The standby replica. The nightly backup. The backup stored offsite by a third-party vendor. The log files that recorded the data being written.

GDPR's Article 17—the "right to erasure"—requires that organizations delete personal data upon request. The regulation is clear. The implementation is a nightmare. Finding every copy of a specific user's data across every system that might have touched it is, for any organization of meaningful size, an exercise in probabilistic archaeology. The organization might find most copies. It will not find all of them. The backup tape in the offsite vault, written six months ago, contains the data. The organization may not even know that vault exists—the contract was signed by someone who has since left the company.

Crypto-erasure transforms this operational nightmare into a key management operation. Figure 5.2 shows the sequence.

Crypto-Erasure

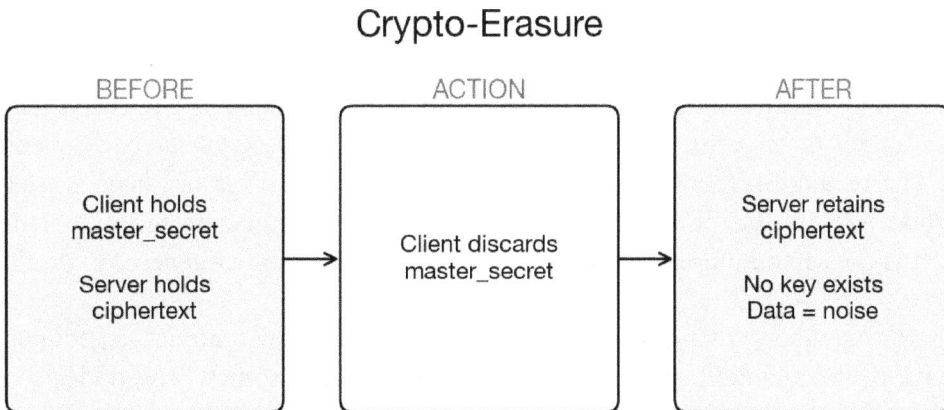

Figure 5.2: Crypto-Erasure Sequence. Discarding the master secret renders all stored ciphertext permanently unreadable without requiring any server-side action.

If the user's data is encrypted with keys derived from the user's master secret, and the master secret is discarded, then every record encrypted under that secret becomes computationally indistinguishable from random noise.[4] The ciphertexts remain on disk. The

---

4   "Computationally indistinguishable from random" is the formal IND-CPA (indistinguishability under chosen-plaintext attack) guarantee provided by the AEAD ciphers used here. An adversary without the key cannot distinguish a ciphertext from a random string of the same length with probability mean-

backups still contain them. The replicas still hold them. But without the keys, the ciphertexts are not data. They are noise. The information is destroyed without the ciphertext being located, because the information was never in the ciphertext alone—it was in the ciphertext combined with the key. Remove the key and what remains is meaningless.

```
function crypto_erase(master_secret):
    // The client discards the master secret
    secure_erase(master_secret)

    // All records derived from this secret are now permanently
unreadable:
    //   - record identifiers cannot be recomputed
    //   - encryption keys cannot be rederived
    //   - ciphertexts on the server are indistinguishable from
random bytes
    //
    // No server-side action required.
```

The server does not need to participate in the erasure. The server does not need to find the records. The server does not need to know which records belonged to the user. The server holds ciphertexts indexed by opaque identifiers. After the client discards the master secret, those ciphertexts are noise. They can remain on the server indefinitely without constituting a privacy risk. Storage is cheap. Meaningless bytes occupy space but leak nothing.

This has a profound implication for regulatory compliance. An organization that stores user data exclusively in a blind database can respond to a GDPR erasure request by confirming that the user's key material has been discarded. The ciphertext may persist in backups for months or years—that is fine. Without the keys, the backup contains noise. The regulation requires that the data be erased. The data has been erased. The ciphertext has not, but the ciphertext without the key is not data in any meaningful sense. It is the same random bytes that a secure random number generator would produce.

There is a subtlety. Crypto-erasure works only if the key material is genuinely the sole path to the plaintext. If the plaintext was also logged somewhere in cleartext—in an application log, an error message, a debugging trace—then destroying the key does not destroy those copies. The blind database architecture addresses this by ensuring that plaintext never exists on the server. The client encrypts before upload. The server never sees plaintext. There is nothing to log. The only copies of the plaintext exist on client devices, under the client's control. Crypto-erasure, combined with client-side encryption, closes the loop.

---

ingfully better than 1/2. See M. Bellare and C. Namprempre, "Authenticated Encryption: Relations among Notions and Analysis of the Generic Composition Paradigm," ASIACRYPT 2000.

God Mode Elimination

Every conventional database system includes administrative access. The DBA can query any table. The root user can read any row. The cloud provider's infrastructure team can access the virtual machines that run the database. This is considered necessary and is, in traditional architectures, unavoidable. If the server holds the keys and the data, then anyone with sufficient access to the server holds them too.

The blind database eliminates god mode as a structural consequence of its design.

The DBA can log into the database server. The DBA can run queries. The DBA can select every record in every table. What the DBA gets back is record identifiers—opaque hashes—mapped to stored values—encrypted ciphertexts prefixed with random nonces. The DBA can read all of it. The DBA understands none of it.

There is no key to retrieve from a key management service. There is no HSM to query. There is no decryption function to invoke on the server. The keys were derived on the client from secrets the server never possessed. The DBA, the sysadmin, the cloud provider's infrastructure team, a state-level adversary who seizes the physical servers—all face the same barrier. They have ciphertext. They do not have keys. The ciphertext is encrypted under AES-256-GCM or ChaCha20-Poly1305. Under the assumption that these ciphers remain secure—an assumption shared by every major standards body and the weight of published cryptanalysis—breaking it without the key is not a practical operation.[5]

This is different from access control, and the difference is important. Access control says: "You are not authorized to read this data." It depends on the system enforcing the authorization. A misconfigured access control list, a privilege escalation vulnerability, a compromised authentication token—any of these bypasses access control. The data remains readable; the restriction on who may read it has been circumvented.

Operational blindness says: "This data is not readable." It does not depend on enforcement. It depends on mathematics. There is no privilege to escalate because there is no privilege that grants decryption capability. There is no access control list to misconfigure because the access control list is irrelevant—even the most privileged account on the system cannot decrypt records without keys that exist only on client devices.

Consider what this means for a subpoena. In a traditional architecture, a legal demand served on the database operator compels the operator to produce records. The operator has the records. The operator has the keys or the ability to decrypt. The operator complies. The records are disclosed.

In a blind database architecture, the same legal demand produces a different result. The operator can comply fully—here is every record in the database. What the compelling authority receives is record identifiers and ciphertexts. To obtain plaintext, the

---

5   AES-256-GCM provides IND-CPA (indistinguishability under chosen-plaintext attack) and INT-CTXT (integrity of ciphertext) security under standard assumptions. The best known attack on AES-256 is a biclique attack with complexity 2254.4, which is a negligible improvement over brute force. See A. Bogdanov, D. Khovratovich, and C. Rechberger, "Biclique Cryptanalysis of the Full AES," ASIACRYPT 2011. ChaCha20-Poly1305 has comparable security margins; see D. J. Bernstein, "ChaCha, a variant of Salsa20," 2008, and Y. Nir and A. Langley, RFC 8439, "ChaCha20 and Poly1305 for IETF Protocols," 2018.

authority must identify specific users and compel *them* to provide key material. This is not obstruction. The operator has disclosed everything it possesses. What the operator possesses is ciphertext. The architecture ensures that mass disclosure—give us every user's records in readable form—is computationally infeasible without the users' key material. Targeted disclosure—decrypt this specific user's records—requires targeting that specific user, which requires identifying them first, which the operator cannot do because the record identifiers are opaque.

The architecture does not prevent lawful investigation. It prevents fishing expeditions. An investigator who knows which user to target and can compel that user to provide credentials can access that user's data. An investigator who wants to scan the entire database looking for persons of interest cannot. This is the same distinction drawn in Chapter 1 between targeted investigation and mass surveillance, enforced by mathematics rather than policy.

Composition: The User Service on a Blind Database

Chapter 3 described an anonymous identity architecture—the User Service that issues unlinkable, site-specific tokens so that users can authenticate without being tracked across sites. That architecture has a vulnerability noted at the time: the User Service holds a database of identity mappings. The operator of the User Service could, in a traditional architecture, read those mappings. The operator could see which users have accounts on which sites. The operator could build a surveillance graph from the data it stores.

If the User Service stores its identity mappings in a blind database, the operator cannot read which users have accounts on which sites.

The construction is direct. When a user establishes a mapping between their identity and a site-specific token, the client derives a record identifier from the user's master secret and the site identifier:

```
record_id = HASH(master_secret, "identity_mapping", site_id)
key = KDF(master_secret, record_id, "encrypt")
ciphertext = AEAD_encrypt(key, nonce, identity_mapping_payload)
server.store(record_id, nonce || ciphertext)
```

The User Service stores the record. The User Service cannot read the record. The User Service cannot determine which site the mapping pertains to. The User Service cannot correlate mappings across sites because the record identifiers are derived from master secrets it does not hold. Two records belonging to the same user look no more related than two records belonging to different users.

A breach of the User Service now yields encrypted blobs. A subpoena yields encrypted blobs. An acquisition by a hostile entity yields encrypted blobs. In all cases, the identity mappings remain confidential because the keys that protect them never existed on the server.

This is what composition looks like in this architecture. The identity layer from

Chapter 3 provides unlinkable authentication. The blind database from this chapter provides unreadable storage. Neither alone achieves the full privacy goal. Together, they close each other's gaps. The anonymous identity layer prevents cross-site tracking during authentication. The blind database prevents surveillance of stored identity mappings. The combination ensures that the User Service facilitates identity without accumulating knowledge about the identities it facilitates.

Prior Art and Design Rationale

Prior systems that tried to protect stored data from the server failed in ways that shaped this architecture's design choices.

CryptDB, developed at MIT, pioneered the idea of running queries over encrypted data.[6] The server could perform SQL operations—comparisons, joins, ordering—on ciphertexts, using property-preserving encryption (PPE) schemes that deliberately leak enough mathematical structure for the operations to work. The appeal was obvious: keep your existing database, keep your existing queries, just encrypt everything. The problem was that the deliberate leakage turned out to be far more revealing than the designers anticipated. Subsequent analysis demonstrated that an attacker with access to the encrypted database and modest auxiliary information could reconstruct large portions of the plaintext.[7] The lesson is direct: encryption that preserves queryable properties preserves attackable properties. The blind database avoids this entirely by eliminating server-side queries. There is nothing to preserve because there are no operations to support.

Mylar, also from MIT, extended the approach to web applications—end-to-end encryption with the server mediating encrypted content between users.[8] The architecture was ambitious: users could share encrypted documents, and the server would facilitate the sharing without reading the contents. Grubbs, Ristenpart, and others subsequently published an attack showing that a malicious server—the exact threat model Mylar was supposed to defend against—could recover plaintext by manipulating the key-sharing protocol.[9] The system's complexity created attack surface. The blind database takes the opposite approach: the server has no role in key distribution, no role in mediating shared access, and therefore no mechanism through which a malicious server can manipulate the cryptographic protocol.

Keybase came closest to the blind database's philosophy before Zoom acquired it in

6   R. Popa, C. Redfield, N. Zeldovich, and H. Balakrishnan, "CryptDB: Protecting Confidentiality with Encrypted Query Processing," SOSP 2011.

7   M. Naveed, S. Kamara, and C. Wright, "Inference Attacks on Property-Preserving Encrypted Databases," CCS 2015. Demonstrated that order-preserving and deterministic encryption schemes leak enough structure to recover plaintext from encrypted columns using publicly available auxiliary data.

8   R. Popa, E. Stark, J. Helfer, S. Valdez, N. Zeldovich, M. Kaashoek, and H. Balakrishnan, "Building Web Applications on Top of Encrypted Data Using Mylar," NSDI 2014.

9   P. Grubbs, R. McPherson, M. Naveed, T. Ristenpart, and V. Shmatikov, "Breaking Web Applications Built On Top of Encrypted Data," CCS 2016. Showed that a malicious server operator—the primary threat Mylar was designed to resist—could recover plaintext by exploiting the multi-key search mechanism.

2020.[10] Keybase provided client-side encryption tied to publicly verifiable social identities—you could encrypt a message to someone's Twitter handle, and the encryption happened entirely on your device. The key insight Keybase validated was that ordinary users would accept client-side encryption if the application handled key management transparently. What Keybase did not do was build a general-purpose blind storage layer. It was an application, not an architecture. The blind database is the storage primitive that an application like Keybase would build on.

The **Signal Protocol's Sealed Sender** feature addresses a different but related problem: metadata.[11] Standard encrypted messaging protects message content but reveals sender and recipient to the server. Sealed Sender encrypts the sender's identity so the server delivers messages without knowing who sent them. This is metadata reduction in production, at scale, used by hundreds of millions of people. It demonstrates that practical systems can reduce what the server learns beyond just content. The blind database's operational blindness is a stronger version of the same impulse applied to storage rather than messaging—the server knows neither the content nor the meaningful identity of the records it holds.

Oblivious RAM (ORAM) is the theoretical answer to access pattern leakage—the one category of information the blind database openly acknowledges it does not protect.[12] ORAM protocols allow a client to read and write to remote storage without the server learning which locations were accessed. The constructions are mathematically rigorous and practically devastating. The best schemes impose logarithmic overhead per access, requiring $O(\log N)$ actual operations per read or write and continuous server-side reshuffling. For a billion-record database, each access triggers dozens of operations, most of them decoys. This is why ORAM remains largely academic despite decades of research. The blind database accepts access pattern leakage as a known tradeoff rather than paying a cost that would make the system unusable at scale.

The design rationale comes down to one choice: where does the complexity live? CryptDB and Mylar tried to keep the server smart—to preserve server-side functionality while adding encryption. Both failed because a smart server is an attackable server. ORAM tries to make the server oblivious through protocol machinery, and succeeds theoretically at a cost that makes deployment impractical. The blind database puts the work on the client. The client derives keys, encrypts, decrypts, maintains its own indexes, and handles its own search. The server is a durable key-value store. Nothing more.

What you gain is a small attack surface, simple security analysis, and an architecture whose guarantees follow from standard cryptographic assumptions rather than novel constructions. What you give up is server-side intelligence—no queries, no search, no

---

10   Keybase, Inc. Acquired by Zoom Video Communications, May 2020. Keybase's client-side encryption architecture is described in its published protocol documentation at https://book.keybase.io.

11   Joshua Lund, "Technology Preview: Sealed Sender for Signal," Signal Blog, October 29, 2018. Describes the cryptographic mechanism by which Signal hides the sender's identity from the server during message delivery.

12   O. Goldreich and R. Ostrovsky, "Software Protection and Simulation on Oblivious RAMs," Journal of the ACM 43(3), 1996, pp. 431-473. The foundational result establishing that any RAM program can be simulated obliviously with $O(\log^3 N)$ overhead, later improved to $O(\log^2 N)$ and $O(\log N)$ by subsequent work.

aggregation, no joins. For a general-purpose analytics platform, that is a fatal limitation. For a system whose purpose is to store data that belongs to users and should be readable only by users, it is the point.

What This Does Not Protect Against

The blind database is a strong construction within a defined scope. Honesty about the boundaries of that scope is as important as the construction itself. There are four categories of threat that the blind database does not address.

Client compromise. The entire security model depends on the client holding secrets the server does not possess. If the client is compromised—through malware, a stolen device, a phishing attack that captures the master secret—the attacker obtains the same key material the legitimate user holds. The attacker can derive record identifiers, request ciphertexts from the server, derive decryption keys, and read every record the user has stored. The blind database protects data from the server. It does not protect data from an attacker who has become the client.

This is not a flaw in the architecture. It is a boundary condition. No storage encryption scheme protects against compromise of the key holder. A bank vault does not protect against someone who has the combination. The blind database places the user's data under the user's control, which means the user's security posture—device security, credential hygiene, resistance to social engineering—becomes part of the system's overall security. This is a transfer of responsibility, not an elimination of risk.

Key loss and the recovery problem. If the user loses the master secret and has no recovery mechanism, the data is gone. The encryption is working as designed—without the key, the ciphertext is noise. But the user who has lost their password, lost their device, or otherwise lost access to their key material has also lost access to their data. Permanently.

The security levels described earlier provide partial mitigation. Recoverable records survive password changes because their derivation does not depend on the password. But if the user loses access to their username and server salt—if they forget their credentials entirely—even recoverable records become inaccessible. The unrecoverable level is, by design, unrecoverable. There is no backdoor, no recovery key held by the operator, no secret override. That is the point. It is also the risk.

Applications built on a blind database must design recovery paths carefully. Multi-device key synchronization, social recovery schemes (where trusted contacts each hold a share of the key material), paper backup keys—these are application-level solutions to a problem the architecture intentionally creates. The architecture chooses to make data inaccessible without the key rather than provide a server-side recovery mechanism that would reintroduce god mode. Recovery is the user's responsibility. If the user fails at it, the data is lost.

Access pattern leakage. The server cannot read the contents of records. The server can observe which record identifiers are accessed and when. This is metadata, and metadata carries information.

If the server observes that record identifier X is accessed every weekday at 9:00 AM from the same IP address, the server learns something about the user's habits. If record identifier X is accessed immediately after a specific external event—a news story, a market movement, a political announcement—the server can correlate the access with the event. If record identifiers X, Y, and Z are always accessed together, the server can infer that they are related, even though it cannot read their contents.

These are real leakages. For most threat models, they are secondary to content disclosure—knowing that someone accessed a record at 9:00 AM is less damaging than knowing the record contains a medical diagnosis. But for high-threat-model scenarios—journalists protecting sources, dissidents evading surveillance, whistleblowers communicating with investigators—access pattern leakage can be significant.

Mitigations exist. Oblivious RAM (ORAM) protocols allow clients to access records without revealing which records they accessed, by mixing real accesses with decoy accesses and reshuffling storage. The cost is substantial—typically a 10x to 100x overhead in both bandwidth and latency. Padding requests to uniform sizes prevents the server from distinguishing request types by size. Cover traffic—accessing records at random intervals regardless of need—obscures timing patterns. Each mitigation adds cost. For most applications, the content protection provided by the base architecture is sufficient. For high-sensitivity applications, the mitigations are available and the costs are quantifiable.

Denial of service. The server is trusted for availability. If the server refuses to return records, the client cannot access its data. The server cannot read the data, but the server can withhold it. This is a fundamental limitation of any architecture that uses a remote server for storage: the server can always choose not to serve.

The blind database does not protect against an operator who decides to hold data hostage, a government that orders the server shut down, or an infrastructure failure that makes the server unreachable. These are availability threats, not confidentiality threats. The architecture is designed to protect confidentiality. Availability requires different mechanisms: replication across independent operators, client-side caching of critical records, decentralized storage protocols. These are complementary to the blind database, not part of it.

The four limitations share a characteristic: none of them are unique to the blind database. Client compromise threatens any system where users hold secrets. Key loss threatens any system where users manage their own keys. Access pattern leakage affects any client-server system where the server handles requests. Denial of service affects any system that depends on remote infrastructure. The blind database does not introduce these problems. It inherits them from the operational environment in which any real system must function.

What the blind database does is eliminate the problems that traditional databases introduce: server-side content disclosure, structural leakage from property-preserving encryption, god mode access, and the operational impossibility of complete data deletion. Within its scope, the architecture provides genuine, mathematically grounded protection. Outside its scope, the threats remain and must be addressed by other means. The honest accounting of both is the basis for informed engineering decisions.

Recommended Cryptographic Primitives

The architecture is agnostic to specific algorithms as long as they satisfy the required security properties. The following choices reflect current best practice:

Function	Recommended Primitive	Notes
Record ID hash	SHA-256	Collision-resistant, widely available, fast
Key derivation	HKDF-SHA256 (RFC 5869)	Extract-then-expand; handles non-uniform input
Symmetric encryption	AES-256-GCM or ChaCha20-Poly1305	Both are AEAD; ChaCha20 preferred on devices without AES-NI
Nonce generation	Cryptographic RNG	192-bit (24-byte) nonces for XChaCha20; 96-bit for AES-GCM

libsodium provides constant-time, audited implementations of all of these across every major platform. Using libsodium (or its bindings—sodium in JavaScript, pynacl in Python, sodiumoxide in Rust) avoids the most common implementation pitfalls: non-constant-time comparisons, nonce reuse, improper key handling, and side-channel vulnerabilities in software AES implementations.

Two implementation notes. First, all comparisons of hashes, MACs, and ciphertexts must be constant-time. A comparison that short-circuits on the first differing byte leaks information about the compared values through timing. libsodium's sodium_memcmp handles this. Language-level equality operators do not. Second, nonces must never be reused with the same key. For AES-256-GCM with its 96-bit nonce, the birthday bound limits safe usage to approximately 2^{32} encryptions per key before the probability of nonce collision becomes non-negligible. For XChaCha20-Poly1305 with its 192-bit nonce, random nonce generation is safe for a practically unlimited number of encryptions. If record update frequency is high, the larger nonce space is the safer choice.

Summary

The blind database is not a novel cryptographic construction. Client-side encryption is well understood. Key derivation functions have been standardized for decades. AEAD ciphers are the default in modern protocol design. The individual components are unremarkable.

What is interesting is the architectural decision to compose them in a way that eliminates server-side intelligence entirely. The server is not a database in the traditional sense. It is a key-value store that makes no assumptions about and has no access to the meaning of what it stores. This is a deliberate retreat from the trend of the past forty years, which has been to make servers smarter, more capable, more powerful in their ability to process the data they hold.

That trend made sense when the primary concern was functionality. It makes less sense when the primary concern is privacy. Every capability the server gains is a capability that can be exploited by an attacker, compelled by a government, or abused by an insider. The blind database asks: what is the minimum the server must know to provide the service? The answer, for storage, is nothing. The server must be available. The server must be durable. The server must be fast enough. The server does not need to understand what it stores. The understanding can live entirely on the client, where it is protected by keys the server never holds.

The constraints this imposes on application design are real. Server-side search is gone. Server-side aggregation is gone. Ad-hoc queries across the full dataset are gone. These are genuine losses. But the question is not whether the losses exist. The question is whether the losses are acceptable given what is gained. For applications that store user-owned data—medical records, financial documents, personal messages, identity mappings, credentials—the tradeoff is straightforward. The user needs storage and retrieval. The user does not need the server to search their records. The user's client can search locally. The server's inability to search is the server's inability to surveil. The constraint is the protection.

The previous chapter asked what a solution must achieve. This chapter has presented one that achieves it. The server stores data it cannot read, indexed by identifiers it cannot interpret, encrypted under keys it cannot derive. Deletion is key destruction. God mode is structurally absent. The operator's blindness is not a bug to be patched or a limitation to be worked around. It is the architecture working as intended.

Identity is now private. Storage is now blind. The next problem is accountability: how do you distinguish a human from a bot when the identity system is anonymous and the database cannot be inspected? The next chapter examines why this is difficult, and the chapter after that presents the Proof of Human architecture.

CHAPTER 6

The Accountability Problem

An online identity costs nothing to create and nothing to replace.

The previous two chapters solved a storage problem: how to keep user data on a server without the server being able to read it. The cryptographically blind database stores ciphertext it cannot decrypt, indexed by keys it cannot derive. The operator's blindness is the security property. That architecture protects data at rest.

It does nothing about the entity interacting with the system.

A blind database that cannot identify its users cannot distinguish a human from a bot. It cannot distinguish one human from the same human operating fifty accounts. It cannot distinguish a legitimate user from a synthetic identity manufactured to defraud other users. The storage architecture is necessary but insufficient. The trust model is incomplete without a mechanism for accountability—a way to establish that the entity on the other end of an interaction is singular, human, and has something to lose.

This chapter examines why that mechanism does not yet exist. Not because no one has tried, but because every attempt has answered the wrong question.

The Scale of Automated Abuse

The problem begins with economics. Creating an online identity costs nothing. Creating a thousand costs nothing multiplied by a thousand, which is still nothing. The marginal cost of an additional fake account on any major platform is zero in terms of resources and zero in terms of consequence. When an account is banned, the operator creates another. The ban lands on a mask, not a face.

The asymmetry is fundamental. A platform that bans an account bears the cost of detection, investigation, and enforcement. The operator who created the account bears no cost at all. The next account is free. The platform's enforcement cost scales linearly with the number of fake accounts. The attacker's creation cost is effectively zero. In any sustained conflict where one side's costs scale and the other's do not, the outcome is determined before the conflict begins.

The scale is difficult to overstate. Estimates of automated account activity range from single digits (platform self-reports) to thirty percent or higher (independent analyses), and the gap between these estimates itself illustrates how contested the measurement is. The exact figure matters less than the structural observation: when identity is free and disposable, the equilibrium quantity of fake identities is limited only by the attacker's motivation and the platform's detection capacity. Motivation is high. Detection capacity is demonstrably insufficient.

Bot networks operate at industrial scale. A single operator can manage thousands of accounts simultaneously, each with a generated profile photo, a plausible posting history, and behavioral patterns that mimic human activity closely enough to evade automated detection. These accounts are deployed for spam, for market manipulation, for political influence operations, for review fraud, for social engineering attacks, for any purpose where the appearance of human consensus or human identity has economic value.

Sybil attacks—named after the case study of a person with multiple identities—exploit the assumption that each account represents a distinct individual. Voting systems, reputation systems, consensus mechanisms, review platforms: all assume that participants are who they claim to be, or at minimum that each participant is a separate entity. When one operator controls thousands of identities, these systems are compromised at their foundation. The vote is stuffed. The consensus is manufactured. The reviews are fiction.

The disposability of identity is the core vulnerability. Blocking accomplishes nothing when the entity behind a blocked account can instantiate a replacement in seconds. Reporting accomplishes nothing when the report removes a mask from someone wearing an infinite supply. Every enforcement action targets the identity rather than the person. The person is untouched. The parade of disposable facades continues indefinitely.

This would be concerning enough if the accounts were text-only. Voice synthesis has made it worse. Current voice synthesis systems can produce convincing clones from as little as thirty seconds of sample audio—extracted from a social media video, a voicemail greeting, a conference recording. Family members report difficulty distinguishing the clone from the original. The Federal Trade Commission has documented billions in losses from imposter scams, and the figure climbs as the synthesis tools become cheaper, faster, and more accessible.

Video synthesis follows the same trajectory. A person's face and voice can be rendered in real-time video, saying things the person never said, endorsing products the person has never used. The synthetic likeness is deployed to defraud strangers who trust the face. When the fraud is reported and the content removed, the operator uploads it again from a new account. The cycle continues until the reporter exhausts themselves.

The catch compounds the problem. Answering a scam call provides audio that can be cloned for future scams. Appearing on video provides footage for future deepfakes. Existing online creates the raw material for exploitation, and withdrawal from online interaction—the only technically safe response—means abandoning the communication infrastructure that modern life depends on.

The question that emerges from this landscape is straightforward: how do you verify that the entity on the other end of an interaction is a real, singular human being? The question has been asked before. The answers have failed, one after another, in ways that are instructive.

CAPTCHA: Training Its Own Replacement

CAPTCHAs were designed precisely to distinguish humans from machines. The Completely Automated Public Turing test to tell Computers and Humans Apart presented challenges that were easy for humans and hard for software: distorted letters, image grids, puzzle-solving tasks. The difficulty curve was calibrated to exclude automated systems while admitting human users with only minor friction.

For a period, the tests worked. Then the same human attempts at solving CAPTCHAs became training data for machine learning systems. Every time a human identified a traffic light in a grid of photographs, that selection became a labeled training example. The aggregate of millions of human solutions taught computer vision systems to recognize exactly the objects that CAPTCHAs used as challenges. The test for humanity generated the training set for its obsolescence.

Today, artificial intelligence completes CAPTCHA challenges faster and more accurately than humans. The irony is structural, not incidental. The mechanism by which CAPTCHAs verified humanity—presenting tasks that required human perception—was the mechanism by which they produced the data that made human perception unnecessary. The system trained its own replacement.

Websites still deploy CAPTCHAs because the alternatives are worse and because CAPTCHAs raise the cost of automated attacks from zero to trivially above zero. The gates they guard are open. The mechanism survives because of institutional inertia, not because it accomplishes its stated purpose.

The progression illustrates a general principle. Any test of humanity that can be expressed as a task will eventually be performed better by machines than by humans. The task itself becomes the training objective. The harder the CAPTCHA, the more valuable the training signal when a human solves it. The mechanism contains the seed of its own defeat. This is not a failure of CAPTCHA engineering. It is a consequence of defining humanity as task performance in a world where task performance is precisely what machine learning systems optimize.

Biometrics: Permanence as Vulnerability

Biometric verification was proposed as an unforgeable alternative. Fingerprints, facial geometry, voice patterns, iris scans: physical characteristics that are unique to each individual and, in theory, impossible to replicate. The premise held only until replication became feasible.

Fingerprints can be lifted from surfaces and cast in silicone. The attack is not hypothetical; it has been demonstrated repeatedly in both research settings and criminal investigations. Facial recognition can be defeated by masks, by photographs, by three-dimensional prints of a target face. Voice cloning, as noted, requires only thirty seconds of sample audio. Iris scans can be defeated by high-resolution photographs of the target's eye.

Each biometric modality has a corresponding attack vector, and the cost of executing the attack is consistently lower than the cost of deploying the biometric. This is not a temporary state of affairs awaiting better biometric technology. It is a structural asymmetry: biometrics are observable physical properties, and observable properties can be captured and replayed.

The deeper problem is permanence. A password, when compromised, can be changed. A fingerprint cannot. Once a biometric is compromised—through a database breach, through physical capture, through the thirty seconds of video that enables voice cloning—the user cannot issue themselves a new one. The compromise is permanent. A single breach exposes the user for life.

This makes biometric databases uniquely dangerous. A breach of a password database is serious but recoverable: users change their passwords. A breach of a biometric database is irreversible. The fingerprints, voiceprints, and facial geometry data in that database cannot be rotated, reissued, or replaced. Every user in the breached database has had an immutable credential permanently compromised.

The permanence that makes biometrics seem reliable—the fingerprint is always your fingerprint—is the property that makes them catastrophically vulnerable. Permanence means no recovery from compromise. No recovery from compromise means a single failure is terminal.

Reputation Systems: Measuring Transmissibility, Not Trust

Reputation systems attempt to infer trustworthiness from behavioral history. Users accumulate scores based on their interactions. High-scoring users are trusted. Low-scoring users are suspect. New users face suspicion until they accumulate enough positive interactions to establish standing. The approach seems reasonable. It fails for reasons that are structural rather than incidental.

Reputation systems measure success within a selection environment. They do not measure the underlying property they claim to represent. The distinction matters.

Content spreads on social platforms through dynamics that have nothing to do with accuracy or reliability. High-status accounts are copied because they are high-status, regardless of what they say. Content that has already gained attention attracts more attention, regardless of whether it deserves it. Simple, emotionally resonant messages outcompete nuanced analysis because simplicity and emotion transmit more effectively than complexity and equanimity. These are transmission biases—properties of the selection environment rather than properties of the content being selected.

The result is predictable. Reputation scores reflect success at gaming the selection environment, not underlying trustworthiness. The dynamic is a specific instance of a broader phenomenon: when a metric becomes a target, it ceases to be a good metric. Reputation scores become targets the moment they carry consequences, and they carry consequences by design—that is their purpose.

As the gap between what earns reputation and what deserves reputation widens, quality contributors face a choice: optimize for the broken metric or exit. Most exit. The system equilibrates at the quality level of those willing to play the game, which is the quality level of those with incentives to manipulate.

The mechanism is identical to adverse selection in markets. Producing genuine trustworthiness is expensive: it requires consistent good-faith behavior over time. Manufacturing the appearance of trustworthiness is cheap: it requires gaming the scoring algorithm. When the scoring system cannot distinguish the genuine article from the manufactured appearance, cheap signals flood the market. Producers of the genuine article face higher costs for an outcome indistinguishable from the cheap version. Rationally, they reduce their investment or exit. The market settles at the quality level of the manipulators.

Reputation systems do not fail because bad actors exploit them. Reputation systems fail because the selection environment makes exploitation the dominant strategy. The physics is the problem. No amount of algorithmic refinement fixes a system where the metric being optimized is structurally decoupled from the property being measured.

Economic Stake: Testing Wealth, Not Humanity

Economic stake approaches attempt to create accountability through financial commitment. If creating an account costs money, the reasoning goes, spammers cannot afford to create accounts at scale. The mechanism prices out abuse by making abuse expensive.

The mechanism also prices out poverty.

A financial barrier that excludes bad actors based on willingness to pay simultaneously excludes legitimate users based on ability to pay. A ten-dollar account creation fee is trivial for a well-funded bot operator who can absorb the cost across a high-volume fraud operation. The same fee is prohibitive for a user in a developing economy where ten dollars represents a day's wages.

The system selects for wealth rather than humanity. Those with resources can create many accounts and treat the cost as overhead. Those without resources cannot create any. The barrier is regressive: it imposes the heaviest burden on those least able to bear it while posing the least obstacle to those with the most resources.

Economic stake tests economic status. It does not test human status, singular identity, or accountability. A well-funded attacker who pays the fee is no more accountable than an attacker who does not, because the payment creates no link between the account and a persistent identity. The money is spent. The account, if banned, is gone. The attacker pays again. The cost is absorbed. Nothing has been proven except the ability to spend money.

Knowledge-Based Verification: Secrets in the Breach Era

Knowledge-based verification relies on secrets that only the legitimate user should know. The name of your first pet. The street you grew up on. Your mother's maiden name. These questions were designed in an era when personal information was genuinely personal—scattered across paper records in filing cabinets that no one would bother to search.

The era ended. The questions now appear as data fields in breach after breach, aggregated and sold in bulk to anyone interested. Social Security numbers, purchase histories, security question answers: all catalogued and available for less than the cost of a meal. The secret that was once told to no one is now in a database alongside your date of birth, your home address, and the answers to every security question you have ever set.

Knowledge-based verification fails because its foundational assumption—that certain personal information is secret—is empirically false. The assumption was reasonable when it was made. It is not reasonable now. The breach era has converted personal secrets into public data. Any verification mechanism that depends on the secrecy of personal information depends on a condition that no longer holds.

The failure is not limited to traditional security questions. Any knowledge-based approach faces the same structural problem. Shared secrets, personal details, private experiences: all are vulnerable to extraction, aggregation, and sale. The economic incentive to collect and monetize personal information is enormous and the defenses against it are consistently inadequate. The secrets were never secret in any robust sense. They were merely obscure, and obscurity is not a security property—it is a temporary condition that erodes under sustained economic pressure.

Hardware Tokens: Proving Possession, Not Humanity

Hardware tokens shift the trust anchor from knowledge to possession. A physical device generates time-sensitive codes or provides cryptographic attestation that the specific device is present. This works for proving device possession. It does not work for proving humanity.

A bot can operate a hardware token as easily as a human can. The token attests that the device is present. It does not attest that a human is operating the device. A script that reads a hardware token's output and submits it to an authentication endpoint is using the token exactly as designed. The proof of device access is real. The proof of humanity is absent.

Hardware tokens solve a different problem—they protect against remote credential theft by requiring physical proximity to the device. This is a genuine security improvement for authentication. It is orthogonal to the question of whether the entity authenticating is human.

AI Fingerprinting and Watermarking: Identifying Tools, Not Accountability

The latest proposed solution is AI fingerprinting. If synthetic content is the concern, the reasoning goes, then identifying synthetic content is the answer. Watermark the outputs of AI systems. Detect the fingerprints that reveal machine generation. Label everything so users know what is real and what is synthetic.

The proposal addresses the wrong problem.

When a person's face appears in a fraudulent video, the harm is the fraud. A fraudulent video created by a human artist, frame by frame, would be equally harmful. A fraudulent video composited from existing footage without any AI involvement would be equally harmful. The tool used to produce the fraud is irrelevant to the harm caused by the fraud. The harm is the deception, the exploitation, the absence of accountability for the person who created and deployed it.

AI fingerprinting identifies the tool. It provides no information about accountability. A synthetic video with a perfect AI watermark is no more and no less harmful than an identical synthetic video without one. The watermark tells you what software was used. It does not tell you who used it, whether they had a right to use the likeness they synthesized, or whether there exists any mechanism to hold them accountable.

The approach is orthogonal to the problem. It feels like action while addressing nothing. It is the equivalent of responding to mail fraud by requiring all printers to embed invisible serial numbers in their output. Knowing which printer produced a document does not identify the person who wrote the fraudulent content, does not create accountability for the fraud, and does not prevent the next fraud from being committed on a different printer.

The Pattern Across Failures

The failed approaches share a structural deficiency. Each addresses a proxy variable rather than the actual problem.

The approaches are not merely inadequate today. They are on trajectories that make them more inadequate over time. Each year, machines solve puzzles better, biometrics are replicated more cheaply, breaches expose more secrets, and bot networks manufacture reputation more convincingly. The gap between proxy and reality widens as attack capabilities improve.

The failure is not a matter of insufficient engineering effort. These are not problems that better implementations will solve. The approaches fail because they measure the wrong thing. No amount of refinement to a CAPTCHA system changes the fact that it tests task performance rather than humanity. No improvement to a biometric scanner changes the fact that it reads observable physical properties that can be captured and replayed. The deficiency is in the question being asked, not in the precision of the answer.

The Actual Question

The question that matters has three parts.

Is the entity singular? Does this identity represent one person, or is it one of thousands controlled by a single operator? Singularity means one persistent identity per person. Not a swarm of disposable accounts. Not a fresh mask for every interaction. One identity that persists across time and whose history follows the person who holds it.

Is the entity human? Is this a biological person, or is it a script, a bot, a language model generating plausible text? Humanity in this context is not a philosophical question about consciousness. It is a practical question about whether there exists a biological person whose intentions and decisions drive the actions taken under this identity.

Does the entity have stake? Does the identity cost something to the person holding it, such that losing it represents a real consequence? An identity with no cost is an identity with no accountability. The entity must have something to lose—not money, but the identity itself. If the identity is expensive to establish and cannot be trivially replaced, then actions taken under that identity carry consequence. If the identity is disposable, consequence is impossible. Stake is what converts identity from a label into a commitment. Without it, banning an account is a meaningless gesture—the operator discards the banned identity and creates a new one at no cost. With it, losing an identity means losing whatever investment went into establishing it, which changes the calculus of abuse from costless to consequential.

These three properties—singularity, humanity, and stake—are the actual requirements. Every failed approach addresses at most one, and most address none.

CAPTCHAs attempt humanity verification. They do not establish singularity or stake. Even if CAPTCHAs worked, a human operator managing a thousand accounts would pass a thousand CAPTCHAs and retain a thousand disposable identities with no accountability.

Biometrics attempt singularity through physical uniqueness. They fail at the implementation level (replication attacks) and create catastrophic risk at the architectural level (permanent compromise). They do not establish stake because biometric verification, once passed, does not create ongoing consequence for the identity.

Reputation systems attempt to create stake through accumulated history. They fail because the metric being accumulated is decoupled from the property being measured, and because reputation can be manufactured at scale through the same bot networks the system is supposed to exclude.

Economic barriers attempt to create stake through financial cost. They fail because the cost falls on a dimension—wealth—that is uncorrelated with legitimacy and negatively correlated with equitable access.

Hardware tokens and AI fingerprints do not attempt any of the three properties. They answer different questions entirely.

Requirements for a Solution

The analysis of failed approaches defines the constraints that a working solution must satisfy. These constraints are not aspirational. They are the conditions required by the problem structure.

Verify humanity without surrendering identity. The mechanism must confirm that a biological human exists behind the identity without requiring that human to disclose who they are. Biometrics fail this requirement because they bind identity to the physical body and create surveillance infrastructure. The solution must prove "a human" without proving "which human."

Establish singularity without central registration. The mechanism must ensure one identity per person without requiring a central authority that maintains a registry of all humans and their corresponding identities. Centralized registries are surveillance infrastructure by definition. They create a single point of compromise that maps every person to every identity. The solution must enforce singularity through a mechanism that no single entity can observe or control.

Create stake without testing wealth. The identity must be costly to obtain and expensive to replace, but the cost cannot be financial. Financial cost selects for wealth. The cost must be temporal, procedural, or structural—something that is expensive in a way that money cannot shortcut. The identity must take time and effort to establish, such that losing it is a genuine consequence regardless of the holder's financial resources.

Resist the attacks that defeated predecessors. The mechanism cannot depend on secrets that can be breached (eliminating knowledge-based approaches). It cannot depend on physical characteristics that can be captured and replayed (eliminating biometrics). It cannot depend on puzzles that machines will learn to solve (eliminating CAPTCHAs). It cannot depend on device possession that bots can replicate (eliminating hardware tokens). It cannot depend on behavioral patterns that can be manufactured at scale (eliminating reputation systems).

Function without technical sophistication from the user. The mechanism must work for everyone, not just people with technical expertise. A system that requires understanding of cryptographic protocols to use is a system that excludes the population most vulnerable to the attacks it is supposed to prevent.

Degrade gracefully under attack. When the mechanism is attacked—and it will be attacked—the failure mode must be denial of service to the attacker, not compromise of legitimate users. A system where attacks degrade the attacker's position without affecting legitimate participants has the correct failure mode. A system where attacks compromise the integrity of all participants has the wrong one.

Preserve privacy as a structural property. The mechanism must not create a new surveillance infrastructure in the process of solving the accountability problem. Trading privacy for accountability is not a solution; it is a different problem. The system must prove that a human exists, that the human is singular, and that the human has stake—and it must accomplish all three without learning or storing anything that identifies the human behind the identity. This is the hardest constraint, because accountability and privacy appear to be in tension. Every intuitive approach to accountability—registries, identity documents, biometric databases—works by creating a record that links actions to persons. That link is simultaneously the accountability mechanism and the surveillance mechanism. Any solution that satisfies this constraint must find a way to create consequence without creating linkage. That such a thing is possible is not obvious. That it is necessary is clear from the failures catalogued in this chapter.

No single point of trust. The mechanism must not depend on any single entity—no single company, no single government, no single server—to function honestly or remain uncompromised. Any architecture that requires trusting a single party to verify humanity has created a chokepoint that can be corrupted, coerced, or compromised. The verification must be distributed in a way that prevents any individual participant from controlling, observing, or subverting the process.

These requirements are demanding. They rule out every existing approach to human verification. They rule out biometric databases, identity registries, financial barriers, reputation scores, and challenge-response tests. They rule out anything that creates a mapping between real-world identity and online identity, because that mapping is the surveillance infrastructure that the privacy architecture exists to prevent.

They also describe something that is architecturally achievable. The next chapter presents a proof-of-human mechanism that satisfies all of them—a system that verifies humanity, enforces singularity, and creates stake without requiring the user to reveal who they are, without requiring a central authority to maintain a registry, and without creating any data structure that an attacker or an operator could use to de-anonymize participants.

The accountability problem is not that we cannot build systems with accountability. The problem is that every system built so far has answered the wrong question, tested the wrong property, or created a surveillance liability that undermines the privacy it was supposed to protect. The right question has three words: singular, human, stake. The right answer must address all three without compromising any of the privacy guarantees that the preceding chapters established.

CHAPTER 7

Proof of Human Architecture

Proving you are human should not require proving who you are.

The previous chapter catalogued a graveyard of approaches to human verification. CAPTCHAs trained the systems they were designed to exclude. Biometrics created permanent vulnerabilities from immutable credentials. Reputation systems measured transmissibility rather than trustworthiness. Economic barriers tested wealth rather than humanity. Each approach answered the wrong question. The right question has three parts: Is the entity singular? Is the entity human? Does the entity have stake?

This chapter presents an architecture that answers all three without creating a surveillance infrastructure in the process. The mechanism is a composite score—a single number between zero and one—that accumulates evidence of humanity from multiple independent signals, stores cryptographic proofs rather than raw data, and travels with the user's anonymous identity without revealing who the user is. The architecture does not attempt to achieve certainty. It achieves cost. Specifically, it makes forging a high score so expensive that the economics of large-scale abuse collapse.

The Logarithmic Effort Scale

The humanness score operates on a scale from 0.0 to 1.0. No combination of signals ever reaches 1.0, because certainty about human identity is not achievable and designing a system that claims otherwise would be dishonest. The score is asymptotic. It approaches one but never arrives.

The critical property of the scale is not the number itself but the cost function behind it. Each increment in score requires roughly an order of magnitude more effort to forge than the previous increment.[1] A score of 0.1 represents approximately ten dollars of effort to synthesize falsely. A score of 0.2 represents approximately one hundred dollars. A score of 0.3 represents approximately one thousand. The progression continues:

Score	Approximate Cost to Forge
0.0	Free
0.1	~$10
0.2	~$100

---

1   The logarithmic cost model is a design target, not a formally proven bound. The relationship between score increments and forgery cost depends on the independence of signal sources and the current economics of identity fabrication. The specific dollar figures are illustrative calibration points derived from market surveys of identity-forgery services, not from a mathematical proof.

0.3	~$1,000
0.4	~$10,000
0.5	~$100,000
0.6+	~$1,000,000+

Money is a proxy here, not the mechanism. The system does not charge fees. The dollar figures are calibration targets illustrating the logarithmic structure, not empirical measurements of specific attack costs.[2] They represent the approximate labor, infrastructure, and time required to fabricate the underlying signals convincingly. An attacker forging a score of 0.3 needs a verified email address, a verified phone number, a payment instrument linked to a financial identity, a postal address that receives mail, and enough behavioral history to pass pattern analysis. Each signal adds cost. The cost compounds because the signals are independent—forging one does not help forge the others.

The logarithmic structure means that early gains are cheap and later gains are prohibitively expensive. This is deliberate. A new user should be able to reach a useful score quickly—email verification, phone verification, a few weeks of normal activity. Getting from 0.15 to 0.20 should be straightforward for a legitimate user and moderately expensive for an attacker. Getting from 0.45 to 0.50 should be effortless for a legitimate user who has been active for months and ruinously expensive for an attacker who must synthesize months of consistent behavioral patterns across multiple independent signal types.

The practical consequence is that sites can set score thresholds calibrated to their risk tolerance. Viewing public content might require 0.1 or no threshold at all. Posting content might require 0.3. Sending direct messages to strangers might require 0.5. Moderating a community might require 0.6. Each threshold implicitly defines the minimum investment an attacker must make to abuse that capability, and the investment required for higher thresholds exceeds what bot operators can sustain at scale. A single fake identity with a score of 0.5 might be economically feasible. A thousand of them is not.

This is the structural difference from economic stake approaches that test wealth. The cost here is not money. The cost is time, consistency, and the independent fabrication of multiple signal types that resist simultaneous forgery. A wealthy attacker can write a check. A wealthy attacker cannot fabricate six months of consistent typing patterns that match human behavioral distributions while simultaneously maintaining a verified postal address that receives physical mail.

Signal Taxonomy

The score is computed from nine signal types, each with a defined weight and decay behavior. The weights reflect the difficulty of forging each signal, not its importance to

---

2   Forgery cost estimates are based on observed pricing for identity components in underground markets as of 2024: bulk email accounts at $0.01–$0.10 each, verified phone numbers at $2–$5, synthetic financial identities at $50–$200. See Anderson, R. *Security Engineering*, 3rd ed., Wiley, 2020, ch. 12, for a survey of identity fraud economics.

any particular application. A signal that is easy to forge gets a low weight. A signal that requires sustained effort or physical-world verification gets a high weight.

Signal Type	Weight	Decay Behavior
Email verification	0.02	None
Phone verification	0.03	None
Payment instrument	0.05	None
Postal mail verification	0.05	None
Device attestation	0.04	6-month half-life
Typing patterns (30 days)	0.08	Continuous refresh
Activity patterns (1 year)	0.15	Continuous refresh
Human-in-loop verification	0.10	1-year half-life
Government ID (optional)	0.20	None

The signals divide into three categories by nature: point-in-time verifications, continuous behavioral signals, and decaying attestations.

Point-in-time verifications—email, phone, payment instrument, postal mail, government ID—are events that occur once and are recorded. An email was verified. A payment instrument was linked. A postal address received a mailed code. These signals do not decay because the verification event itself does not expire; what was demonstrated remains demonstrated. Their weights are low because each individual verification is relatively easy to forge. An email address costs nothing. A phone number costs a few dollars. A payment instrument requires a financial identity, which costs more but is still within reach.

The cumulative effect is what matters. Any single point-in-time verification is cheap. Obtaining all of them simultaneously, each linked to an identity that must be consistent across all verifications, is expensive. A burner email is trivial. A burner email, a burner phone, a payment instrument tied to a verifiable financial identity, and a postal address that receives physical mail—all linked to the same anonymous identity—is a significantly larger investment.

Continuous behavioral signals—typing patterns and activity patterns—are the most valuable signals in the taxonomy and the hardest to forge. They are computed locally on the user's device from ongoing interaction data: keystroke timing, mouse movement patterns, scroll behavior, session duration and frequency, the cadence of interaction over days and weeks and months.

Typing patterns carry a weight of 0.08 and require thirty days of accumulated data. The analysis is not keystroke logging. The client computes statistical features—inter-key intervals, key-hold durations, digraph timing, error-and-correction patterns—and produces a behavioral fingerprint. The fingerprint captures the rhythm of a particular human's interaction without recording what they typed. After thirty days, the fingerprint stabilizes enough to provide meaningful evidence of humanity.

Activity patterns carry a weight of 0.15 and require a full year of data. This is the heaviest-weighted non-governmental signal because it is the hardest to forge. A year of consistent human-like interaction—with natural variation in session timing, seasonal patterns in activity, the irregular cadences that characterize biological life rather than automated processes—is extraordinarily difficult to synthesize. A bot can mimic human typing for an hour. Mimicking human life patterns across a year, with consistent individual variation that does not regress toward statistical averages, is—under the assumption that current behavioral modeling techniques hold—an unsolved problem at scale.[3]

Both behavioral signals use continuous refresh rather than decay. They do not expire; instead, the model is continuously updated with recent data. If the behavioral patterns change dramatically—because a bot has taken over an account that was once human-operated, for instance—the score reflects the change. The signal is current because the computation is current.

Decaying attestations—device attestation and human-in-loop verification—provide evidence that loses value over time. Device attestation confirms that the user's device has specific hardware security properties (a secure enclave, a trusted platform module) and that the device itself has not been compromised. The attestation decays with a six-month half-life because devices change, and because an attestation about a device that was secure six months ago is weaker evidence than one from last week.

Human-in-loop verification is a catch-all for challenge-response mechanisms that require real-time human presence: video verification with a live operator, interactive challenges that require adaptive human reasoning, or other mechanisms that confirm a human is actively present. These carry a weight of 0.10 and decay with a one-year half-life. They are valuable when fresh and diminish as the verification recedes into the past.

Government ID carries the highest individual weight at 0.20 and is explicitly optional. Some users will provide government identification. Many will not, and the architecture must function without it. A user who provides every other signal but declines government ID can still achieve a meaningful score. Government ID is weighted heavily because it is among the most expensive signals to forge—obtaining a fraudulent government-issued identity document requires significant criminal infrastructure—but its optionality is a design requirement, not an afterthought. A system that requires government ID is a system that excludes people without government ID, and the people most in need of the protections this architecture provides—dissidents, refugees, abuse survivors, the undocumented—are often precisely the people who cannot or should not be required to present government identification.

The weights sum to 0.72 across all nine signals. This is deliberate. Even if every signal is present and active with no decay, the maximum score does not reach 1.0. The ceiling is below one because the taxonomy is not exhaustive and because claiming that any fixed set of signals achieves certainty would be false. If new signal types are added in the future, the maximum score rises but remains below one. The asymptote is a structural commitment to honesty about the limits of verification.

---

3   Monrose, F. and Rubin, A. "Keystroke dynamics as a biometric for authentication." *Future Generation Computer Systems* 16, no. 4 (2000): 351–359. Behavioral biometrics remain an active research area. While individual session forgery is feasible, long-duration behavioral consistency across multiple signal types has not been demonstrated by adversarial systems at the time of writing.

Proofs, Not Data

Every component of this privacy architecture applies the same principle: store the minimum information required for function, and store it in a form that cannot be repurposed. The storage problem chapter established this for general data. Proof of Human applies it to behavioral and verification signals.

The server does not store the user's email address. It stores a cryptographic proof that an email address was verified, bound to the user's anonymous identity, at a specific time. The proof confirms that the verification event occurred. It does not contain the email address, the domain, or any information from which the email address could be reconstructed.

The server does not store keystroke timings. It stores a proof that a behavioral analysis was performed on thirty days of typing data, that the analysis produced a fingerprint consistent with a singular human operator, and that the fingerprint met the threshold for the typing-pattern signal. The raw keystrokes never leave the client. The statistical features computed from the keystrokes never leave the client. Only the conclusion—"this data is consistent with a singular human"—is transmitted, and it is transmitted as a signed attestation, not as the underlying evidence.

The signal record structure reflects this principle:

```
signal_record = {
    signal_type:  "typing_patterns",
    proof:        cryptographic_attestation,
    weight:       0.08,
    timestamp:    unix_epoch_seconds,
    decay_params: {
        type:        "continuous_refresh",
        last_refresh: unix_epoch_seconds
    }
}
```

The proof field contains a cryptographic attestation—a hash-based commitment or, for stronger guarantees, a zero-knowledge proof—that binds the signal type, the verification result, and the timestamp to the user's identity without containing the raw signal data. An email verification proof is a signed statement: "An email address was verified for identity X at time T." Not "The email address user@example.com was verified for identity X at time T." The distinction is the difference between a proof and a record. A record contains data. A proof confirms a property of data that no longer exists in the system.

This is not a minor architectural detail. It is the mechanism by which the system avoids creating a new surveillance infrastructure. Every failed approach to human verification created a database of sensitive information as a side effect: biometric databases that could not survive breach, knowledge databases that were breached routinely, behavioral profiles that advertising networks would pay to acquire. Proof of Human stores proofs. The proofs confirm properties. The underlying data does not exist on any server. A breach of the proof database yields a collection of attestations: "Someone verified an email. Someone demonstrated human typing patterns. Someone verified a postal address." The attestations are useless without the underlying data, which was never stored.

Consider the contrast with current practice. Every major platform already collects the behavioral signals that Proof of Human uses—keystroke timing, mouse movements, session patterns, device fingerprints—stored on platform servers and fed into advertising and analytics systems. What this architecture changes is not the collection but the storage: proofs are transmitted, data is not.

This is less surveillance than current practice, not more.

Score Computation

The score computation is a weighted sum of active signals with decay applied.

Proof of Human: Score Accumulation

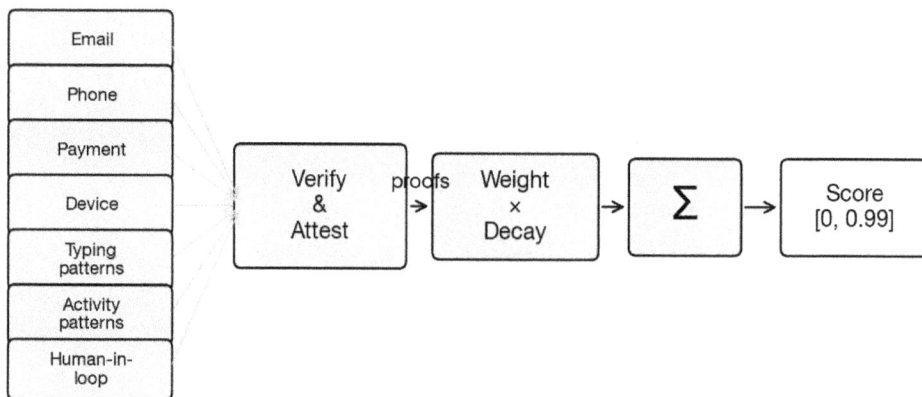

$$\text{score} = \min(0.99, \ \Sigma \ \text{weight}_i \cdot \text{signal}_i \cdot \text{decay}_i)$$

Figure 7.1: **Signal Flow from Source to Score.** The following diagram traces a single signal from source through verification, score computation, and proof storage. Notice what crosses each boundary: raw data stays on the client, only proofs reach the server, and only a score reaches consuming sites.

The pseudocode below makes the computation explicit:

```
function compute_score(signal_records, current_time):
    total = 0.0

    for record in signal_records:
        weight = record.weight

        // Apply decay based on signal type
        if record.decay_params.type == "none":
            decay_factor = 1.0
```

```
        else if record.decay_params.type == "half_life":
            elapsed = current_time - record.timestamp
            half_life = record.decay_params.half_life_seconds
            decay_factor = 0.5 ^ (elapsed / half_life)

            // Signal contributes negligibly after sufficient
decay
            if decay_factor < 0.01:
                continue

        else if record.decay_params.type == "continuous_refresh":
            elapsed_since_refresh = current_time - record.decay_
params.last_refresh
            refresh_window = record.decay_params.refresh_window_
seconds

            if elapsed_since_refresh > refresh_window:
                // Refresh window expired; signal is stale
                continue
            else:
                decay_factor = 1.0

        total = total + (weight * decay_factor)

    // Score never reaches 1.0
    return min(total, 0.99)
```

The computation is straightforward because the complexity lives in the signal verification, not in the aggregation. Each signal independently establishes a proof. The score computation simply sums the weighted, decay-adjusted contributions. The min cap at 0.99 enforces the asymptotic property: no combination of signals produces a score of 1.0.

Several properties of this computation matter.

Additivity. Signals contribute independently. The score from an email verification plus the score from a phone verification equals the sum of their weights. There is no interaction term, no bonus for combining signals, no penalty for missing one. This simplicity is intentional. Complex scoring functions create opacity that undermines trust. A user who can add up their signal weights and predict their score trusts the system more than a user facing a black-box algorithm.

Decay as memory. Decaying signals model the reasonable intuition that evidence of humanity should be recent. A device attestation from two years ago is weaker evidence than one from yesterday. The half-life mechanism captures this: a six-month half-life means the signal contributes half its weight after six months, a quarter after a year, an eighth after eighteen months. After several half-lives, the contribution rounds to zero and the signal effectively expires. The user must re-verify to restore the contribution.

Continuous refresh as presence. Behavioral signals do not decay in the half-life sense; they require ongoing presence. If a user stops interacting with the system, their behavioral signals stale out when the refresh window expires. This models the observation that behavioral evidence of humanity is only meaningful if the behavior is current. A typing pattern from a year ago proves that a human was present a year ago. It says nothing about who or what is operating the account today.

No cliff effects. The scoring function is smooth. No single signal causes a dramatic score change. Losing one signal reduces the score by that signal's weight. Gaining one signal increases it by that signal's weight. There are no thresholds internal to the scoring function, no sudden jumps, no discontinuities. The thresholds are set by consuming sites, not by the score computation itself.

The Retrieval Protocol

The humanness score must be retrieved and presented to consuming sites without creating a linkable trail. If the same score retrieval could be observed across multiple sites, an attacker could use the retrieval pattern to correlate identities—defeating the anonymous identity architecture from Chapter 3.

Retrieval uses a challenge-response protocol with ephemeral keys:

```
function retrieve_score(client_secret, identity_service):

    // Step 1: Service issues challenge
    challenge = identity_service.generate_challenge()
    key_identifier = challenge.key_id

    // Step 2: Client derives ephemeral key from secret
    ephemeral_key = hash(client_secret, key_identifier, current_
nonce)

    // Step 3: Client computes response
    response = hmac(ephemeral_key, challenge.payload)

    // Step 4: Service verifies response
    identity_service.verify(key_identifier, response)

    // Step 5: Service returns signal proofs
    signal_proofs = identity_service.get_proofs(key_identifier)

    // Step 6: Client computes score locally
    score = compute_score(signal_proofs, current_time())

    // Step 7: Client discards ephemeral key
    discard(ephemeral_key)

    return score
```

The ephemeral key is derived from the client's secret and the challenge. It is used once and discarded. The identity service never receives the client's secret—it receives only the HMAC response, which proves knowledge of the secret without revealing it. This follows the standard zero-knowledge pattern[4]: the verifier learns that the client knows the secret but learns nothing about the secret itself.

The score computation happens on the client. The identity service returns signal proofs—the attestations described in the previous section—and the client aggregates them into a score. The service does not compute the score. This matters because it means the service cannot manipulate scores selectively. It returns the same proofs regardless of which site the score will be presented to. The client performs the aggregation. The client produces the number.

The client then presents the score to the consuming site as part of the anonymous identity token described in Chapter 3. The token contains a site-specific identifier, the humanness score, a timestamp, and a signature from the identity service attesting that the score was computed from valid proofs. The site receives the score. The site does not receive the proofs, the signal types, the timestamps, or any other information about how the score was derived.

Composition with Anonymous Identity

The proof-of-human score does not exist in isolation. It is bound to the anonymous identity architecture from Chapter 3.

When a user authenticates, the client computes a site-specific token that is unlinkable across sites. The humanness score travels with that token. The bank sees a high score. The social network sees a high score. Neither can link them to the same person.

The composition works because the score is a property of the identity, not a property of the person. The identity service knows that a particular set of proofs yields a particular score. The consuming site knows that a particular site-specific token has a particular score. Nobody in the system can connect the proofs to the site-specific token to the actual human. The identity service does not know which sites the user visits. The consuming site does not know what proofs the user has accumulated. The user's privacy is preserved while the score's utility is maintained.

The practical effect is that the humanness score functions as a portable trust signal without functioning as a tracking mechanism. A user with a score of 0.45 presents that score—or a score derived from the same proofs—to every site they visit. Each site sees a number. No site sees the same identifier. The score is useful because it communicates trustworthiness. The score is safe because it communicates nothing else.

This composition is not automatic. It requires that the token construction includes the score in a way that the identity service can sign without learning the site-specific token, and that the consuming site can verify without learning the identity-service-side

---

4   Goldwasser, S., Micali, S., and Rackoff, C. "The knowledge complexity of interactive proof systems." *SIAM Journal on Computing* 18, no. 1 (1989): 186–208. The HMAC-based challenge-response described here provides a weaker property than full zero-knowledge proof—specifically, it demonstrates knowledge of a secret without revealing it, but does not achieve simulation-based zero-knowledge in the formal sense.

identifier. The cryptographic mechanisms for achieving this—blind signatures, commitment schemes, selective disclosure proofs—are established techniques.[5] The implementation details belong in the technical appendix. The architectural point is that the composition works: humanness verification and anonymous identity are not in tension. They are complementary.

What Sites See

A consuming site receives three things when a user authenticates: a site-specific identifier that is stable across sessions but unlinkable to identifiers on other sites, a humanness score between 0.0 and 0.99, and a timestamp indicating when the score was last computed.

The site does not receive the user's email address, phone number, typing patterns, device information, postal address, government ID status, or any other underlying signal. The site does not learn which signals contributed to the score or how much each contributed. The site does not learn whether the user has a government ID or declined to provide one. The site receives a number and a signature attesting that the number was honestly computed from validated proofs.

This is sufficient for the site's needs. A site that requires a score of 0.3 for posting does not need to know whether the user achieved 0.3 through email plus phone plus payment plus postal verification, or through email plus typing patterns plus activity patterns. The site needs to know that forging a score of 0.3 costs on the order of one thousand dollars of effort—a calibration target, not a proven bound. The underlying signal composition is irrelevant to the site's risk calculation.

The minimalism is not merely a privacy benefit. It is a simplification benefit. Sites integrate with a single number. They do not parse signal types, evaluate decay parameters, or implement signal-specific verification logic. The complexity of the signal taxonomy, the decay functions, the proof storage, and the score computation is encapsulated entirely within the proof-of-human infrastructure. Sites see a number. Sites set a threshold. Everything else is hidden.

Threshold Governance

Sites set their own thresholds. The proof-of-human architecture does not dictate what score is required for any particular action. It provides the score. The site decides what to do with it.

This separation is deliberate. Different sites have different risk profiles. A public forum tolerating occasional spam might set a posting threshold at 0.15. A banking application might require 0.5 for transactions above a certain amount. A platform that

5   Chaum, D. "Blind signatures for untraceable payments." *Advances in Cryptology—CRYPTO '82*, edited by D. Chaum, R. L. Rivest, and A. T. Sherman, Plenum Press, 1983, pp. 199–203. Selective disclosure credentials build on this foundation; see Camenisch, J. and Lysyanskaya, A. "An efficient system for non-transferable anonymous credentials with optional anonymity revocation." *EUROCRYPT 2001*, pp. 93–118.

has experienced coordinated harassment campaigns might temporarily raise thresholds to 0.6. The thresholds are policy decisions, not cryptographic properties.

The architecture enables this flexibility by providing a continuous score rather than a binary human/not-human determination. Binary determinations force a single global threshold: everyone above the line is in, everyone below is out. Continuous scores allow each site to draw its own line. The score is a shared language. The threshold is a local decision.

Sites can also implement graduated access rather than binary access. A new user with a score of 0.10 might be able to read content and leave reactions. At 0.20, they can post comments. At 0.35, they can create new threads. At 0.50, they can send direct messages. Each capability tier implies a minimum investment to abuse, and the investment required for high-tier capabilities exceeds what casual abuse operations can sustain.

Decay in Practice

Decay functions serve a specific purpose: they ensure that the score reflects current evidence rather than historical evidence. A user who verified a device two years ago and has not interacted since should not carry a score that implies ongoing human presence.

Device attestation decays with a six-month half-life. After six months, the signal contributes half its original weight (0.02 instead of 0.04). After a year, one quarter (0.01). After two years, the contribution is negligible. The user's device may have changed, been compromised, or been disposed of. The attestation's declining contribution reflects this uncertainty.

Human-in-loop verification decays with a one-year half-life. A video verification or interactive challenge that was performed a year ago contributes half its weight. The implicit question—"Is a human still operating this identity?"—is less confidently answered as time passes since the last direct verification.

Continuous-refresh signals do not decay in the half-life sense. Instead, they require ongoing data. Typing patterns must be refreshed with recent typing data. Activity patterns must be refreshed with recent activity. If the user stops providing fresh behavioral data, the signal's refresh window expires and the signal drops from the score entirely. This is appropriate: behavioral evidence of humanity is only meaningful if the behavior is current.

The decay mechanisms create a natural incentive for continued legitimate use. A user who remains active maintains their score effortlessly—their behavioral signals refresh automatically, their device attestations renew periodically, and their point-in-time verifications remain valid. A dormant account's score naturally declines as decaying signals expire and behavioral signals stale out. Reactivating the account requires re-establishing the decayed signals, which requires the presence of the actual human who originally established them.

This property is valuable because it limits the market for aged accounts. In current systems, aged accounts with established reputations are bought and sold as tools for abuse. A five-year-old account with a high reputation score can be purchased and immediately deployed for fraud. In this architecture, an account whose human operator has not interacted recently has a decayed score that reflects the absence of its operator. Purchasing the account does not purchase the score. The score must be rebuilt by the new operator, which requires establishing behavioral signals from scratch—which takes months.

Weight Tuning

The signal weights presented in this chapter are calibrated to current forgery economics. They are not permanent. The cost of forging specific signals changes as technology, markets, and attack techniques evolve. If phone number verification becomes trivially cheap to forge—through widespread availability of virtual phone numbers, for instance—the weight assigned to phone verification should decrease. If new signal types become available that provide strong evidence of humanity at low privacy cost, they should be added with appropriate weights.

Weight tuning is a governance function, not a cryptographic function. The mathematics of the score computation does not determine the weights. The weights are chosen by the operators of the proof-of-human infrastructure based on empirical assessment of forgery costs. This means that the weights are a locus of power, and the governance of that power matters.

The architecture does not prescribe a specific governance model for weight adjustment. It establishes constraints that any governance model must satisfy: weight changes must be transparent (users must be able to see current weights and how they affect their scores), weight changes must be gradual (sudden changes that invalidate existing scores undermine trust), and the total weight budget must remain below 1.0 (the asymptotic property is a design invariant, not a tunable parameter).

Multiple competing proof-of-human verifiers are an architectural possibility and a governance safeguard. If a single verifier's weight assignments become adversarial—inflating the weight of signals that advantage certain populations or disadvantage others—competing verifiers with different weight assignments provide an alternative. Sites choose which verifier's scores to accept, or accept scores from multiple verifiers. Competition constrains capture. Monopoly invites it.

Recommended Cryptographic Primitives

Function	Primitive
Signal proofs	Hash-based commitments (SHA-256); SNARKs for stronger guarantees
HMAC	HMAC-SHA256
Key derivation	HKDF-SHA256

Score attestation signatures   Ed25519

The proof storage and retrieval protocol uses standard primitives available through lib-sodium. The computational requirements are modest—the most expensive operations are the HMAC computations during retrieval and the signal verification during accumulation. Score computation itself is simple arithmetic over weighted sums.

Prior Art and Design Rationale

The proof-of-human architecture did not emerge from a vacuum. Several systems have attacked the same problem—distinguishing humans from machines at scale—and each made design tradeoffs that illuminate why this architecture looks the way it does.

Worldcoin is the most visible recent attempt. Founded by Sam Altman in 2019, the project uses custom hardware—a device called the Orb—to scan a person's iris and produce a unique biometric hash.[6] The goal is noble enough: one verified human, one credential, worldwide. The problem is the method. Iris scans are immutable biometric data derived from a physical feature that cannot be changed if the database is compromised or the governance shifts. Worldcoin's design philosophy is the precise opposite of this chapter's: it achieves singularity through biometric certainty, accepting the surveillance risk that entails. We achieve singularity through accumulated economic cost, accepting the uncertainty that entails. The surveillance risk is more dangerous, because a biometric database is a permanent liability while an imperfect score is a temporary inconvenience.

Hashcash, proposed by Adam Back in 1997, is the intellectual ancestor of every economic-deterrent approach to spam and abuse, including this one.[7] Back's insight was that requiring a computational proof of work—a partial hash collision that takes measurable CPU time to compute—attaches a cost to sending email without requiring identity or payment. One email costs a fraction of a second. A million spam emails cost days of computation. The idea is elegant and the math is sound. It failed in practice for two reasons: the cost was borne by legitimate senders as well as spammers (an accessibility problem), and the rise of botnets made computation cheap for attackers who stole it from compromised machines. Proof of Human borrows Hashcash's core principle—make abuse expensive through accumulated cost—but shifts the cost from computation to signal diversity. The expense of forging a high score is not CPU cycles but the independent fabrication of multiple verification signals over time. This is harder to steal than computation, because behavioral consistency over months cannot be outsourced to a botnet.

Privacy Pass, developed by researchers at Cloudflare, comes closest to what this

---

6   Worldcoin Foundation. "Worldcoin Whitepaper." 2023. Developed by Tools for Humanity; whitepaper published by the Worldcoin Foundation. For critical analysis of the biometric approach, see Gebru, T. and Torres, É.P. "The TESCREAL Bundle: Eugenics and the Promise of Utopia through Artificial General Intelligence." *First Monday*, vol. 29, no. 4, April 2024.

7   Back, A. "Hashcash—A Denial of Service Counter-Measure." Technical report, 1997. Revised 2002. The proof-of-work concept was later adopted by Bitcoin (Nakamoto, 2008) but the original application was anti-spam email filtering.

architecture attempts.[8] Privacy Pass issues anonymous tokens to users who have passed a verification challenge. The tokens are unlinkable—a site that redeems a token cannot trace it back to the challenge that generated it, and two sites redeeming tokens from the same user cannot link those redemptions. The cryptographic approach uses blind signatures, the same primitive this architecture relies on for score attestation. Where Privacy Pass differs is scope: it provides a binary signal (passed/did not pass a single challenge), while Proof of Human provides a continuous score accumulated from multiple independent signal types over time. Privacy Pass answers "was this user human at one moment?" Proof of Human answers "how much sustained evidence of humanity has this identity accumulated?" The continuous score enables graduated access policies that a binary token cannot support.

reCAPTCHA v3, Google's current bot-detection system, also produces a continuous score between 0.0 and 1.0 without requiring the user to solve a challenge.[9] The resemblance to Proof of Human's score is superficial. reCAPTCHA v3 computes its score from behavioral surveillance—tracking mouse movements, browsing patterns, cookie history, and interaction data across every site that embeds the reCAPTCHA script. The user pays not with effort but with privacy. Google learns how every user interacts with every participating site. reCAPTCHA v3 demonstrates that continuous scoring works. It also demonstrates exactly the surveillance architecture this chapter is designed to avoid. In Proof of Human, behavioral signals are analyzed locally, raw data never leaves the client, and the server stores proofs, not behavioral profiles. The difference is not incidental. It is the point.

These four systems define the design space. Worldcoin proves identity through biometrics and accepts surveillance risk. Hashcash attaches cost through computation and loses to stolen resources. Privacy Pass issues anonymous binary tokens and cannot support graduated trust. reCAPTCHA v3 produces continuous scores through behavioral surveillance.

Proof of Human occupies a position none of them hold: continuous scoring from multiple independent signals, accumulated over time, stored as proofs rather than data, without behavioral surveillance by any central party. The logarithmic effort scale and signal-accumulation-without-surveillance combination is novel to this design. The weight calibrations are not proven bounds—they are empirical targets based on current forgery economics, and they will need adjustment as those economics change. The structural combination—asymptotic scoring, proof-not-data storage, signal independence, and local behavioral analysis—has not been attempted by prior systems, and the design rationale follows directly from the failures catalogued above.

---

8   Davidson, A., Goldberg, I., Sullivan, N., Tankersley, G., and Valsorda, F. "Privacy Pass: Bypassing Internet Challenges Anonymously." *Proceedings on Privacy Enhancing Technologies* 2018, no. 3 (2018): 164–180. The protocol uses blind RSA signatures (later updated to use VOPRF) to issue unlinkable anonymous tokens.

9   Google. "reCAPTCHA v3: Returning a Score." developers.google.com, 2018. For analysis of the surveillance implications, see Englehardt, S. and Narayanan, A. "Online Tracking: A 1-million-site Measurement and Analysis." *ACM CCS 2016*, pp. 1388–1401, which documents the scope of Google's cross-site behavioral data collection.

What This Does Not Protect Against

Honesty about limitations is a design requirement, not a courtesy. The proof-of-human architecture has boundaries, and stating them clearly is necessary for any honest assessment of what the system achieves.

Determined adversaries with sufficient budget can forge high scores. The logarithmic effort scale makes high scores expensive, not impossible. A state-level actor or a well-funded criminal organization willing to invest a million dollars can plausibly forge a score of 0.6 or higher for a single identity. The architecture makes this expensive enough to prevent abuse at scale—forging a thousand high-scoring identities costs a thousand times as much—but it does not prevent a single well-funded fake identity from passing thresholds. No system does. The question is not whether a sufficiently motivated attacker can defeat the system. The question is whether the system changes the economics enough to prevent industrialized abuse. The answer is yes, but "preventing industrialized abuse" is a weaker claim than "preventing all abuse."

Weight tuning is governance, not cryptography. The security of the score depends on the weights being calibrated correctly. If the weight for email verification were set to 0.50 instead of 0.02, the entire effort scale would collapse—a trivially forgeable signal would provide half the maximum score. The cryptographic components of the system are mathematically verifiable. The weight assignments are judgment calls. Judgment calls require trust in the entity making them. The architecture distributes this trust through transparency and competition among verifiers, but it does not eliminate it. Some amount of trust in governance is irreducible.

Not all humans can provide all signals. A person without a phone number cannot contribute the phone verification signal. A person without a bank account cannot contribute the payment instrument signal. A person without a fixed postal address cannot contribute the postal verification signal. A person with certain motor disabilities may produce typing patterns that do not match the statistical expectations of the behavioral analysis.

This is an accessibility concern, not a theoretical one. The architecture mitigates it through weight distribution—no single signal is required for a useful score, and the signal taxonomy includes multiple paths to accumulation—but mitigation is not elimination. A person who can provide only email verification and activity patterns reaches a maximum score of 0.17 even after a full year of consistent use. If a site sets a threshold of 0.30 for basic participation, that person is excluded. The exclusion is not intentional, but unintentional exclusion is still exclusion.

The governance of minimum thresholds must account for accessibility. Sites that set thresholds must consider which populations those thresholds exclude and whether the exclusion is proportionate to the risk being mitigated. The architecture provides the score. The site sets the threshold. The responsibility for equitable threshold-setting falls on the site, and acknowledging that responsibility is part of deploying the system honestly.

The score could enable new forms of discrimination. A humanness score is a number attached to an identity. Numbers attached to identities have a historical tendency to become instruments of sorting, stratification, and exclusion. Credit scores were designed to predict loan default risk and became gatekeepers for housing, employment, and insurance. A humanness score designed to prevent bot abuse could, through similar drift, become a prerequisite for participation in public life.

The architectural safeguards—asymptotic scoring, optional signals, competing verifiers, transparent weights—reduce this risk but do not eliminate it. The score could become a social sorting mechanism if institutions treat it as a measure of human worth rather than a measure of forgery cost. The architecture cannot prevent misuse of a number by institutions that receive it. It can constrain the number's range (0.0 to 0.99), prevent it from encoding specific personal information (proofs, not data), and ensure that its composition is transparent (published weights, auditable computation). Whether these constraints are sufficient depends on the social and regulatory environment in which the system operates, which is outside the architecture's control.

Behavioral analysis is not infallible. The typing-pattern and activity-pattern signals depend on statistical models of human behavior. These models have false-positive and false-negative rates. Some bots produce behavioral patterns that are sufficiently human-like to pass. Some humans produce behavioral patterns that are sufficiently unusual to fail. The architecture treats these signals as evidence with weights, not as binary determinations, which limits the impact of individual misclassifications. But misclassifications occur, and a user whose legitimate behavioral patterns are flagged as non-human has a degraded score and a legitimate grievance.

Collusion between signal providers undermines independence. The effort-compounding property of the score depends on signals being independently verifiable. If the entity that verifies email addresses also verifies phone numbers and also performs device attestation, then compromising that single entity compromises multiple signals simultaneously. The forgery cost drops from the sum of independent forgery costs to the cost of compromising one provider. The architecture assumes that signal verification is distributed across independent providers. If that assumption fails—through market consolidation, through collusion, through a single provider accumulating verification monopoly—the effort scale degrades.

These limitations are real. Acknowledging them does not weaken the architecture. It defines its scope. The proof-of-human system makes industrialized abuse prohibitively expensive, establishes meaningful stake for individual identities, and does both without creating a surveillance infrastructure. It does not achieve perfection. It achieves a substantial improvement over a status quo where identity is free, abuse is costless, and accountability is structurally impossible.

Summary

The proof-of-human architecture reduces to four components: a signal taxonomy that defines what counts as evidence of humanity, a proof-storage model that records verification events without recording verified data, a score computation that aggregates weighted, decaying signals into a single number, and a retrieval protocol that delivers the score to consuming sites without creating a linkable trail.

The signal taxonomy establishes nine signal types spanning point-in-time verifications, continuous behavioral analysis, and decaying attestations. The weights reflect forgery cost. The taxonomy is extensible—new signals can be added with appropriate weights as new verification methods become available.

The proof-storage model ensures that the system accumulates evidence without accumulating data. Every signal is recorded as a cryptographic attestation that a verification occurred, not as the underlying information that was verified. A breach of the proof database reveals that verifications happened. It does not reveal what was verified.

The score computation sums weighted signals with decay applied. The function is transparent, additive, and capped below 1.0. No combination of signals achieves certainty. Under our calibration model, every increment in score costs roughly an order of magnitude more to forge than the previous increment.

The retrieval protocol uses ephemeral keys and challenge-response authentication to deliver proofs to the client without creating persistent session data on the server. The client computes the score locally. The score travels with the anonymous identity token. The consuming site receives a number. The consuming site does not receive the identity, the proofs, or the signals.

The previous chapter asked three questions: Is the entity singular? Is the entity human? Does the entity have stake? The architecture answers all three. Singularity is maintained through the cryptographic binding of signals to a single anonymous identity—forging a second identity requires forging a second complete set of independent signals, at full cost for each. Humanity is verified through behavioral analysis that tests properties machines cannot easily replicate at scale. Stake is created through the accumulation of effort that cannot be quickly replaced—an identity with months of behavioral history and multiple verified signals represents an investment that burning the identity destroys.

The architecture does this without biometric databases, without identity registries, without financial barriers, and without storing any data that would enable surveillance if breached or compelled. The proofs exist. The data does not. The score is useful. The score is safe. The privacy architecture's integrity is preserved while the accountability gap is closed.

What the architecture does not address is communication. The user can authenticate anonymously. The user can store data in ways the operator cannot read. The user can demonstrate humanity without surrendering identity. But when the user sends a message, the infrastructure that carries the message learns that a conversation is happening. Authentication is private. Storage is private. Metadata is not. That is the next problem.

CHAPTER 8

The Metadata Problem

Content encryption is solved. The mathematics works. The mathematics has never been the problem.

The problem is everything else. The server that delivers your encrypted message cannot read its contents, but it knows who sent the message, who received it, when it was sent, how large it was, and how often these two parties communicate. It knows these things because it must know them to function. A server that does not know where to deliver a message cannot deliver the message. A server that does not know who is requesting stored messages cannot authenticate the request. The operational requirements of message delivery create metadata as a structural byproduct, and that metadata accumulates on servers that can be subpoenaed, hacked, or compelled to cooperate.

The encrypted messaging industry has spent a decade convincing users that their conversations are private. The conversations are. The fact that the conversations occurred is not. The distinction between these two things is the subject of this chapter.

What Metadata Reveals

The relationship graph of a messaging system is a complete record of who communicates with whom. Every message creates an edge in this graph. Over time, the graph accumulates structure that is more revealing than any individual message could be.

Alice messages Bob every morning at 7:15 AM. The pattern reveals that they begin each day in contact. Charlie messages Diana seventeen times in a single hour, then not at all for three weeks. The pattern reveals a crisis followed by resolution or rupture. A cluster of twenty accounts all message the same central account within a five-minute window. The pattern reveals an organization coordinating. None of these inferences require reading a single word of content. All of them are available to anyone who can observe the metadata.

The inference extends beyond relationships. Message timing correlates with sleep schedules, work hours, and time zones. An account that sends messages at 3 AM local time on a regular basis is either an insomniac or located in a different time zone than claimed. Message sizes correlate with content types: a 47-byte message is a brief acknowledgment; a 4.7-megabyte message is a document or image. The metadata sketches the shape of the content without exposing the content itself.

Organizations are particularly exposed. Corporate hierarchy appears in communication patterns: who messages whom, who serves as a hub, who is peripheral. The formal org chart may say one thing; the communication graph says another, and the communication graph is more accurate. A reporter's source list appears in their contact history. A dissident network appears in the cluster of connections between accounts that share no public affiliation. A law firm's client relationships appear in the messaging patterns between attorneys and external parties.

The metadata also reveals absence. If two people who should be communicating are not, that is information. If a team that normally coordinates falls silent, that is information. If a source who contacted a journalist weekly stops contacting them after a particular date, that is information. The graph records what happens and what stops happening.

Intelligence agencies understood this decades before the public did. The NSA's collection programs focused on metadata precisely because metadata is structured, queryable, and sufficient. Former NSA director Michael Hayden stated publicly: "We kill people based on metadata."[1] The statement was not hyperbole. Relationship graphs, location data, and communication timing patterns are the inputs to targeting decisions. The content of the calls is secondary. The pattern of the calls is primary.

The Reality Winner Case

The gap between content security and metadata security is not theoretical. It has produced criminal convictions.

In May 2017, a twenty-five-year-old NSA contractor named Reality Winner printed a classified intelligence report describing foreign interference in an American election.[2] She believed the public should know. She mailed the document to a news organization that had published classified material before and had built its reputation on protecting sources.

The news organization contacted the NSA to verify the document's authenticity. In doing so, they shared a copy of the printed document. That copy contained invisible yellow dots—printer microdots deposited by the printer on every page, encoding the date, the time, and the printer's serial number.[3] The dots were too small for the human eye to

---

1   Michael Hayden, remarks at Johns Hopkins University Foreign Affairs Symposium, April 1, 2014. The event, titled "The Price of Privacy: Re-Evaluating the NSA," was held at Shriver Hall. The full quote, in context of defending NSA collection programs: "We kill people based on metadata." The statement was made publicly, on video, in response to a question about the distinction between metadata collection and content surveillance. Hayden served as NSA Director from 1999 to 2005 and CIA Director from 2006 to 2009.

2   *United States v. Reality Leigh Winner*, Case No. 1:17-cr-00034-JRH-BKE (S.D. Ga. 2017). The FBI affidavit in support of the arrest warrant details the investigative sequence: printer steganography analysis, audit log correlation, email metadata review, and geographic matching. Winner pleaded guilty on June 26, 2018, and was sentenced to sixty-three months in federal prison.

3   Machine Identification Code (MIC) steganography, also known as printer tracking dots, embeds a pattern of sub-millimeter yellow dots on every printed page. The pattern encodes the printer's serial number, date, and time of printing. The technology was developed by Xerox and Canon in the mid-1980s and first publicly reported in 2004 based on information from Xerox researcher Peter Crean. The Electronic Frontier Foundation decoded the Xerox DocuColor dot patterns and published a decoding guide in October 2005.

detect. They were not too small for the NSA's forensic analysis.

The printer's serial number, combined with the NSA's own access logs, identified which contractor had used which printer at which time. The timestamp on the microdots matched the access log entry. Winner's work email showed she had been in contact with the news organization. The postmark on the mailed envelope read Augusta, Georgia—where Winner lived and worked.

The investigation took less than a week. She was arrested at her home on a Saturday. She received sixty-three months in federal prison—the longest sentence ever imposed for an unauthorized disclosure of classified information to the media.

No encrypted message was broken. No ciphertext was decrypted. No content was intercepted in transit. The content of the leaked document was never the forensic issue. Winner was identified, arrested, and ultimately convicted through four layers of metadata: physical metadata (printer microdots), access metadata (print job logs), communication metadata (email records showing contact with the news organization), and geographical metadata (the postmark on the envelope). Each layer was generated automatically, as a byproduct of normal system operation, by infrastructure designed to record without anyone specifically requesting that it record. The surveillance was architectural. The metadata was sufficient.

The news organization was experienced and security-conscious. Its staff used encrypted communication tools. They had protocols for handling sensitive material. None of this protected the source, because the protocols addressed content security while the vulnerability was relationship security. The encrypted channel protected what was said. It did not protect the fact that someone was saying it.

Content Security vs. Relationship Security

The Winner case illustrates a general principle. Content encryption and relationship security address different threat models, and solving one does not advance the other.

Content encryption prevents an adversary from reading the substance of a communication. It answers: if someone intercepts this message, can they understand it? The answer, with modern end-to-end encryption, is no. This is a genuine and important protection.

Relationship security prevents an adversary from determining that a communication occurred between two specific parties. It answers: if someone observes the infrastructure, can they determine that Alice communicated with Bob? The answer, with every major messaging platform currently deployed, is yes.

The distinction matters because investigators frequently do not need to know what was said. They need to know that communication occurred. The fact that a government employee messaged a journalist tells a story. The fact that an employee accessed a sensitive file and then immediately contacted an external address tells a story. The timing, the parties, the frequency—these are the evidentiary elements that establish probable cause, support warrants, and sustain convictions. The content, when eventually obtained, often serves only to confirm what the metadata already suggested.

Law enforcement has adapted to this reality. Agencies subpoena metadata because it is available, because it is often sufficient, and because the legal standards for obtaining metadata are frequently lower than the standards for obtaining content. A pen register order—which compels a provider to disclose communication metadata—requires a lower evidentiary threshold than a wiretap order, which compels disclosure of content. The legal framework treats metadata as less sensitive than content. The investigative reality is that metadata is often more useful.

Why Existing Approaches Fail

Several technical approaches to metadata protection exist. Each imposes costs that limit adoption, and none eliminates the problem.

Anonymity Networks

Anonymity networks—Tor being the most widely deployed—route traffic through multiple relays to obscure the origin and destination of communications. A message from Alice to Bob passes through three or more intermediate nodes, each of which knows only the previous hop and the next hop but not the full path. The design prevents any single relay from knowing both the sender and the recipient.

The protection is real but comes at a cost: latency. Each additional relay adds network delay. Messages that take milliseconds on a direct connection take seconds through an anonymity network. For web browsing, this is tolerable. For real-time messaging—the kind of communication people actually use for day-to-day coordination—seconds of latency per message degrades the experience to the point of abandonment. Users tolerate the latency for high-stakes communication and abandon it for everything else, which means everything else continues to generate metadata on conventional infrastructure.

There is a deeper limitation. Anonymity networks protect individual messages in transit but do not protect the long-term communication pattern. If Alice connects to the Tor network every Tuesday at 9 PM and Bob's server receives a connection from the Tor network every Tuesday at 9:02 PM, a sufficiently resourced observer can correlate the timing. Traffic analysis at the network edges—watching who enters the anonymity network and when, and who exits and when—can defeat the anonymity that the routing provides. The more messages Alice and Bob exchange, the more data points the observer has, and the stronger the correlation becomes.

Mix Networks

Mix networks address the timing correlation problem directly. Messages entering a mix node are collected into batches, shuffled, and released at random intervals. If Alice's message enters the mix at 9:00 and exits at 9:01, an observer can correlate input and output. If messages are batched and shuffled, exiting hours later in random order, the correlation becomes computationally difficult.

The protection is stronger than what anonymity networks provide. The cost is correspondingly higher: hours of latency per message. You cannot hold a conversation when each message takes hours to deliver. Mix networks are suitable for asynchronous communication—email, dead drops, delayed notifications—but not for the real-time messaging that constitutes the vast majority of interpersonal communication. An architecture that protects only asynchronous communication leaves the real-time communication that people actually depend on fully exposed.

Federated Systems

Federated messaging systems distribute the infrastructure across multiple independent servers rather than concentrating it in one. Matrix, XMPP, and similar protocols allow anyone to operate a server, and users on different servers can communicate with each other. The metadata is fragmented: each server sees only its portion of the relationship graph.

The fragmentation reduces the power of any single operator or any single subpoena. No one server holds the complete picture. But the metadata still exists—it is scattered rather than eliminated. A determined investigator serves subpoenas on multiple servers and reassembles the graph. A state-level adversary that monitors network traffic between federated servers can observe the inter-server communication patterns and reconstruct much of the global graph without any server's cooperation.

Federation is a meaningful improvement over centralization. It is not a solution to the metadata problem. It raises the cost of metadata collection from trivial (one subpoena to one company) to moderate (multiple subpoenas to multiple operators, plus traffic analysis). Against a resourced adversary—a national intelligence agency, a well-funded law enforcement operation—the cost increase is insufficient.

Sealed Sender and Similar Mitigations

Some messaging systems have implemented partial metadata protections. Signal's sealed sender feature encrypts the sender's identity so that the server does not know who sent a given message, only who should receive it. This is a genuine improvement: the server's relationship graph becomes directional rather than bidirectional. The server knows that Bob received a message but not that Alice sent it.

The limitation is that the server still knows the recipient. It must, because the server must deliver the message to the correct account. Over time, the pattern of messages received by Bob—their timing, frequency, and correlation with Alice's online presence—can allow the server to infer the sender despite the sealed sender protection. The mitigation makes inference harder. It does not make inference impossible.

The Good Police Work Principle

The same principle that applied to identity in Chapter 2 and storage in Chapter 5 applies to communication metadata. The goal is not to make investigation impossible. The goal is to require that investigation begin with a specific hypothesis about a specific individual.

Current messaging architecture permits mass surveillance of metadata. A single subpoena served on a centralized messaging provider can yield the relationship graph of millions of users. The provider's servers contain the complete communication history: who messaged whom, when, how often, for how long. An investigator with a warrant naming Alice can obtain Alice's metadata. An investigator with a server subpoena can obtain everyone's metadata and then search it for persons of interest. The architecture enables the latter because the metadata exists in concentrated, queryable form.

The distinction is structural, not legal. Targeted investigation requires knowing who to investigate before obtaining evidence. Mass surveillance obtains evidence first and searches it for persons of interest afterward. Current messaging systems enable mass surveillance not because any law permits it—though many laws do—but because the architecture makes the metadata available in bulk. The metadata exists on the server. The server can be compelled. The compulsion yields everything.

The architectural goal is to make the mass query unanswerable. An investigator who knows Alice's identity and has a warrant should be able to investigate Alice—to serve process on Alice, to examine Alice's devices, to request Alice's cooperation. An investigator who has a server subpoena should not be able to obtain the relationship graphs of all users, because the server should not possess them. The server's inability to answer the mass query is not a failure. It is the security property.

The server's lack of capability became the user's protection. The same principle must extend to metadata. A server that does not store relationship data cannot be compelled to produce it. A server that never knows the full communication path cannot reveal it. The architectural absence of capability must become the structural presence of protection.

The Architectural Source of the Problem

The metadata problem originates in a design assumption so fundamental that it is rarely questioned: communication requires a mediator.

Alice wants to send a message to Bob. In every major messaging system deployed today, Alice sends the message to a server, and the server delivers it to Bob. The server is the mediator. The mediator must know who is sending, who is receiving, and when the exchange occurs. These facts are required for the mediator to perform its function. The metadata is not a side effect of poor engineering. It is a structural requirement of mediated communication.

The mediator's knowledge is comprehensive. It sees every message's sender, recipient, timestamp, and size. Over time, it accumulates the complete relationship graph of its user base: every connection, every conversation, every pattern of interaction. This graph is stored on infrastructure the mediator controls, backed up according to the mediator's policies, retained for as long as the mediator chooses or the law requires, and available to any legal process the mediator is subject to.

The server stores messages for offline recipients—because users expect to receive messages even when they are not actively connected. The server manages encryption key exchange—because the sender needs the recipient's public key to encrypt. The server authenticates users—because the system must verify that the person claiming to be Bob is actually Bob. Each of these functions requires the server to know something about the relationship between communicating parties. Each function generates metadata as a structural byproduct.

The question is whether these functions can be decomposed and reorganized so that no single entity accumulates the complete picture. Can messages be delivered without a central mediator knowing both endpoints? Can offline delivery work without a server that knows the recipient's identity? Can key exchange occur without a central directory that maps identities to keys?

These are architectural questions, not cryptographic ones. The cryptography for content protection is sufficient. What is needed is a communication architecture that does not concentrate metadata in subpoenable locations.

Requirements for a Solution

The analysis produces a set of constraints that any metadata-resistant communication architecture must satisfy.

Real-time messaging. People will not accept hours or even minutes of delay for ordinary communication. Any solution that imposes latency beyond what users experience with current messaging applications will not be adopted, regardless of its security properties. A system that is secure but unusable protects no one because no one uses it. The solution must support conversational messaging with latency measured in seconds at most.

Decentralization. Any central server becomes a single point of metadata accumulation and a single point of subpoena. The architecture must distribute the communication function so that no single operator, no single server, no single entity possesses the relationship graph. This does not mean no servers. It means no server that knows enough to reconstruct the global communication pattern.

Ephemerality. Stored metadata is retrievable metadata. The architecture must minimize or eliminate persistent records of communication events. Messages in transit generate transient state; that state should not survive the completion of delivery. A system that routes messages through intermediaries must ensure those intermediaries do not retain logs of what they routed. The absence of records is not a policy choice—policies can be changed, logs can be secretly retained. The absence must be structural: the intermediaries should not possess the information in a form that could be logged even if they wanted to.

Sender anonymity. The infrastructure that delivers a message to the recipient should not know who sent it. The sender's identity should be available only to the intended recipient, encrypted within the message payload, invisible to every intermediary.

Receiver anonymity. The infrastructure that accepts a message from the sender should not know who will ultimately receive it. This is harder than sender anonymity because the system must somehow get the message to the right place without knowing where the right place is in terms of user identity. It requires decoupling the routing address from the user's identity.

Resistance to traffic analysis. Even without explicit metadata records, a sufficiently resourced observer who monitors network traffic can infer communication patterns from timing, volume, and connection patterns. The architecture must provide some degree of resistance to this class of analysis—through cover traffic, timing obfuscation, or routing structures that decorrelate observable network events from actual communication events.

No trust in infrastructure. The security properties must not depend on the good behavior of any server, relay, or intermediary. Any node in the system might be compromised, operated by an adversary, or subject to legal compulsion. The architecture must ensure that no single compromised node—and ideally no small coalition of compromised nodes—can reconstruct the metadata that the system is designed to protect.

These requirements are demanding. They rule out every centralized messaging architecture. They rule out simple federation, which scatters metadata but does not eliminate it. They rule out anonymity networks that sacrifice real-time performance. They rule out mix networks that sacrifice latency for stronger anonymity.

They describe something that does not yet exist in deployed form: a communication system that achieves the real-time performance users expect, the end-to-end encryption the industry has already delivered, and the metadata protection that neither the industry nor the research community has yet made practical.

The content encryption movement proved that a critical capability could be removed from servers—the ability to read messages—without destroying the messaging experience. The question is whether another critical capability can be removed: the ability to know who is communicating with whom. The next chapter presents an architecture—HermesP2P—designed to answer that question. The server that cannot read your messages should also not know who you are messaging. Both absences are protections. Both must be architectural.

CHAPTER 9

HermesP2P Architecture

Your encrypted message is private. The fact that you sent it is not.

Chapter 8 established that metadata—who communicated with whom, when, from where—reveals as much as content.

The architecture presented in this chapter eliminates the mediator. Messages flow through a peer-to-peer network where no single node possesses the complete communication path. The name invokes Hermes, the Greek intermediary who carried messages between realms without retaining them. The design embodies the same principle: messages pass through the network and cease to exist. Nodes hold messages only long enough to forward them. Nothing is archived. Nothing persists. The infrastructure facilitates communication without recording that communication occurred.

HermesP2P: Onion Routing

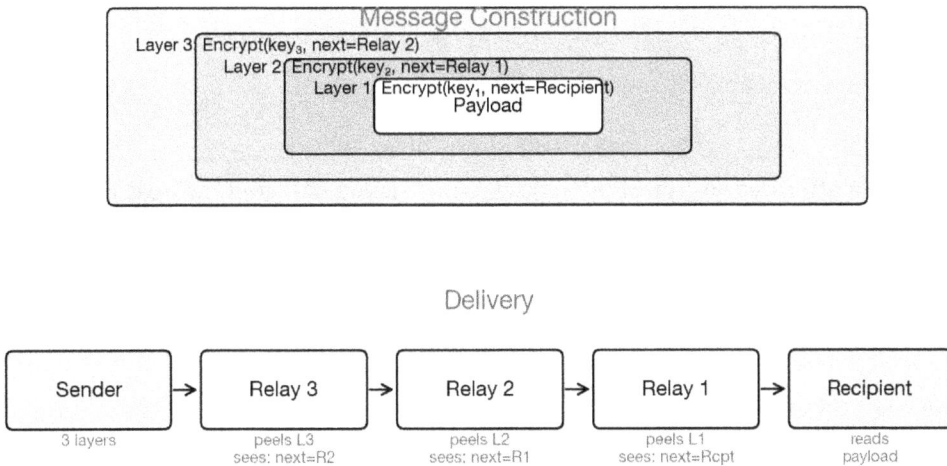

Figure 9.1: Onion Routing Message Flow. Each relay peels one encryption layer and learns only the previous hop and the next hop. Nothing more.

Onion Routing: Hiding the Path

When Alice sends a message to Bob, her client constructs a path through the network: her device, then relay node R1, then relay node R2, then relay node R3, then Bob's device. Each hop in this chain is encrypted separately, in layers. R1 receives a package encrypted with R1's public key. Inside that package is another package encrypted with R2's public key. Inside that is a package encrypted with R3's public key. Inside that is the message encrypted for Bob. Each relay decrypts one layer, discovers the address of the next hop, and forwards the remainder. No relay except Alice knows the complete path. No relay except Bob can read the message content.

The construction is straightforward. The sender builds from the inside out, starting with the innermost layer—the payload for the final recipient—and wrapping outward, one encryption layer per relay.

```
function construct_onion(message, recipient_key, relay_path):
    // Start with the innermost layer: the actual message for the
recipient
    current = encrypt(recipient_key, message)

    // Wrap outward through the relay path, last relay first
    for i in reverse(relay_path):
        relay_address = relay_path[i].address
        relay_key = relay_path[i].public_key
        // Each layer contains the next hop address and the inner
package
        current = encrypt(relay_key, relay_address_next ||
current)

    return current
```

The variable relay_address_next is the address of the node that should receive the inner package after decryption. For the outermost layer, the next address is R2. For the next layer in, the next address is R3. For the innermost relay layer, the next address is Bob's routing address. Each relay sees exactly one address: where to send the package next.

A relay processing an incoming onion layer performs a single operation:

```
function process_relay(encrypted_package, my_private_key):
    // Decrypt one layer
    decrypted = decrypt(my_private_key, encrypted_package)

    // Extract the next destination and the remaining package
    next_hop = decrypted[0:ADDRESS_LENGTH]
    remaining = decrypted[ADDRESS_LENGTH:]

    // Forward without retention
    send(next_hop, remaining)
```

```
// Discard all state related to this message
clear(decrypted, encrypted_package)
```

The relay learns exactly three things: that it received a package from the previous node, that it should forward something to the next node, and the size of the package. It does not learn who originated the message, who will ultimately receive it, what the message says, or how many layers remain. The decryption reveals one address and one opaque blob. The relay forwards the blob to the address and forgets the transaction.

R1 knows that Alice sent something and that R2 should receive something. R1 does not know about R3 or Bob. R2 knows that R1 sent something and R3 should receive something. R2 does not know about Alice or Bob. R3 knows that R2 sent something and that Bob's routing address should receive something. R3 does not know about Alice or R1. The complete path exists only in Alice's client, which selected the relays and constructed the layers.

The path selection itself matters. Alice's client selects relays from a pool of available nodes, ideally choosing nodes operated by different parties in different jurisdictions. If Alice selects three relays all operated by the same entity, that entity can correlate traffic across all three hops and reconstruct the full path. The protocol cannot prevent this at the cryptographic level—it is a network topology problem. The mitigation is a diverse relay pool with enough independent operators that random selection is unlikely to land on a colluding set.

Recommended Primitives

The encryption at each layer uses X25519 for key agreement and ChaCha20-Poly1305 for authenticated symmetric encryption. Each layer's encryption uses a fresh ephemeral key, so that even if a relay's long-term private key is later compromised, previously relayed traffic cannot be retrospectively decrypted. This is forward secrecy applied per hop.[1] The Sphinx packet format provides a well-studied construction for this pattern[2], with the additional property that the packet maintains a constant size at each hop, preventing relays from inferring their position in the chain based on packet size.

Message Structure

Every message in the network follows a common structure regardless of channel type. The structure has three components: an envelope visible to the network, the onion layers that the relays process, and an encrypted payload that only the recipient can read.

```
{
```

---

[1]   Forward secrecy per hop follows from the use of ephemeral X25519 key pairs at each relay. After the shared secret is derived and used, the ephemeral private key is discarded. Compromise of a relay's long-term key does not reveal past session keys. This is the same construction used in TLS 1.3 (RFC 8446, Section 7.4.2).

[2]   Danezis, G. and Goldberg, I. "Sphinx: A Compact and Provably Secure Mix Format." *Proceedings of the 2009 IEEE Symposium on Security and Privacy*, pp. 269-282. Sphinx provides bitwise unlinkability between incoming and outgoing packets at each hop, constant packet size, and replay protection.

```
"envelope": {
  "version": 1,
  "message_id": "random_128_bit_identifier",
  "size": 1024,
  "created": 1703880000
},
"layers": [
  {
    "encrypted_for": "relay_1_ephemeral_public_key",
    "ciphertext": "..."
  }
],
"payload": {
  "content": "encrypted_message_bytes",
  "content_type": "text/plain",
  "ttl": 3600,
  "timestamp": 1703880000,
  "nonce": "random_192_bit"
}
}
```

The envelope is unencrypted. It contains the protocol version, a random message identifier used for deduplication (so nodes do not re-forward messages they have already seen), the padded size of the message, and a creation timestamp. The message identifier is random and carries no information about the sender or recipient. It exists solely so that a node receiving the same message twice—which will happen in a gossip network—can recognize the duplicate and discard it.

The layers field contains the outermost onion layer. As each relay processes the message, it decrypts this field, extracts the next hop, and replaces the field with the inner layer before forwarding. By the time the message reaches the recipient, the layers field contains the final encrypted payload.

The payload field is encrypted for the ultimate recipient. It contains the message content, a content type indicator, a time-to-live (TTL) value in seconds, and a timestamp. The TTL governs how long the network will continue to propagate and store the message. When the TTL expires, nodes discard the message. The timestamp allows the recipient to assess message freshness and provides replay protection—a message with a timestamp far in the past is suspect.

Padding is applied at the envelope level. All messages are padded to one of a small number of fixed sizes (1 KB, 4 KB, 16 KB, 64 KB) to prevent message size from leaking information about content type or length. A one-word acknowledgment and a paragraph of text are both transmitted as 1 KB packets. This wastes bandwidth. It is the cost of preventing size-based inference.

Channel Types

The network supports three channel types, each designed for a different communication pattern. The types differ in who can read messages, how messages propagate, and what cryptographic operations are involved. They share the same underlying message structure and routing infrastructure.

Public Channels

A public channel is a broadcast medium. Anyone can subscribe. Anyone can read. Messages propagate through the gossip protocol to all subscribed nodes. The channel is identified by a deterministic hash of its name, so any node that knows the channel name can compute the channel identifier and subscribe.

```
PublicChannel = {
    "channel_id": hash("channel_name"),
    "poh_threshold": 0.3,
    "description": "plaintext_description",
    "created": 1703880000
}
```

The `poh_threshold` field specifies the minimum Proof of Human score required to post to this channel. Any node can read messages on the channel, but posting requires attaching a PoH attestation that meets or exceeds the threshold. The threshold is set by the channel creator and propagated as part of the channel metadata.

Messages posted to public channels are signed by the sender's pseudonymous identity key. The signature serves two purposes: it allows recipients to verify that the message was not tampered with in transit, and it allows recipients to associate multiple messages from the same pseudonym over time. The pseudonym is a public key that serves as the sender's identity on this channel. It is derived from the anonymous identity layer described in Chapter 3 and is unlinkable to identities on other channels or platforms.

A public channel message includes the PoH attestation:

```
PublicMessage = {
    "channel_id": hash("channel_name"),
    "sender_pubkey": "ed25519_public_key",
    "content": "plaintext_or_formatted_message",
    "poh_attestation": {
        "score": 0.45,
        "issuer_signature": "ed25519_signature",
        "issued_at": 1703870000
    },
    "signature": "ed25519_signature_over_all_fields",
    "timestamp": 1703880000,
    "ttl": 86400
}
```

Nodes that receive a public channel message validate the sender's signature, verify the PoH attestation against the channel's threshold, and then decide whether to store and forward the message. Messages that fail validation are dropped silently.

Private Channels

A private channel restricts readership to members who share a symmetric encryption key. Messages are encrypted with the channel key before being released into the network. They propagate through the same gossip mechanism as public channel messages—any node will forward them—but only nodes that possess the decryption key can read the content.

```
PrivateChannel = {
    "channel_id": "random_256_bit_identifier",
    "symmetric_key": "chacha20_256_bit_key",
    "members": ["pubkey_1", "pubkey_2", "pubkey_3"]
}
```

Membership is defined by possession of the symmetric key. There is no membership list stored on the network. The members field in the schema above exists only in each member's local client configuration. If Alice, Bob, and Carol share the channel key, they are members. If Dave obtains the key—whether through invitation or compromise—Dave becomes a member. The system has no mechanism to distinguish authorized key possession from unauthorized key possession, because from the protocol's perspective, there is no difference. The key is the membership credential.

This has implications for revocation. If a member should be removed, the remaining members must generate a new channel key and distribute it among themselves, excluding the departing member. The old channel ID is abandoned. Messages encrypted under the old key remain readable by the former member. Messages encrypted under the new key are not. Revocation is key rotation, not access control list modification.

Messages on private channels are encrypted before signing:

```
PrivateMessage = {
    "channel_id": "random_256_bit_identifier",
    "ciphertext": encrypt(channel_key, {
        "sender_pubkey": "ed25519_public_key",
        "content": "message_content",
        "signature": "ed25519_signature",
        "timestamp": 1703880000
    }),
    "ttl": 3600
}
```

The sender's identity and the message content are inside the encrypted payload. Network nodes that forward the message see only the channel identifier, the ciphertext, and the TTL. They cannot determine who posted the message or what it says. They cannot even determine the number of members, because the channel identifier is random and the encrypted messages are indistinguishable from random data to non-members, under the standard assumption that ChaCha20-Poly1305 ciphertext is semantically secure.[3]

---

3   Bernstein, D.J. "ChaCha, a variant of Salsa20." https://cr.yp.to/chacha.html, 2008. ChaCha20-Poly1305 is an IETF-standardized AEAD cipher (RFC 8439) with no known attacks faster than

Direct Messages

Direct messages route to a specific recipient using onion routing. The sender encrypts the message for the recipient's public key, wraps it in onion layers through a selected relay path, and releases it into the network. The message hops through intermediate relays until it reaches a node connected to the recipient. The recipient decrypts and reads.

```
DirectMessage = {
    "recipient_address": "derived_ephemeral_address",
    "onion_layers": "encrypted_relay_layers",
    "payload": encrypt(recipient_public_key, {
        "sender_pubkey": "ed25519_public_key",
        "content": "message_content",
        "sender_signature": "ed25519_signature",
        "timestamp": 1703880000
    }),
    "ttl": 300
}
```

The `recipient_address` is not the recipient's long-term public key. It is an ephemeral address derived from the recipient's key schedule—a rotating address that changes periodically. The recipient publishes (or makes discoverable through the DHT) a current routing address that other nodes can use to reach them. The address rotates on a schedule known only to the recipient, so that an observer who learns the routing address at time T cannot use it to identify the recipient at time T+1.

The sender encrypts the payload for the recipient's long-term public key, ensuring that only the intended recipient can read the content. The sender's identity is inside the encrypted payload, visible only to the recipient. The network sees the ephemeral routing address and the onion layers. It does not see who sent the message or who will read it.

Direct messages typically carry a shorter TTL than channel messages. They are intended for a specific recipient, and if the recipient is not reachable within the TTL window, the message expires. This is a genuine limitation: offline delivery is harder in a peer-to-peer network than in a centralized system where the server holds messages indefinitely. The tradeoff is explicit. A server that holds messages for offline delivery is a server that knows who has pending messages and can be compelled to disclose that information. The TTL-limited model accepts delivery failure as preferable to metadata retention.

Gossip Protocol: Message Propagation

Public and private channel messages propagate through a gossip protocol. The mechanism is epidemic: each node that receives a valid message forwards it to a subset of its peers, and those peers forward to their peers, until the message has reached all subscribed nodes or its TTL has expired.

---

brute-force key search on the full 256-bit key space.

HermesP2P: Gossip Propagation

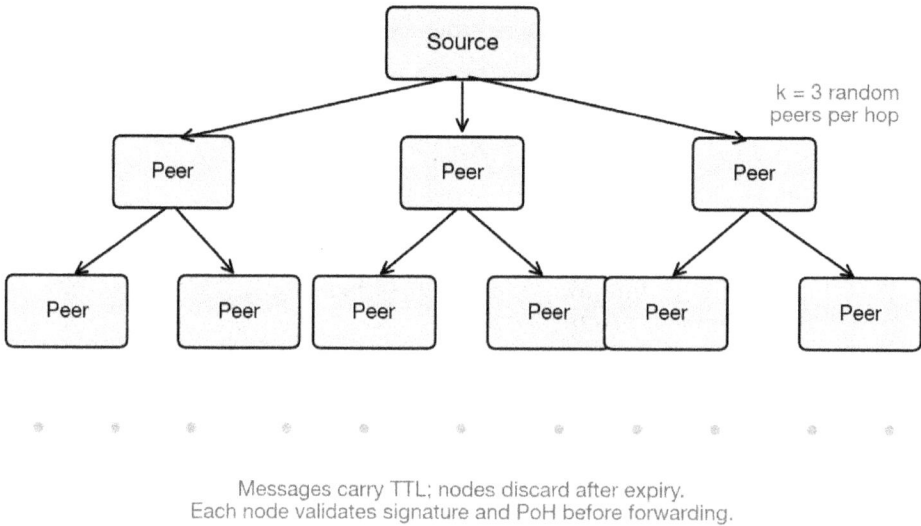

Messages carry TTL; nodes discard after expiry.
Each node validates signature and PoH before forwarding.

Figure 9.2: Gossip Protocol Message Propagation. Node A originates the message and forwards it to a random subset of peers. Each receiving node decrements the TTL, checks for duplicates, and fans out to its own peers. The message spreads epidemically until it reaches all subscribed nodes or the TTL expires.

The protocol operates as follows:

```
function on_message_received(message, source_peer):
    // Step 1: Deduplication
    if message.message_id in seen_messages:
        return   // already processed

    // Step 2: Validate structure
    if not valid_envelope(message):
        return   // malformed

    // Step 3: For public channels, validate signature and PoH
    if message.channel_id in public_channels:
        if not verify_signature(message):
            return   // invalid signature
        if not verify_poh(message, public_channels[message.
channel_id].poh_threshold):
            return   // insufficient humanness score

    // Step 4: Check TTL
    if message.timestamp + message.ttl < current_time():
        return   // expired
```

```
// Step 5: Store in local buffer
seen_messages.add(message.message_id, expiry=message.ttl)
message_buffer.store(message)

// Step 6: Forward to k random peers (excluding source)
peers = select_random_peers(k, exclude=[source_peer])
for peer in peers:
    send(peer, message)
```

The parameter k—the fanout—determines how aggressively messages spread. A higher k means faster propagation and more redundancy, at the cost of more bandwidth. A lower k means slower propagation and less bandwidth consumption, at the risk of messages failing to reach all subscribers. Typical values for k range from 3 to 7, depending on network size and message volume.

The seen_messages set is a deduplication filter, typically implemented as a Bloom filter or a bounded hash set that retains message identifiers for the duration of the message's TTL. When a node receives a message it has already seen, it drops the duplicate without forwarding. This prevents messages from circulating indefinitely and consuming bandwidth exponentially.

The message_buffer is a TTL-limited store. Messages live in the buffer until their TTL expires, at which point they are deleted. There is no archival. There is no long-term storage. The buffer exists to serve messages to peers who request recent channel history (for example, a node that was temporarily offline and reconnects). Once the TTL expires, the message is gone. The default state is deletion.

The gossip protocol is probabilistic. There is no guarantee that every message reaches every subscriber. In practice, with sufficient fanout and network connectivity, message delivery rates are high—mathematical models of epidemic protocols show that with k $>=$ $\ln(N)$ + c (where N is the network size and c is a small constant), the probability of reaching all nodes approaches 1. But "approaches 1" is not "equals 1." Some messages will be lost, particularly during network partitions or when the recipient's peers are all temporarily offline. This is a property of the architecture, not a bug. Guaranteed delivery requires a persistent store that knows who has and has not received each message—which is exactly the metadata the architecture is designed to eliminate.

Proof of Human as Spam Resistance

Public channels face a problem that private channels and direct messages do not: anyone can post. Without some mechanism to limit participation, a public channel becomes a target for spam. A single operator running a thousand bot accounts can flood any public channel with noise, drowning legitimate conversation.

The architecture's answer is the Proof of Human mechanism described in Chapter 7. Public channels specify a minimum PoH threshold. To post, a sender must attach a PoH attestation—a signed claim from the identity layer that the sender has accumulated a humanness score at or above the threshold. Nodes that receive public channel messages verify this attestation before storing or forwarding the message. Messages from senders below the threshold are dropped.

The economics are the point. A PoH score of 0.3 represents roughly $1,000 in effort to forge (see Chapter 7's effort scale). A bot operator who wants to flood a channel with spam must invest $1,000 per bot identity that meets the threshold. A thousand bots require a million dollars. The attack does not become impossible. It becomes expensive. And expensive attacks are attacks that most adversaries do not undertake.

The threshold is tunable per channel. A casual discussion channel might set the threshold at 0.15—tens of dollars to forge, sufficient to deter trivial bot swarms. A channel used for coordination among journalists or activists might set the threshold at 0.4 or higher, requiring substantial accumulated evidence of humanity. The channel creator sets the threshold based on their assessment of the threat model.

This mechanism does not prevent a determined, well-funded adversary from participating. Nothing does. What it prevents is the cheap, scalable abuse that renders public forums unusable. The marginal cost of an additional fake identity goes from zero to a figure that scales with the channel's threshold. That shift in economics—from free to costly—is the entire protection.

Composition with Anonymous Identity

If participants authenticate via the Anonymous Identity architecture described in Chapter 3, their messaging pseudonyms are unlinkable to identities on other platforms.

The connection works as follows. A user's identity on a HermesP2P channel is an Ed25519 public key derived from their site-specific anonymous token. The derivation is deterministic for a given user on a given channel, so the pseudonym is stable within the channel—other members recognize returning participants. But the derivation uses the channel identifier as an input, so the same user on a different channel produces a different pseudonym. An observer who knows a user's pseudonym on Channel A cannot determine that user's pseudonym on Channel B, because the derivation is a one-way function of inputs that include the channel identifier.

This means that a prominent voice on a public discussion channel, a member of a private coordination channel, and a participant in direct message conversations may all be the same person, and no one—not even the network infrastructure—can establish that linkage. The unlinkability is cryptographic, not policy-based.[4] It does not depend on the user remembering to use different names or the platform promising not to correlate accounts. Under the assumption that the channel-keyed derivation function is a secure pseudorandom function—a standard property of HMAC-based constructions—the correlation is computationally infeasible.[5]

---

[4]   The unlinkability property follows from the standard construction: the pseudonym on each channel is derived as PRF(master_secret, channel_id), where PRF is a pseudorandom function. An adversary who observes pseudonyms on two different channels cannot determine whether they belong to the same user without inverting the PRF, which is computationally infeasible under standard assumptions.

[5]   Preimage resistance of SHA-256 is a standard assumption in modern cryptography. The best known preimage attack on SHA-256 requires approximately 2256 operations. See Rogaway, P. and

Node Discovery and Network Bootstrap

A peer-to-peer network must solve the bootstrap problem: how does a new node find its first peers? There is no central server to connect to. The network exists only as the set of nodes that are currently participating. A node that knows no other nodes cannot participate.

The solution is pragmatic rather than elegant. New nodes connect to a small set of bootstrap nodes—well-known addresses published in the client software, in community directories, or shared through out-of-band communication. The bootstrap nodes are not special in protocol terms. They are ordinary nodes that have volunteered to serve as initial contact points. They introduce the new node to a handful of their own peers. Those peers introduce the new node to additional peers. Within a few rounds of introduction, the new node has a diverse set of connections and no longer depends on the bootstrap nodes.

The bootstrap nodes represent a centralization risk. If all bootstrap nodes are operated by the same entity, or if all are subject to the same jurisdiction, that entity or jurisdiction can deny new users access to the network. The mitigation is diversity: multiple independent bootstrap nodes operated by different parties in different jurisdictions, with the ability for users to configure custom bootstrap nodes. The protocol does not depend on any specific bootstrap node. It depends on the new user being able to reach at least one node that is already connected.

After initial bootstrap, peer discovery continues through gossip. Nodes periodically exchange peer lists with their neighbors, learning about new nodes and dropping nodes that have become unreachable. The network topology is dynamic, self-healing, and resistant to the loss of any individual node. There is no authoritative directory. The network's knowledge of itself is distributed across all participants.

The bootstrap problem is real and should not be minimized. A user in a restrictive network environment—behind a national firewall, on a network that blocks known bootstrap addresses—may be unable to join the network at all. This is a deployment challenge, not a protocol design flaw, but the distinction is cold comfort to the user who cannot connect. Techniques borrowed from censorship-circumvention tools (domain fronting, pluggable transports, bridge relays) can help, but they add complexity and operational overhead. The honest assessment is that network bootstrap in adversarial environments remains difficult.

Traffic Analysis: What the Architecture Does Not Hide

The onion routing and gossip protocol protect against passive, centralized metadata collection. No single node in the network possesses the complete relationship graph. No single node can be subpoenaed to produce a comprehensive record of who communicated with whom. This is a substantial improvement over centralized messaging, where

---

Shrimpton, T. "Cryptographic Hash-Function Basics." *Fast Software Encryption*, 2004, for formal definitions.

a single legal demand yields the entire graph.

It is not a complete defense. Several classes of analysis remain viable against a sufficiently resourced adversary, and the limits are real.

Timing Correlation

An adversary who can observe both endpoints of a communication—Alice's device sending a message and Bob's device receiving a message a short time later—can correlate the timing and infer that Alice communicated with Bob. The onion routing hides the path through the network but does not hide the fact that traffic entered the network at Alice's end and exited at Bob's end.

The correlation becomes stronger with more observations. A single coincidence in timing is weak evidence. A pattern of coincidences—Alice sends at 9:00:00, Bob receives at 9:00:02, repeatedly—is strong evidence. The more messages Alice sends to Bob, the more data points the adversary accumulates, and the higher the confidence of the correlation.

This attack requires real-time observation of specific endpoints. It does not scale the way log analysis does. An adversary cannot perform timing correlation retroactively on historical data, because the data was never recorded.[6] The adversary must be watching both endpoints simultaneously, which requires knowing (or guessing) who to watch before the communication occurs. This is a fundamentally different capability from querying a server's logs after the fact.

Volume Analysis

Even without identifying specific communications, an adversary who monitors a node's network traffic can observe patterns. A node that generates a burst of traffic every weekday at 9 AM is probably operated by someone with a regular schedule. A node whose traffic volume spikes immediately after a public event may be commenting on that event. Traffic volume and timing patterns reveal behavioral information even when the content and endpoints are hidden.

Global Adversary

A nation-state with visibility into network infrastructure across many jurisdictions can observe traffic entering and exiting the network at multiple points. The more points the adversary monitors, the more correlations become possible. Against an adversary who can see all traffic everywhere, the protections of onion routing diminish because the adversary observes the intermediate relays as well as the endpoints.

This is not a solvable problem with routing alone. It is a fundamental property of any network that uses the existing internet as its transport layer. The packets must traverse physical infrastructure. Whoever controls that infrastructure can observe the

---

6   This distinction—prospective vs. retrospective surveillance—is central to Tor's threat model. See Dingledine et al. 2004, Section 3.1: Tor explicitly does not defend against a global passive adversary but does raise the cost of targeted surveillance from "query the logs" to "watch the network in real time."

packets. Encryption hides the content. It does not hide the fact that packets are moving, their sizes, their timing, or the IP addresses of the nodes sending and receiving them.

Cover Traffic as Mitigation

The standard mitigation for traffic analysis is cover traffic: nodes send a constant stream of messages regardless of whether actual communication is occurring. Real messages are indistinguishable from cover traffic because both look like encrypted packets of the same size sent at the same rate. An adversary who observes the node's traffic cannot determine when real communication occurs because the traffic pattern does not change.

The cost is substantial. Cover traffic means every node in the network is sending data continuously—consuming bandwidth, consuming battery on mobile devices, consuming data plan allowances. The bandwidth overhead is proportional to the cover traffic rate, and meaningful protection requires a rate high enough that real messages are a small fraction of total traffic.

In practice, most users will not accept this cost. A mobile user on a metered data plan will not enable a feature that consumes gigabytes of bandwidth per month to send kilobytes of actual messages. This is not a technical judgment. It is an economic one. The protection is available to those who choose to accept the cost. Most will not.

Cover traffic is effective but expensive, and the expense means it will be used by a small minority of privacy-conscious users rather than the general population. For those users, timing correlation becomes significantly harder. For the majority, timing correlation remains a viable attack. The architecture makes this a user choice rather than a system default because imposing the cost on all users would reduce adoption to the point where the network itself becomes unviable.

Prior Art and Design Rationale

The underlying techniques are not novel. Onion routing has existed since the mid-1990s. Gossip protocols are older than the internet. What matters is how these mechanisms integrate with the identity architecture established in Chapters 3 and 7, how the channel model supports different communication patterns, and where the protections end.

HermesP2P is not the first system to attempt private messaging over a decentralized network. Several serious projects have attacked the same problem, each with real engineering talent behind it, and each hitting a specific wall. Understanding those walls is necessary for understanding the choices made here.

Tor is the obvious starting point.[7] Tor provides anonymity through onion routing with a volunteer relay network, and it works—millions of people use it daily. The Tor network's design is well-studied and its threat model is precisely documented, which is more than most privacy tools can claim. HermesP2P borrows the core insight: layered encryption through a multi-hop path so that no single relay knows both endpoints. But Tor optimizes for low-latency interactive use (web browsing), which makes it vulnerable

---

7   Dingledine, R., Mathewson, N., and Syverson, P. "Tor: The Second-Generation Onion Router." *Proceedings of the 13th USENIX Security Symposium*, 2004.

to timing correlation attacks. An adversary who can observe traffic entering and leaving the Tor network can correlate flows by volume and timing.[8] Tor's designers know this and state it plainly in their threat model. HermesP2P's messaging use case tolerates higher latency, which opens design space for timing obfuscation that Tor's interactive model cannot afford.

Vuvuzela and **Stadium** took a different approach entirely.[9][10] These systems, developed at MIT and Stanford respectively, provide provable metadata-hiding guarantees by requiring all participants to send messages in synchronized rounds, with cover traffic filling every slot. The result is mathematically elegant: an adversary learns nothing about who communicated with whom. The cost is bandwidth. Every participant sends a message in every round, whether they have anything to say or not. The bandwidth overhead scales with the number of participants, not the number of actual messages. For a research prototype, this is acceptable. For a deployed system that needs to run on mobile devices over metered connections, it is a hard stop. HermesP2P makes cover traffic optional and user-controlled rather than mandatory, accepting weaker guarantees in exchange for deployability.

Pond, designed by Adam Langley at Google, was the most thoughtfully designed secure messaging system never to achieve adoption.[11] Langley's design document remains worth reading. Pond used a mix network with Tor for transport, forward-secret ratcheted encryption, and careful metadata minimization. It was discontinued in 2015—not from technical failure but from the adoption problem that plagues all privacy tools: the system is useless until your contacts are on it, and your contacts will not join until it is useful. Pond required dedicated servers operated by trusted parties, creating a deployment bottleneck. HermesP2P's peer-to-peer model avoids the server dependency, though it inherits its own bootstrap challenges.

Briar is the closest deployed system to what HermesP2P describes.[12] Built for journalists and activists operating under surveillance, Briar routes all traffic through Tor, supports store-and-forward messaging, and can operate over local WiFi or Bluetooth when internet access is unavailable. Briar is real software used by real people in real danger, which earns it a respect that whitepapers cannot claim. Its limitation is its dependency on Tor. Briar inherits Tor's timing-analysis vulnerabilities and Tor's network reachabil-

---

8   Murdoch, S.J. and Danezis, G. "Low-Cost Traffic Analysis of Tor." *Proceedings of the 2005 IEEE Symposium on Security and Privacy*, pp. 183-195. Demonstrates that Tor's low-latency design permits timing correlation by an adversary observing both ends of a circuit.

9   van den Hooff, J., Lazar, D., Zaharia, M., and Zeldovich, N. "Vuvuzela: Scalable Private Messaging Resistant to Traffic Analysis." *Proceedings of the 25th ACM Symposium on Operating Systems Principles (SOSP)*, 2015.

10   Tyagi, N., Gilad, Y., Leung, D., Zaharia, M., and Zeldovich, N. "Stadium: A Distributed Metadata-Private Messaging System." *Proceedings of the 26th ACM Symposium on Operating Systems Principles (SOSP)*, 2017.

11   Langley, A. "Pond." https://github.com/agl/pond. Discontinued 2015. The design document at https://pond.imperialviolet.org remains one of the clearest articulations of secure messaging tradeoffs in the literature.

12   Briar Project. https://briarproject.org. Peer-to-peer encrypted messaging designed for activists, journalists, and anyone who needs a safe way to communicate. Routes traffic through Tor; supports direct WiFi/Bluetooth transport.

ity constraints. In countries that block Tor, Briar becomes difficult to use. HermesP2P's transport layer is not tied to Tor, which provides flexibility at the cost of losing Tor's large and established relay network.

Loopix uses a mix network architecture with Poisson-distributed cover traffic to provide strong anonymity guarantees with tunable latency.[13] Messages are delayed at each mix node according to an exponential distribution, which destroys the timing correlations that plague Tor. The cover traffic is generated stochastically rather than in synchronized rounds (unlike Vuvuzela), which reduces bandwidth overhead. The tradeoff is latency: messages may take seconds to minutes to traverse the mix network, depending on the parameterization. For email-like communication, this is fine. For interactive messaging, users expect sub-second delivery, and Loopix's design makes that difficult to guarantee without weakening the timing protections.

Each of these systems identified the correct problem: metadata is the vulnerability. Each hit a wall. HermesP2P's design responds to those specific walls: onion routing for asynchronous messages rather than interactive streams (permitting timing jitter Tor cannot add), optional cover traffic rather than mandatory (trading provable guarantees for practical bandwidth budgets), fully peer-to-peer operation (avoiding Pond's deployment bottleneck), transport-layer independence (avoiding Briar's Tor dependency), and tolerance for seconds of latency rather than demanding sub-second delivery (accepting Loopix's insight about mixing without its cost to interactive use).

Whether these are the right choices depends on the threat model. Against a passive adversary collecting metadata from a central server, the protections are strong. Against a global adversary performing real-time traffic analysis, the protections are partial. The prior art makes clear that no deployed system has solved the global adversary problem at consumer-acceptable cost. HermesP2P does not claim to have solved it either.

What This Does Not Protect Against

The architecture eliminates centralized metadata accumulation. It makes mass surveillance expensive by removing the database that mass surveillance depends on. It forces investigation to be targeted rather than retrospective. These are genuine and substantial protections against the threats that most users actually face.

The architecture does not provide absolute anonymity. The following threats remain.

Timing correlation by network-edge observers. An adversary monitoring Alice's network connection and Bob's network connection simultaneously can correlate message timing. The onion routing hides the path but not the endpoints. Against an adversary with sufficient network visibility, the protection of intermediate relays degrades. Cover traffic mitigates this but at a cost most users will not pay.

Endpoint compromise. If Alice's device is compromised—through malware, through physical access, through a vulnerability in the operating system—the adversary reads messages before encryption and after decryption. No network-layer protection helps

13   Piotrowska, A.M., Hayes, J., Elahi, T., Meiser, S., and Danezis, G. "The Loopix Anonymity System." *Proceedings of the 26th USENIX Security Symposium*, 2017.

when the endpoint is hostile. Device security is a different problem from network security. The architecture protects communication in transit and at rest on the network. It does not protect the devices that originate and terminate communication.

Offline delivery challenges. A peer-to-peer network with TTL-limited messages cannot reliably deliver to recipients who are offline for extended periods. A centralized server stores messages until the recipient connects. HermesP2P does not, because a store-and-forward node that holds messages for a specific recipient is a node that knows the recipient has pending messages—which is metadata. The tradeoff is explicit: reliable offline delivery requires someone to hold the message, and holding the message generates metadata. The architecture accepts delivery failure as the lesser harm. For users who are consistently online, this is not a practical problem. For users who connect intermittently—mobile users with poor connectivity, users in regions with unreliable infrastructure—message loss is a real limitation.

The bootstrap problem. A new user who cannot reach any existing node cannot join the network. Bootstrap nodes mitigate this but introduce a centralization point. A censoring regime that blocks known bootstrap addresses can prevent its citizens from joining. Censorship-circumvention techniques exist but add complexity. The problem is not solved; it is managed.

Sybil attacks on relay selection. If an adversary operates a large fraction of the relay nodes in the network, random relay selection may choose a path consisting entirely of adversary-controlled nodes. The adversary can then correlate traffic across all hops and reconstruct the full communication path. The mitigation is a large and diverse relay pool. The vulnerability is proportional to the adversary's share of the network.

Compulsion of individual participants. The architecture ensures that no infrastructure operator possesses the relationship graph. It does not protect against legal or extralegal compulsion of Alice or Bob individually. An adversary who compels Alice to unlock her device has access to Alice's message history as stored on her device. The architecture ensures that compelling the network yields nothing. It cannot ensure that compelling the endpoint yields nothing, because the endpoint must hold plaintext to be useful to its owner.

Putting It Together

The complete communication flow integrates the components described above. Alice wants to send a direct message to Bob.

1. Alice's client derives Bob's current ephemeral routing address from Bob's published key schedule.

2. Alice's client composes the message and encrypts it for Bob's long-term public key. The encrypted payload includes Alice's pseudonymous sender identity and her signature, visible only to Bob after decryption.

3. Alice's client selects three relay nodes from the network's peer pool, choosing nodes operated by different parties.

4. Alice's client constructs the onion layers: encrypts the payload and Bob's routing address for R3's key, wraps that in an encryption for R2's key with R3's address, wraps that in an encryption for R1's key with R2's address.

5. Alice's client sends the outermost package to R1.

6. R1 decrypts one layer, discovers R2's address, forwards the remainder to R2, and discards all state.

7. R2 decrypts one layer, discovers R3's address, forwards the remainder to R3, and discards all state.

8. R3 decrypts one layer, discovers Bob's routing address, forwards the remainder toward Bob, and discards all state.

9. Bob's client receives the package, decrypts it with his private key, reads the message, and verifies Alice's signature.

At no point in this process does any single node possess both the sender's identity and the recipient's identity. Alice knows the full path but is the sender. Bob knows the message content and Alice's pseudonym but does not know the relay path. Each relay knows only its immediate predecessor and successor. The relationship between Alice and Bob is visible only to Alice and Bob.

For public channel messages, Alice constructs the message with her PoH attestation, signs it, and releases it to her connected peers. The gossip protocol carries it across the network. Each node validates the signature and PoH threshold before forwarding. The message reaches all subscribers. No central server recorded that Alice posted it.

For private channel messages, Alice encrypts with the shared symmetric key, then releases to the gossip network. The encrypted blob propagates to all nodes, but only channel members can decrypt. The channel's existence and membership are invisible to the network.

Design Decisions and Their Costs

Every design decision in this architecture trades one property for another. The tradeoffs are deliberate, and understanding them is necessary for evaluating whether the architecture is appropriate for a given use case.

Ephemerality over reliability. Messages expire. The network does not guarantee delivery. Centralized systems guarantee delivery by storing messages persistently, which creates the metadata the architecture is designed to eliminate. The cost of ephemerality is message loss when the recipient is unreachable within the TTL window.

Decentralization over performance. Messages route through multiple relays, adding latency. Each hop adds network round-trip time. A direct message through three relays takes roughly three times longer than a direct connection. For text messaging, the additional latency is measured in hundreds of milliseconds—noticeable but tolerable. For real-time voice or video, the latency may be prohibitive without careful relay selection.

Privacy over accountability on private channels. The network cannot determine who is a member of a private channel or who posted a particular message to it. This means the network also cannot moderate private channels, enforce content policies, or respond to abuse reports. Private channel governance is entirely the responsibility of the members who hold the key. The network provides the pipe. What flows through the pipe is not the network's concern and not within the network's capability to observe.

Bandwidth over metadata protection. Padding messages to fixed sizes, running the gossip protocol, and optionally generating cover traffic all consume bandwidth that a centralized system would not require. The bandwidth overhead is the cost of distributing the communication function across a network that retains nothing.

These tradeoffs are not regrettable compromises. They are the architecture. A system that guaranteed delivery would require persistent state. A system that minimized latency would require direct connections that reveal endpoints. A system that moderated private channels would require the ability to read them. The properties that the architecture lacks are the properties it must lack in order to provide the protections it provides. The constraints are not limitations of the engineering. They are consequences of the physics.

Recommended Cryptographic Primitives

The architecture relies on a small set of well-studied cryptographic primitives:

Function	Primitive
Identity keys	Ed25519
Key agreement	X25519
Symmetric encryption	ChaCha20-Poly1305
Onion packet format	Sphinx
Hashing	SHA-256
Channel key derivation	HKDF-SHA256

All primitives are available in libsodium, which provides consistent, audited implementations across platforms. The choice of ChaCha20-Poly1305 over AES-256-GCM is deliberate: ChaCha20 performs well in software without hardware acceleration, which matters for a network where nodes run on diverse hardware including mobile devices and low-power machines.

Summary

HermesP2P eliminates the central mediator from messaging. Messages route through a peer-to-peer network using onion encryption that hides the communication path from every relay. Public channels propagate via gossip with PoH-based spam resistance. Private channels encrypt with shared symmetric keys where membership requires possession of the channel key. Direct messages use ephemeral routing addresses and recipient-specific encryption. Messages carry TTLs and expire. Nothing persists.

The architecture makes passive, centralized surveillance impractical because there is no center to surveil. It makes retroactive investigation infeasible in the sense that there are no logs to query—not because querying is computationally hard, but because the data was never recorded. It forces any investigation to be targeted, prospective, and expensive—requiring real-time observation of specific endpoints rather than retrospective analysis of stored data.

The architecture does not defeat a global adversary with the resources to monitor a significant fraction of network infrastructure. It does not protect compromised endpoints. It does not guarantee delivery to offline recipients. It does not solve the bootstrap problem in censored environments. These limitations are stated rather than hidden because an architecture that overstates its protections is worse than one that understates them. The user who believes they are protected when they are not is in greater danger than the user who knows the limits.

What the architecture provides is the elimination of the metadata accumulation that current messaging systems generate as a structural byproduct of their design. Against data brokers, hackers, abusive ex-partners, employers, stalkers, and legal fishing expeditions—the adversaries that most people actually face—the absence of persistent metadata is substantial protection. The messages pass through and disappear. The infrastructure remembers nothing. The relationship between sender and recipient exists only on their own devices, under their own control, subject to their own decisions about retention.

The server that cannot read your messages should also not know who you are messaging. This architecture ensures it does not, because no such server exists.

Identity is private. Storage is blind. Communication is ephemeral. The next problem is multi-party coordination: when a workflow spans multiple organizations, how do you prevent each intermediary from accumulating a surveillance record of the complete transaction? The next chapter examines the intermediary problem.

CHAPTER 10

The Intermediary Problem

Every multi-party workflow leaks. Not because the parties are malicious, not because the systems are poorly designed, but because coordination requires information to flow between participants, and every participant along the way retains a copy of what it saw. The result is that any transaction involving more than two parties distributes a complete record of the transaction across entities that have no obligation to protect it and every incentive to exploit it.

The previous chapters addressed problems where one party held data it should not have been able to read. The storage problem was about a server that could see everything in its database. The metadata problem was about a network that could observe everything in transit. This chapter addresses a different structural failure: when multiple parties must cooperate to accomplish a task, the act of cooperation itself creates a composite surveillance record that no single party requested and no single party controls.

The Data Leakage Matrix

Consider a purchase. Not a cash transaction at a counter, but the kind of transaction the internet economy runs on: a buyer selects an item from a seller, pays through a processor, and receives the item through a carrier. Four parties, each performing a legitimate function, each accumulating information as a byproduct of that function.

The payment processor sees the buyer's identity, billing address, card number, transaction amount, and the merchant's identity. The processor also sees the buyer's spending history across every merchant the buyer has ever patronized with that card. Each transaction adds to a longitudinal profile. The processor can determine whether a given purchase is typical or anomalous, can infer income brackets from spending patterns, can detect relationship changes from shifts in joint-account behavior. The processor needs the transaction details to authorize the payment. The processor does not need to retain a permanent cross-merchant behavioral profile, but retention is profitable, so retention is what happens.

The store sees the item selected, the shipping address, the payment authorization, and whatever browsing history preceded the purchase. The store knows which marketing funnel brought the buyer, how long the buyer deliberated, which alternatives the buyer considered. If the buyer has an account, the store sees the complete purchase history. The store shares this information with advertising networks that aggregate it with information from other stores, constructing a behavioral profile that no single store could build alone but that the advertising ecosystem assembles from the fragments each store provides.

The shipping carrier sees the physical parameters: origin address, destination address, package weight, declared value, delivery timing. The carrier observes the rhythm of deliveries over time—frequency, destinations, seasonal patterns. Weight and declared value narrow the range of possible contents. Origin narrows the range further. A carrier that handles enough volume can infer product categories from physical characteristics alone.

If the buyer shares a financial account with a spouse or partner, the account statement reveals the transaction. The line item shows the merchant name and amount. A purchase intended as a surprise is visible in the routine review of shared finances. If the buyer shares an email account, the order confirmation arrives in the shared inbox. If the household uses a voice assistant, the device announces shipping updates to anyone present. If the household uses a doorbell camera, the delivery is recorded with the merchant's name visible on the packaging.

Each of these exposures is a structural consequence of how the system is built, not a failure of any particular component. The payment processor cannot authorize a transaction without knowing the transaction details. The carrier cannot deliver a package without knowing the destination. The store cannot fulfill an order without knowing what was ordered. The information flows because the coordination requires it. The problem is what happens after the coordination is complete: the information persists, aggregates, and propagates to parties who were never part of the original transaction.

The leakage matrix for a single purchase looks like this:

Party	Sees
Payment processor	Buyer identity, billing address, card number, amount, merchant ID, spending history
Store	Items selected, shipping address, payment token, browsing history, purchase history
Shipping carrier	Origin, destination, weight, declared value, delivery pattern
Shared financial account	Merchant name, amount, date
Shared email	Full order confirmation, itemized receipt
Voice assistant	Shipping notifications, merchant name
Doorbell camera	Delivery event, package markings

No single party sees everything. But the union of what all parties see is everything. The buyer's identity, the item purchased, the price paid, the destination, the timing, the behavioral context—the complete record exists, distributed across entities that will never coordinate to delete it and that individually lack the incentive to protect it.

This is one transaction. The problem compounds across transactions. The payment processor that sees a single purchase also sees every purchase. Over months and years, the processor constructs a spending biography: where the buyer shops, how much the buyer spends, how the buyer's patterns shift with seasons and life events. The store that sees one order also sees every return visit. The carrier that delivers one package observes the full delivery calendar. Each party's view, narrow in isolation, becomes comprehensive through repetition. The leakage is not a snapshot. It is a time-lapse.

The Pattern Extends

Commerce is the obvious case, but the structural problem is not specific to commerce. It appears wherever parties coordinate through shared intermediaries. The intermediary sees both sides of the interaction because seeing both sides is how it provides its service.

Customer relationship management. A business subscribes to a CRM platform and uploads customer contacts, interaction histories, sales pipelines, internal notes. The platform stores this data, indexes it, provides search and analytics, integrates with other services. The platform sees every customer the business has, every deal in progress, every note about every relationship. The platform's stated function is to help the business manage relationships. The platform's structural position gives it complete visibility into those relationships.

Analytics services. A website integrates a third-party analytics platform. The platform receives a record of every visitor: pages viewed, time spent, clicks, scrolls, referral sources, device characteristics, geographic location. The analytics service sees the complete behavioral stream of every user of every website that integrates its code. Across millions of sites, the service constructs behavioral profiles of individual users that span their entire web activity—not because any single site intended to share that information, but because the analytics code on each site reports to the same central service.

Legal tools. A law firm adopts a document review platform for litigation support. The platform processes privileged communications, confidential strategy documents, witness statements, and internal analyses. The platform's function is to search and organize these documents. The platform's structural position gives it access to information protected by attorney-client privilege—information whose exposure could compromise cases and harm clients.

Healthcare applications. A patient uses a health tracking application that integrates with their provider's electronic health records system. The application sees symptoms, medications, vital signs, and diagnostic results. The application vendor sees the patient's complete health trajectory. If the application integrates with a pharmacy, the pharmacy sees the prescriptions. If it integrates with an insurance portal, the insurer sees the claims. Each integration adds a party to the coordination, and each party retains what it sees.

Human resources platforms. A company uses an external HR system for payroll, benefits administration, and performance management. The platform sees every employee's compensation, tax information, Social Security number, health insurance selections, performance reviews, and disciplinary records. The platform is a single point of compromise for information that could enable identity theft, employment discrimination, and targeted social engineering against every employee of every company it serves.

The pattern is the same in every case. The intermediary accumulates comprehensive information as a structural byproduct of providing its service. The accumulation is not incidental. The accumulation is the service. The intermediary cannot search documents it cannot read. It cannot analyze behavior it cannot observe. It cannot manage relationships it cannot see. The intermediary's access to information is what makes it useful. That access is also what makes it dangerous.

And because the surveillance is a prerequisite, no amount of policy restraint or regulatory pressure can remove it without either breaking the service or changing the architecture. You cannot ask a system to stop seeing what it must see in order to operate.

SaaS as Surveillance Infrastructure

The software-as-a-service model has a structural problem that its marketing obscures. When a business subscribes to a SaaS platform, the business believes it is licensing software. What is actually happening is that the business is uploading its operational data to a third party that can read, analyze, and retain everything it receives.

This creates three forms of value extraction that go beyond the subscription fee.

Data monetization. The platform can analyze usage patterns across its customer base and sell aggregate insights. It can identify market trends from CRM data, predict economic shifts from financial data, detect industry movements from hiring data. The customers provided this data to manage their own operations. The platform converts it into a separate revenue stream. The conversion is possible because the platform can read what it stores.

Surveillance advertising. Platforms that offer free or subsidized tiers fund themselves through advertising that targets users based on the data the platform holds. The targeting is precise because the platform sees the user's actual behavior, not an inference from proxy signals. A CRM platform that knows which companies a salesperson is targeting can sell advertising to competitors of those companies. An analytics platform that knows which products a user researches can sell advertising to manufacturers of those products. The advertising revenue depends on the platform's ability to read user data.

Vendor lock-in through data accumulation. The longer a business uses a platform, the more data the platform holds. The data is stored in the platform's proprietary format, indexed by the platform's proprietary systems, integrated with the platform's proprietary ecosystem. Migrating to a competitor means extracting the data—a process the platform has no incentive to make easy and every incentive to make difficult. The data that the business uploaded has become the platform's retention mechanism. Switching costs increase with time not because the software becomes more valuable, but because the data becomes harder to leave.

These three dynamics—monetization, advertising, and lock-in—are not abuses of the SaaS model. They are the SaaS model. They are possible because the platform can read the data. They are profitable because the data is valuable. They persist because the customer has no alternative architecture that provides the platform's functionality without the platform's access.

When a breach occurs, the consequences follow from the access model. The platform stored readable data. The attacker obtained readable data. The breach notification explains that the platform takes security seriously and has engaged forensic investigators. The customers discover that trusting the platform with their data meant trusting the platform's security practices, its employee vetting, its infrastructure choices, its patch management, and the security practices of every third-party service the platform itself integrated with. The chain of trust is as long as the chain of dependencies, and any link's failure compromises the data.

The breach is the dramatic failure, but the routine operation is the deeper problem. Breaches are visible, investigated, disclosed. The ordinary data extraction—the daily monetization, the continuous profiling, the steady accumulation—is invisible, legal, and far more consequential in aggregate. A breach exposes data once. The business model exposes it continuously. The breach makes headlines. The business model makes quarterly earnings.

Secure Multi-Party Computation

The theoretical solution to the intermediary problem exists. Secure multi-party computation (MPC) allows multiple parties to jointly compute a function over their inputs while keeping those inputs private. Each party contributes secret data, the computation executes, the result emerges, and no party learns anything about the other parties' inputs beyond what the output reveals.

The mathematics is proven. Protocols exist for general computation on private inputs. Two parties can determine which of them is wealthier without either revealing their net worth. Multiple hospitals can compute aggregate disease statistics without any hospital revealing individual patient records. An auction can determine the winning bid without revealing losing bids. The theoretical framework is comprehensive and well-established.

The practical barriers are substantial. MPC protocols require multiple rounds of communication between all parties. The computational overhead ranges from modest for simple operations to prohibitive for complex ones. All parties must be online simultaneously for the computation to proceed. The protocols are specific to the computation being performed—a protocol for comparing two values is different from a protocol for computing an average, which is different from a protocol for performing a database join. General-purpose MPC, while theoretically possible, is orders of magnitude slower than plaintext computation for any nontrivial workload.

For narrow, high-stakes applications—key generation ceremonies, threshold signing, specific financial computations—MPC is practical and deployed. For the general case of multi-party coordination that constitutes the internet economy—the millions of transactions per second that involve payments, shipping, inventory, and customer service—MPC is not a viable architecture. The overhead is too high, the latency too great, the engineering complexity too severe.

MPC demonstrates that the intermediary problem is solvable in principle. It does not provide a solution that works in practice at the scale the problem demands. The existence proof matters—it tells us that the mathematics does not forbid what we want. The impracticality matters too—it tells us that solving the problem requires a different approach than computing on encrypted inputs in real time.

Trust Does Not Scale

Before the internet economy, the intermediary problem was managed through trust. You bought gifts at a local store where the owner knew you and had no interest in monetizing your purchase history. You paid with cash, which carried no identity. You handed the package to a neighbor or mailed it through a postal service whose operational culture treated mail as private. The coordination happened through relationships where trust was earned over time, where violations had social consequences, where the parties had ongoing stakes in each other's welfare.

This model does not survive contact with the internet economy. The parties to an online transaction are strangers, connected for a moment, separated by geography and jurisdiction, with no history and no future. The buyer in one country, the seller in another, the payment processor in a third, the carrier in a fourth. No party has earned the trust of any other. No party faces social consequences for violating the others' privacy. No ongoing relationship constrains behavior.

Platforms emerged to fill this trust gap. They became the trusted intermediary—the party that both sides accept because neither trusts the other. The platform mediates disputes, guarantees payments, ensures delivery. The platform sees everything because seeing everything is how it provides the trust that the parties cannot establish directly.

The platforms that mediate trust between strangers have become some of the largest companies in the world. Their position as the intermediary that everyone relies on is the source of both their revenue and their data accumulation. They profit from being necessary. They are necessary because organic trust does not scale to transactions between strangers across the globe.

Asking these platforms to voluntarily reduce their access to data is asking them to dismantle the mechanism that makes them profitable. Privacy policies promise data protection, but privacy policies are contractual, not structural. They describe what the platform says it will do with data it can read. They do not prevent the platform from reading the data. They do not survive a change in corporate ownership, a shift in business strategy, a government subpoena, or a breach that renders the policy irrelevant.

The history of privacy policies is a history of erosion. Policies that initially promised confidentiality are revised to permit sharing. Policies that promised data deletion are revised to permit retention. Policies that promised anonymity are revised to permit re-identification. Each revision is legal. Each revision is disclosed. Each revision expands the platform's access because the platform's incentives point consistently in one direction: more data, more access, more value extraction.

Regulation has attempted to constrain this dynamic. The results are instructive. Data protection laws require consent for data collection, purpose limitation for data use, and deletion on request. The platforms comply—formally. Consent is obtained through click-through agreements that no one reads. Purpose limitation is satisfied by defining the purpose broadly enough to encompass any profitable use. Deletion requests are honored for the specific data the user can identify, while derived data, aggregated profiles, and inferred attributes persist in systems the user cannot name and the regulation cannot reach. The regulation assumes a world where data collection is a discrete event that can be consented to and reversed. The reality is a continuous process of extraction where the valuable outputs are several transformations removed from the original inputs.

Requirements for a Solution

The intermediary problem cannot be solved by better policies, stronger regulations, or more trustworthy intermediaries. Policies depend on compliance. Regulations depend on enforcement. Trust depends on the ongoing good behavior of parties with structural incentives to misbehave. Each of these approaches assumes that the intermediary has access to the data and then attempts to constrain what the intermediary does with that access. The constraint is external to the architecture. It can be circumvented, revised, or ignored.

The structural requirement is different: coordination must happen without any party seeing the complete picture.

This is not a requirement for secrecy. The parties still need to perform their functions. The payment processor still needs to authorize the payment. The carrier still needs to deliver the package. The store still needs to fulfill the order. The requirement is that each party sees only what it needs for its function and nothing more—and that this limitation is enforced by the architecture, not by the party's willingness to comply.

The requirement is architectural blindness, not policy promises.

Specifically, a solution must satisfy the following constraints:

Information fragmentation. The data required for a multi-party workflow must be divided so that no single party—and no single intermediary—holds enough information to reconstruct the complete picture. The payment processor should not know what was purchased. The store should not know the buyer's financial identity. The carrier should not know the contents or the buyer. Each party receives the fragment necessary for its function and nothing else.

No accumulation. The fragments a party receives for one transaction must not be linkable to fragments from other transactions. If a payment processor handles a thousand transactions from the same buyer, the processor should not be able to determine that they came from the same buyer. Linkability enables profiling, and profiling reconstructs the complete picture that fragmentation was designed to prevent.

Architectural enforcement. The fragmentation must be enforced by cryptography, not by policy. A party that receives a fragment should be mathematically unable to recover the information excluded from its fragment. The protection should survive a compromised party, a malicious insider, a government subpoena, and a data breach. If the architecture depends on any party's good behavior, it is a policy solution disguised as an architecture.

Composability. The solution must work for multi-step workflows, not just pairwise interactions. A transaction that involves a buyer, a marketplace, a seller, a payment processor, a fraud detection service, and a shipping carrier must fragment information across all of these parties without any coalition of fewer than all parties being able to reconstruct the complete record.

Performance viability. The solution must operate at the speed and scale of actual internet commerce. A system that is theoretically secure but adds minutes of latency to every transaction is not a solution. It is a research result.

Graceful degradation. The solution must handle the real world, where parties go offline, messages are delayed, and not every participant in a workflow is running the latest privacy-preserving protocol. Interoperability with existing systems is a practical necessity, not an optional feature.

These requirements describe a system where intermediaries coordinate workflow without accumulating surveillance records—where the cooperation happens but the exposure does not. The requirements are demanding. They are also achievable.

The next chapter presents the Cryptogram and Delegator architecture: a system of encrypted task descriptions and blind intermediaries that enables multi-party workflows while ensuring that no party in the chain sees more than its designated fragment. The intermediary still coordinates. The intermediary no longer surveils.

CHAPTER 11

Cryptogram and Delegator Architecture

A payment processor needs your credit card number. A shipping company needs your address. Neither needs what the other has—but in current systems, both get everything.

The previous chapter established the intermediary problem: multi-party workflows distribute a complete surveillance record across every participant, and no amount of policy can prevent parties from reading data they structurally possess. The requirement is coordination without accumulation—an architecture where each party sees only the fragment necessary for its function and where this limitation is enforced by cryptography, not by promises.

This chapter presents that architecture. It consists of two components: a structured workflow document called a cryptogram, and a blind routing service called a delegator. The cryptogram fragments workflow information into sections, each encrypted for a specific recipient. The delegator moves the cryptogram between participants, advancing the workflow step by step, without possessing the keys to read any section. The result is multi-party coordination where the coordinator is structurally blind.

The design is not novel in its cryptographic primitives. Asymmetric encryption has existed for decades. What is novel is the composition: the deliberate fragmentation of workflow information so that no party accumulates the complete picture, enforced at the cryptographic level rather than the policy level. The store cannot see the shipping address because the store cannot decrypt the shipping address—not because the store promised not to look.

The Cryptogram

A cryptogram is a structured document that describes a multi-party workflow. It contains routing metadata—which services participate and in what order—and a set of encrypted sections, each containing the information a specific participant needs to perform its function.

The routing metadata is readable by the delegator. It must be, because the delegator needs to know where to send each section. The content of each section is readable only by the intended recipient. The delegator can see the envelope. The delegator cannot see what is inside.

The schema is straightforward:

```
cryptogram = {
  workflow_id:   unique identifier for this workflow instance,
```

```
        created:        timestamp,

    routing: {
        steps: [
            {
                step_number:    1,
                service:        "payment_processor",
                section:        "payment",
                encrypted_for:  payment_processor_public_key
            },
            {
                step_number:    2,
                service:        "store",
                section:        "order",
                encrypted_for:  store_public_key
            },
            {
                step_number:    3,
                service:        "carrier",
                section:        "shipping",
                encrypted_for:  carrier_public_key
            }
        ],
        current_step:   0
    },

    sections: {
        "payment":      encrypted_blob,    // decryptable only by payment
processor
        "order":        encrypted_blob,    // decryptable only by store
        "shipping":     encrypted_blob     // decryptable only by carrier
    },

    responses: {
        // populated as services complete their steps
        // each response encrypted for the next recipient that needs
it
    }
}
```

The routing block is the delegator's instruction set. It specifies the sequence of services, which section each service receives, and which public key each section is encrypted for. The delegator reads this block to determine what to do next. The sections block contains the actual workflow data, encrypted per-recipient. The responses block accumulates encrypted results as the workflow progresses—each response encrypted for the party that needs it in a subsequent step.

The workflow creator assembles the cryptogram before the workflow begins. The creator knows all the participants and what each needs. The creator encrypts each section with the recipient's public key, constructs the routing table, and hands the complete cryptogram to the delegator. From that point forward, the creator does not need to remain online. The workflow proceeds through the delegator's routing logic.

Multiple parties can contribute sections to the same cryptogram before it enters the routing phase. In the purchase example from the previous chapter, the buyer might contribute the payment section while a gift recipient contributes the product selection section. Each contributor encrypts their section for the appropriate recipient. Neither contributor can read the other's section. The cryptogram carries information from multiple sources, fragmented by design, each fragment locked to its intended reader.

Section Encryption

Each section is encrypted using the recipient's public key. The encryption binds the section to the specific workflow instance, preventing a section from being lifted out of one cryptogram and inserted into another.

```
function encrypt_section(recipient_public_key, plaintext,
workflow_id):
    // Generate ephemeral keypair for this encryption
    ephemeral_public, ephemeral_secret = generate_keypair()

    // Derive shared secret from ephemeral private key and
recipient public key
    shared_secret = key_agreement(ephemeral_secret, recipient_
public_key)

    // Derive encryption key from shared secret, binding to
workflow
    encryption_key = KDF(shared_secret, context = workflow_id)

    // Encrypt with authenticated encryption
    nonce = random_bytes(24)
    ciphertext = authenticated_encrypt(encryption_key, nonce,
plaintext)

    // Bundle ephemeral public key so recipient can derive the
same shared secret
    return {
        ephemeral_public_key: ephemeral_public,
        nonce: nonce,
        ciphertext: ciphertext
    }
```

The recipient decrypts by reversing the process:

```
function decrypt_section(recipient_private_key, encrypted_section,
workflow_id):
    // Derive the same shared secret using recipient's private key
    shared_secret = key_agreement(
```

```
    recipient_private_key,
    encrypted_section.ephemeral_public_key
)

// Derive the same encryption key
encryption_key = KDF(shared_secret, context = workflow_id)

// Decrypt and verify authenticity
plaintext = authenticated_decrypt(
    encryption_key,
    encrypted_section.nonce,
    encrypted_section.ciphertext
)

return plaintext
```

The workflow_id binding in the key derivation step is important. It ensures that the encryption key is specific to this workflow instance. If an attacker captures a section's ciphertext and replays it in a different workflow, the recipient will derive a different key (because the workflow_id differs) and decryption will fail. The section is not just encrypted for the right party—it is encrypted for the right party in the right context.

Each section uses an independent ephemeral keypair. Compromise of one section's ephemeral key does not affect other sections. There is no shared key material between sections except the workflow_id, which is public routing metadata. The sections are cryptographically independent.[1] An attacker who somehow decrypts the payment section learns nothing that helps decrypt the shipping section. The fragmentation is not just logical—it is cryptographic.

The recommended primitives are X25519 for key agreement and ChaCha20-Poly1305 for authenticated encryption, both available through libsodium.[2] These are well-audited, widely deployed, and resistant to timing attacks when implemented through constant-time library functions.[3] The choice of primitives is conventional. The novelty is in how they are composed, not in the primitives themselves.

---

[1]   Cryptographic independence here means that each section is encrypted under an independent ephemeral key. Under the IND-CPA (indistinguishability under chosen-plaintext attack) security model— Definition 3.22 in Katz and Lindell, *Introduction to Modern Cryptography*, 3rd ed. (CRC Press, 2020)— knowledge of one ciphertext provides no advantage in distinguishing the plaintext of another ciphertext encrypted under a different key. IND-CPA security implies security for multiple encryptions (Theorem 3.23 in the same text), so the use of independent ephemeral keys across sections guarantees indistinguishability even when an adversary observes all sections of a workflow simultaneously.

[2]   X25519 is the Diffie-Hellman key agreement function over Curve25519, introduced in Daniel J. Bernstein, "Curve25519: New Diffie-Hellman Speed Records," *Public Key Cryptography—PKC 2006*, Lecture Notes in Computer Science, vol. 3958 (Springer, 2006), 207-228. ChaCha20-Poly1305 is an authenticated encryption construction combining the ChaCha20 stream cipher with the Poly1305 MAC; see Bernstein, "ChaCha, a Variant of Salsa20," *SASC 2008* workshop record, and IETF RFC 8439.

[3]   Constant-time implementation is necessary to prevent timing side-channel attacks, where an adversary infers secret key material by measuring how long operations take. The NaCl/libsodium library is specifically designed to avoid secret-dependent branches and memory access patterns. See Bernstein, Lange, and Schwabe, "The Security Impact of a New Cryptographic Library," *LATINCRYPT 2012*, Lecture Notes in Computer Science, vol. 7533 (Springer, 2012), 159-176.

The Delegator Protocol

The delegator is a routing service. It receives a cryptogram, reads the routing metadata, and forwards encrypted sections to the appropriate services in sequence. The delegator advances the workflow step by step, collecting encrypted responses and passing them to subsequent participants as the routing table dictates.

The delegator's routing loop:

```
function route_workflow(cryptogram):
    while cryptogram.routing.current_step < length(cryptogram.
routing.steps):
        step = cryptogram.routing.steps[cryptogram.routing.
current_step]

        // Extract the encrypted section for this step's service
        encrypted_section = cryptogram.sections[step.section]

        // Collect any encrypted responses from prior steps that
this
        // service needs (specified in routing metadata)
        prior_responses = collect_responses(cryptogram, step)

        // Forward to the service endpoint
        // The delegator sends opaque blobs—it cannot read them
        encrypted_response = send_to_service(
            step.service,
            encrypted_section,
            prior_responses
        )

        // Store the encrypted response for downstream steps
        cryptogram.responses[step.service] = encrypted_response

        // Advance
        cryptogram.routing.current_step += 1

    return cryptogram  // workflow complete
```

The critical property is what the delegator never does. It never possesses a private key for any section. It never decrypts any section. It never decrypts any response. The delegator reads routing metadata—service names, step numbers, section labels—and moves opaque blobs between endpoints. The blobs could contain anything. The delegator does not know and cannot determine their contents.

Each service, upon receiving its encrypted section, decrypts it with its own private key, performs its function, and produces a response. The response is encrypted for the next participant that needs it (or for the workflow originator, if the response is a final result). The service sends this encrypted response back to the delegator, which stores it in the cryptogram's response block and continues to the next step.

Consider the purchase workflow. The delegator sends the encrypted payment section to the payment processor. The processor decrypts, verifies funds, generates an authorization token, encrypts the token for the store, and returns it. The delegator stores the encrypted token and advances. The delegator sends the encrypted order section and the encrypted authorization token to the store. The store decrypts both, fulfills the order, encrypts a fulfillment confirmation for the carrier, and returns it. The delegator stores the confirmation and advances. The delegator sends the encrypted shipping section and the encrypted fulfillment confirmation to the carrier. The carrier decrypts, schedules delivery, and returns a tracking identifier encrypted for the buyer.

At no point did the delegator read a card number, a product description, a shipping address, or a price. The delegator moved envelopes. The delegator knows that an envelope went from the workflow creator to the payment processor, then to the store, then to the carrier. The delegator knows the timing of each step. The delegator knows nothing about the contents.

Cryptogram: Multi-Party Workflow

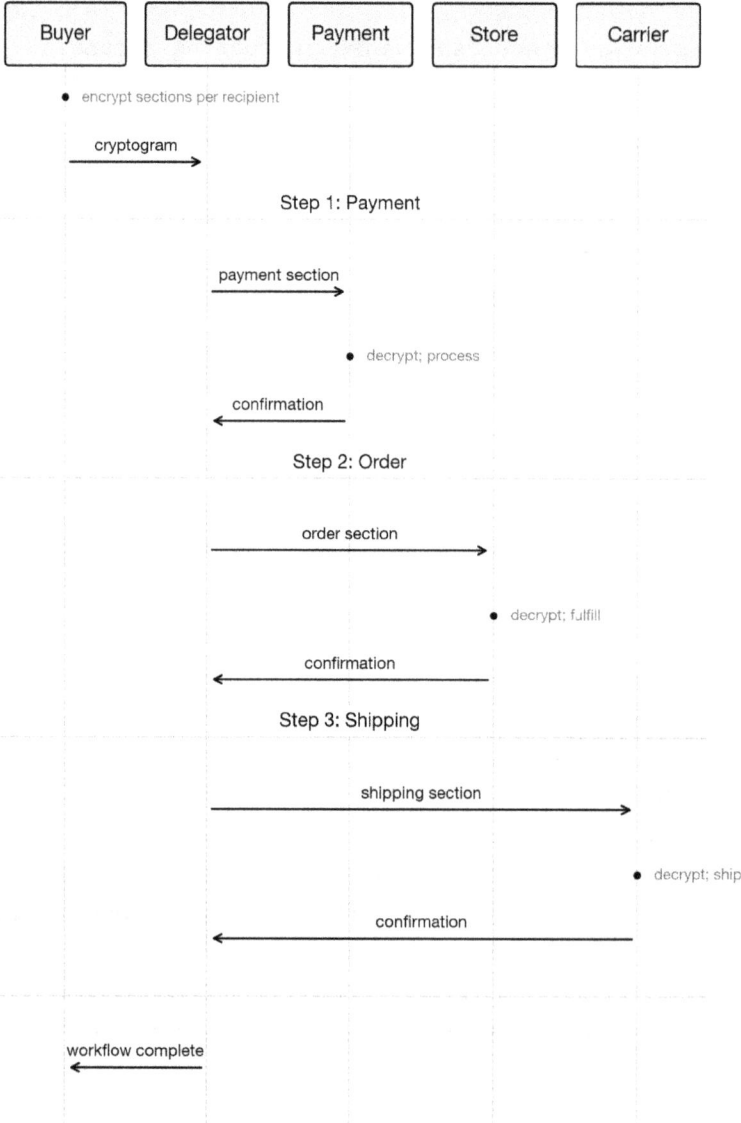

Figure 11.1: Cryptogram Purchase Workflow. The following diagram traces this workflow from start to finish. Each service decrypts only its designated section; the delegator routes opaque blobs without reading them.

The delegator's role is structurally equivalent to a postal worker who picks up a sealed letter, reads the address on the outside, and delivers it. The postal worker does not open the letter. The postal worker could not open the letter even if motivated to do so—the letter is sealed with a lock that only the recipient's key can open. The difference from ordinary mail is that the cryptogram contains multiple letters in one envelope, each sealed for a different recipient, and the delegator delivers them in sequence according to instructions printed on the outside.

Topology Leakage

The delegator cannot read content. The delegator can observe structure. This distinction matters.

The delegator knows the following about every workflow it routes:

- **Participants.** The delegator knows which services are involved in each workflow. It knows that a payment processor, a store, and a carrier participated. It does not know the transaction details, but it knows the parties.

- **Ordering.** The delegator knows the sequence of steps. It knows the payment processor was contacted first, the store second, the carrier third.

- **Timing.** The delegator knows when each step began and ended. It knows the payment processor responded in 200 milliseconds, the store took 3 seconds, the carrier took 10 seconds.

- **Frequency.** Over time, the delegator observes patterns. These four parties coordinate frequently. This workflow type occurs on Friday afternoons. This participant appears in many workflows.

- **Volume.** The delegator knows the sizes of the encrypted sections. A small payment section and a large order section reveal that the order is complex, even though the delegator cannot read the order.

This is topology leakage. It is not content leakage—the delegator does not learn what was purchased, what was paid, or where the shipment went. But topology carries information. A sophisticated adversary with access to the delegator's logs could perform traffic analysis. If only one carrier handles refrigerated shipments, and the delegator observes a workflow involving that carrier, the adversary can infer that the shipment requires refrigeration. If a specific payment processor handles only high-value transactions, its involvement reveals something about the transaction amount. The topology narrows the possibility space even when the content remains hidden.

The tradeoff is explicit. The alternatives are worse along at least one axis:

Fully decentralized coordination eliminates the delegator and its topology leakage. But it requires all parties to know each other, to be online simultaneously, and to manage the coordination complexity themselves. Every participant must know every other participant's endpoint. The coordination burden scales quadratically with the number of parties. For workflows involving five or six services, direct coordination is impractical. The delegator exists because someone has to route, and routing inherently reveals topology.

Trusted intermediaries—the current model—see everything: content and topology. Replacing a content-sighted intermediary with a topology-sighted one is a substantial reduction in exposure. The delegator sees the envelope. The current model sees the letter, the envelope, and every letter that has ever passed through.

Onion-routed coordination could reduce topology leakage by wrapping the cryptogram in layers of encryption and routing it through intermediate relays, as HermesP2P does for messages (Chapter 9). This increases latency and complexity. For workflows where topology sensitivity is high, it is an available mitigation. For most workflows, the topology leakage is an acceptable cost relative to the content protection gained.

The architecture does not pretend topology leakage does not exist. It acknowledges the leakage, quantifies it, and positions it as a conscious tradeoff: the delegator knows who participates and when, but not what they do or what information they exchange. For most threat models, this is a defensible position. For threat models where participation itself is sensitive—a medical specialist's involvement revealing a diagnosis category, for instance—additional measures are required, and the architecture should be layered with onion routing or padded with dummy traffic to obscure the topology.

Ephemeral Workers

The cryptogram pattern works when each step is self-contained: a service receives its section, acts on it, produces a response, and the workflow moves on. Some workflows are not that simple. A step might need to wait for multiple inputs before proceeding. A step might fail and require retry. A condition might need monitoring over a window of time. These patterns require state—and state, as every preceding chapter has established, is where surveillance accumulates.

A coordinator that holds partial results while waiting for additional inputs is a coordinator that accumulates information. A coordinator that remembers which attempts failed and which succeeded is a coordinator that builds a history. The problem is not that state is evil. The problem is that persistent state outlives its usefulness and becomes a liability.

Ephemeral workers solve this by making state temporary by design. An ephemeral worker is a short-lived process provisioned for a specific task with explicit, non-negotiable limits on its existence. When the limits are reached, the worker destroys itself and everything it held.

The schema for an ephemeral worker:

```
ephemeral_worker = {
  worker_id:          unique identifier,
  created:            timestamp,
```

```
  limits: {
    max_operations:        10,      // terminate after this many
operations
    max_duration_seconds: 3600,     // terminate after this many
seconds
    trigger_on_complete:  "next_workflow_step"
  },

  state:                 encrypted_blob,  // current working state,
encrypted
                                          // for the worker's own
ephemeral key
  operations_count:    0,
  status:              "active"
}
```

The limits block encodes the privacy constraints directly into the worker's existence. The worker does not decide when to forget. The worker is structurally incapable of existing beyond its limits. When operations_count reaches max_operations, the worker terminates. When the elapsed time exceeds max_duration_seconds, the worker terminates. Whichever limit is reached first wins. The termination is not optional. It is not a policy the worker follows. It is a condition of the worker's provisioning.

Consider a workflow that requires three approvals before proceeding. A stateless delegator cannot track which approvals have arrived—it has no memory between steps. A permanently stateful coordinator could track the approvals, but it would accumulate the approval history indefinitely, creating a record of who approved what and when. An ephemeral worker resolves the tension:

```
function handle_approval_workflow(delegator, cryptogram, approval_
step):
    // Provision a worker to collect three approvals
    worker = provision_ephemeral_worker(
        max_operations = 3,
        max_duration_seconds = 86400,    // one day to collect all
approvals
        trigger_on_complete = approval_step.next_step
    )

    // Worker receives each approval as it arrives
    while worker.status == "active":
        incoming = delegator.receive_for(worker.worker_id)

        if incoming is approval:
            worker.state = add_approval(worker.state, incoming)
            worker.operations_count += 1

        if worker.operations_count >= worker.limits.max_
operations:
            // All approvals collected—trigger continuation
```

```
        encrypted_result = encrypt_for_next_step(worker.state)
        delegator.advance(cryptogram, encrypted_result)
        worker.destroy()
        return

    if elapsed(worker.created) > worker.limits.max_duration_
seconds:
        // Time expired—workflow fails, worker dies
        worker.destroy()
        return "timeout"
```

The first approval arrives and is held in the worker's state. The second arrives and is held. The worker remembers approvals one and two while waiting for approval three. When approval three arrives, the worker aggregates the result, encrypts it for the next step, hands it to the delegator, and destroys itself. The state existed for the duration of the wait—seconds, minutes, possibly hours—and then vanished. No permanent record of who approved, in what order, or how long each took persists beyond the workflow's completion.

If the third approval never arrives, the worker hits its time limit and terminates. The incomplete state is destroyed. The workflow fails, but it fails cleanly—no partial records linger in a coordinator's memory.

The properties of ephemeral workers are specific and deliberate:

Bounded state lifetime. The worker exists for a known maximum duration and a known maximum number of operations. The state it holds cannot outlive these bounds regardless of what happens.

No history. An ephemeral worker processes a known quantity and then disappears. It does not accumulate experience across workflows. It does not learn from past operations. Each worker is born, performs its task, and dies. The next workflow provisions a new worker with no memory of the previous one.

Bounded compromise damage. If an ephemeral worker is compromised during its brief lifetime, the attacker obtains whatever state the worker currently holds. This is bad but bounded. The attacker does not obtain a history of everything the worker has ever processed, because no such history exists. The damage from compromise is proportional to the current state, not to accumulated history. A compromised permanent coordinator leaks years of data. A compromised ephemeral worker leaks the current operation.

Parallel execution. Multiple workers can handle independent parts of a workflow simultaneously, each with its own limits, none accumulating beyond its scope. A workflow that requires three parallel sub-tasks provisions three workers. Each processes its portion independently. None has visibility into the others.

The limits are not arbitrary. They are derived from the workflow's requirements. A workflow that needs to aggregate ten inputs provisions a worker with capacity for ten. A workflow that should complete within an hour provisions a worker with a one-hour lifetime. A workflow that might never complete provisions a worker that will eventually expire regardless, preventing indefinite accumulation. The limits encode what the workflow needs. Everything beyond those limits is denied.

Retry logic illustrates the value of ephemerality. In a traditional system, a coordinator that retries a failed step retains a record of the failure: the timestamp, the error, the state at the time of failure, the number of attempts. Over time, the coordinator accumulates a detailed failure history for every workflow it has ever managed. This history is useful for debugging. It is also a surveillance record—it reveals which services fail, under what conditions, and for which workflows. An ephemeral worker that handles retries provisions a new worker for each attempt. The new worker has no knowledge of prior attempts. If the step eventually succeeds, the successful result is encrypted and forwarded. If all attempts fail, the worker expires. No failure history persists. The debugging information is lost, and this is a real cost—but the surveillance record is also lost, and this is a real benefit. The tradeoff is explicit.

The architecture makes forgetting the default and remembering the exception. Most coordination steps need no memory beyond the moment. For those steps, ephemeral workers provide coordination without accumulation. For the exceptions that genuinely require memory, the blind database provides persistence without exposure. The architecture does not eliminate all state. It makes state explicit, bounded, and encrypted where it must exist.

Composition with Blind Database

Not all workflows are ephemeral. Some genuinely require persistent state: subscription services that track entitlements over months, approval chains that span weeks, audit trails that must persist for legal compliance. For these workflows, ephemeral workers alone are insufficient. The state must survive beyond any single worker's lifetime.

The solution is to combine ephemeral workers with the Blind Database architecture described in Chapter 5. The delegator stores encrypted workflow state it cannot read. Long-running workflows persist in durable storage while remaining private—the storage layer holds ciphertext it cannot decrypt, and the workflow participants hold keys the storage layer cannot access.

```
function persist_workflow_state(delegator, workflow_id, step_
number, state):
    // Derive a storage identifier from public workflow metadata
    state_id = hash(workflow_id, step_number)

    // Encrypt state for the party that will eventually resume the
workflow
    // The delegator performs this operation but cannot read the
state
    encrypted_state = state    // already encrypted by the worker
before handoff

    // Store in blind database
    blind_store(state_id, encrypted_state)

function resume_workflow(delegator, workflow_id, step_number):
```

```
state_id = hash(workflow_id, step_number)
encrypted_state = blind_retrieve(state_id)

// The delegator returns the encrypted state to the
appropriate party
// Only that party can decrypt it
return encrypted_state
```

This creates a layered approach. For workflows that complete quickly—a purchase authorization, a payment verification, a single-step approval—ephemeral workers hold state briefly and then vanish. For workflows that require persistence—a multi-week approval chain, a subscription lifecycle, a regulatory audit trail—the blind database holds encrypted state that the delegator and the storage layer cannot read. For workflows that require both, ephemeral workers handle the transient coordination while the blind database handles the durable parts.

The combination preserves the core property: no party accumulates readable state it does not need. The ephemeral worker forgets by self-destructing. The blind database persists without understanding. The delegator routes without reading. At each layer, the party performing the function is structurally prevented from seeing beyond its role.

Consider how this applies to the SaaS model that the previous chapter examined. A business using a CRM platform currently uploads customer contacts, interaction histories, and sales pipelines in plaintext. The platform stores, indexes, and processes this data—and sees all of it. Under the cryptogram architecture, the business encrypts each data category for the specific service function that requires it. The search service receives encrypted index fragments that it processes through a function it can execute but whose inputs it cannot read in aggregate. The analytics service receives encrypted summary data that it can compute on but cannot correlate with individual records. The storage service holds encrypted blobs it cannot interpret. No single service sees the complete customer record. The platform as a whole coordinates the workflow—search, analytics, storage, reporting—through a delegator that routes encrypted sections between internal services. The platform still functions. The platform is structurally blind.

This restructuring has a direct consequence for breach impact. When a platform that holds plaintext is breached, the attacker obtains the complete customer database. When a platform that operates on encrypted fragments is breached, the attacker obtains fragments. Even if the attacker compromises the delegator and every internal service simultaneously, each service's fragment is encrypted with different keys held by the business client. The attacker obtains ciphertext from each service, none of which can be decrypted without the client's keys. The breach exposes the platform's infrastructure but not the client's data. The trust model has shifted from "trust the platform not to be breached" to "trust that well-studied cryptographic primitives hold." The latter is a substantially stronger foundation—not because cryptography is infallible, but because its failure modes are public, specific, and subject to decades of adversarial review.[4]

---

4   The confidence in standard cryptographic primitives rests on decades of public cryptanalysis. AES-256 has been subject to intensive analysis since its standardization in 2001 (FIPS 197); the best known attacks reduce the security margin but remain computationally infeasible. The same applies to

Putting the Pieces Together

The complete architecture composes the cryptogram, the delegator, and ephemeral workers into a workflow system where coordination happens and surveillance does not.

The workflow creator assembles a cryptogram: routing metadata specifying the participants and sequence, and encrypted sections containing each participant's designated information. The creator hands the cryptogram to the delegator.

The delegator reads the routing metadata. It forwards the first encrypted section to the first service. The service decrypts, processes, produces an encrypted response. The delegator stores the response and advances to the next step. This continues until the workflow completes.

If a step requires waiting for multiple inputs, the delegator provisions an ephemeral worker. The worker collects inputs within its limits, aggregates a result, encrypts the result for the next step, and destroys itself. The delegator routes the encrypted result forward.

If the workflow must persist across days or weeks, the delegator stores encrypted intermediate state in a blind database. The state is retrievable by identifier but readable only by the party that holds the decryption key. The delegator can resume the workflow later without ever having understood the state it stored.

Each participant sees only its designated fragment. The payment processor sees payment details. The store sees order details. The carrier sees shipping details. No participant sees the other participants' fragments. No participant accumulates a cross-workflow profile. The delegator sees the topology—who participates and when—but not the content. The ephemeral workers see transient state and then forget. The blind database sees ciphertext and cannot interpret it.

The cryptographic primitives are standard. The section encryption uses X25519 key agreement and ChaCha20-Poly1305 authenticated encryption, both available through libsodium. The workflow signatures use Ed25519.[5] The Blind Database uses the key derivation and encryption scheme described in Chapter 5. Nothing here requires exotic cryptography. The protection comes from how the standard primitives are composed, not from the primitives themselves.

The integration with earlier components strengthens the architecture at every layer. Participants in a cryptogram workflow can be identified by their anonymous identity tokens from Chapter 3, unlinkable across workflows. The sections within a cryptogram can be stored in a blind database if durability is required. The cryptogram itself can travel over HermesP2P (Chapter 9) if the parties want to avoid even the topology leakage that a centralized delegator would observe. Each layer of the architecture addresses

---

ChaCha20-Poly1305, the AEAD construction used in this architecture (IETF RFC 8439), which has no known attacks faster than brute-force search on the 256-bit key space. These primitives may eventually fall—to quantum computers or unforeseen mathematical breakthroughs—but they will fall publicly, not quietly.

5   Ed25519 provides 128-bit security for digital signatures with fast verification and deterministic nonce generation, eliminating the class of catastrophic failures caused by weak random number generators that plagued earlier ECDSA deployments. See Bernstein, Duif, Lange, Schwabe, and Yang, "High-Speed High-Security Signatures," *Journal of Cryptographic Engineering* 2, no. 2 (2012): 77-89.

a different concern—identity, storage, transport, coordination—and the layers compose without introducing new trust assumptions. The anonymous identity system ensures participants cannot be correlated across workflows. The blind database ensures persistent state cannot be read by the storage layer. HermesP2P ensures transport metadata cannot be observed. The cryptogram ensures workflow content cannot be read by the coordinator. The protections stack.

Recommended Cryptographic Primitives

Function	Primitive
Key agreement	X25519
Symmetric encryption	ChaCha20-Poly1305 (authenticated)
Sealed boxes	libsodium `crypto_box_seal` (X25519 + XSalsa20-Poly1305)
Workflow signatures	Ed25519
Key derivation	HKDF-SHA256

All primitives are available through libsodium. The section encryption uses ephemeral keypairs per section, ensuring cryptographic independence between fragments.[6] Compromise of one section's key material does not affect any other section.

Prior Art and Design Rationale

The cryptogram architecture is not the first attempt at this problem, and understanding where it sits relative to prior work clarifies both what it accomplishes and what it deliberately leaves on the table.

Secure Multi-Party Computation (MPC) is the theoretical gold standard.[7] First formalized by Andrew Yao in the 1980s, MPC lets multiple parties jointly compute a function over their combined inputs without any party revealing its input to the others. In principle, this solves the coordination-without-disclosure problem completely. In practice, it is expensive. General-purpose MPC protocols require multiple rounds of communication between all parties, and the overhead grows with the complexity of the function being computed. Specialized protocols exist for narrow tasks—private set intersection, joint statistical computation—but a general-purpose MPC system that handles arbitrary multi-step workflows with acceptable latency does not exist in deployable form. The

---

6   The use of ephemeral keypairs per section provides a property analogous to forward secrecy in the TLS context: compromise of a recipient's long-term private key does not retroactively compromise past sessions, provided the ephemeral key material has been destroyed. See Menezes, van Oorschot, and Vanstone, *Handbook of Applied Cryptography* (CRC Press, 1996), Section 12.2.

7   Andrew C. Yao, "Protocols for Secure Computations," *Proceedings of the 23rd Annual IEEE Symposium on Foundations of Computer Science* (1982), 160-164. For a survey of practical MPC developments, see Lindell, "Secure Multiparty Computation," *Communications of the ACM* 64, no. 1 (2021): 86-96.

cryptogram architecture sidesteps the problem MPC solves. Rather than enabling parties to jointly compute on shared secrets, it ensures that secrets are never shared in the first place. There is no joint computation to protect because there is no joint data.

Shamir's Secret Sharing addresses a related but distinct problem.[8] Shamir's scheme splits a single secret into n shares such that any k of them can reconstruct the original, but fewer than k shares reveal nothing. This is useful for threshold access—ensuring that a secret can be recovered if enough trustees cooperate, while remaining safe if some trustees are compromised. It does not solve the compartmentalization problem. In a cryptogram workflow, the payment processor and the shipping carrier are not holding shares of the same secret. They are holding entirely different secrets, each relevant only to their own function. Shamir's scheme protects a single secret against partial loss. The cryptogram protects multiple secrets against cross-party leakage. They are solving different problems with different threat models.

Confidential computing and trusted execution environments (TEEs)—Intel SGX, ARM TrustZone, AMD SEV—take a hardware approach.[9] The idea is to create an isolated enclave within a processor where code and data are protected even from the operating system and the machine's owner. A service running inside an enclave could process sensitive data without the service operator being able to observe it. In theory, this would allow a delegator to process workflow contents inside a hardware enclave, gaining the benefits of content access without the risks. In practice, the security guarantees of TEEs have eroded. A series of side-channel attacks—Spectre, Foreshadow, Plundervolt, and others—demonstrated that the isolation boundaries of SGX enclaves can be breached through timing attacks, power manipulation, and speculative execution exploits.[10] Each attack was patched, and new attacks followed. The fundamental difficulty is that hardware isolation depends on physical properties of silicon that are difficult to verify and easy to probe. TEEs remain useful as a defense-in-depth layer, but building an architecture whose security *depends* on TEE isolation is building on a foundation that has cracked repeatedly under adversarial pressure.

The cryptogram architecture takes a simpler position: do not try to compute on secrets jointly, and do not rely on hardware to enforce isolation. Instead, do not share the secrets at all. The delegator never needs to read the data—it only needs routing metadata, which is unencrypted by design. Each service receives only the fragment it requires, encrypted with standard primitives whose security properties are well-understood and publicly auditable.[11] This approach is less powerful than MPC and less flexible than

---

8   Adi Shamir, "How to Share a Secret," *Communications of the ACM* 22, no. 11 (1979): 612-613.

9   For an overview of trusted execution environments, see Sabt, Achemlal, and Bouabdallah, "Trusted Execution Environment: What It Is, and What It Is Not," *IEEE Trustcom/BigDataSE/ISPA* (2015), 57-64.

10   The erosion of SGX security guarantees is documented across multiple disclosures: Spectre (Kocher et al., 2018), Foreshadow/L1 Terminal Fault (Van Bulck et al., "Foreshadow: Extracting the Keys to the Intel SGX Kingdom," *USENIX Security* 2018), and Plundervolt (Murdock et al., "Plundervolt: Software-based Fault Injection Attacks against Intel SGX," *IEEE S&P* 2020). Each demonstrated a distinct side-channel class breaching enclave isolation.

11   The primitives used here—X25519, ChaCha20-Poly1305, Ed25519, HKDF-SHA256—are all specified in IETF RFCs (7748, 8439, 8032, 5869 respectively) and implemented in libsodium, which has

TEE-based processing. But it is dramatically simpler. It requires no specialized protocols, no hardware trust assumptions, and no multi-round communication between parties. The security argument reduces to: each section is encrypted under a well-studied scheme, and only the intended recipient holds the decryption key. This is a claim that can be verified by anyone who can read a cryptographic specification.

The design rationale is not "we invented something new" but "we composed existing things in a way that eliminates the need for the hard parts." MPC solves the problem of computing on shared secrets—the cryptogram eliminates shared secrets. TEEs solve the problem of trusting a processor you do not control—the cryptogram eliminates the need for the processor to see the data. Shamir's scheme distributes trust in a single secret—the cryptogram distributes different secrets to different parties. In each case, the architecture avoids the harder problem by restructuring the workflow so the harder problem does not arise.

What This Does Not Protect Against

Every security architecture has boundaries, and failing to articulate them honestly converts an engineering limitation into a deception. The cryptogram and delegator architecture has specific limitations that users and implementers must understand.

Topology leakage is real. The delegator knows who participates in each workflow, the ordering of steps, and the timing. This was discussed at length above, but it bears repeating in a summary of limitations because it is the most fundamental one. Content is hidden. Structure is visible. For workflows where participation itself is sensitive—involvement of a particular medical specialist, a particular legal entity, a particular financial institution—the topology may reveal more than the content would. Mitigations exist (onion routing, dummy traffic, timing obfuscation), but they add complexity and latency. The base architecture leaks topology by design.

Workflows requiring long-term mutable state. The ephemeral worker pattern handles transient state. The blind database pattern handles persistent state. But some workflows require long-lived state that is continuously updated by multiple parties—a shared document, a running account balance, a reputation score that evolves over years. These patterns require a coordinator that can read state, modify it, and write it back. The cryptogram architecture does not solve this problem. It pushes the problem to the endpoints: if a service must maintain mutable state, that service must maintain it, and the service can read what it maintains. The architecture limits the number of parties that hold readable state, but it cannot eliminate all readable state from all parties.

Compromised service endpoints. The architecture protects data in transit and ensures that the delegator cannot read content. It does not protect data at the endpoint. When the payment processor decrypts its section, the processor holds plaintext. If the processor is compromised, the plaintext is exposed. The architecture reduces the surface—the processor sees only its fragment rather than the entire workflow—but it does

---

undergone multiple independent security audits. The security argument does not depend on novel constructions or unpublished results.

not eliminate the surface. Each endpoint that decrypts a section is a potential point of compromise for that section's content. The architecture limits the blast radius. It does not eliminate the blast.

Delegator availability as a trust point. The delegator does not hold secrets, but the delegator is a single point of availability. If the delegator goes offline, workflows stall. If the delegator is compromised, the attacker can disrupt workflows (deny service), can observe topology (which was already acknowledged as leaked), and can potentially tamper with routing—directing sections to wrong endpoints or dropping sections entirely. The attacker cannot read section contents even with full delegator compromise, but the attacker can prevent the workflow from completing correctly. Delegator availability and integrity are trust assumptions. They are weaker trust assumptions than the current model—where the intermediary must be trusted with content, topology, and availability—but they are trust assumptions nonetheless.

Collusion between participants. The architecture prevents any single party from seeing beyond its fragment. It does not prevent parties from voluntarily sharing their fragments with each other. If the payment processor and the store collude, they can combine their decrypted sections and reconstruct a more complete picture. The architecture does not and cannot prevent voluntary information sharing between parties that each legitimately possess their own fragment. It prevents the delegator from facilitating such sharing and prevents any party from accessing fragments not designated for it. Collusion between endpoints is outside the architecture's scope.

Metadata at the service level. Even when a service receives only its designated encrypted section, the service observes metadata: the time the request arrived, the IP address it arrived from (the delegator's address, but still), the size of the section, the response time expected. If multiple workflows arrive from the same delegator, the service observes the delegator's traffic patterns. This is a weaker form of the topology leakage problem, now at the service endpoint rather than at the delegator. It is less severe because individual services see only their own traffic, but it exists.

These limitations do not invalidate the architecture. They define its scope. The architecture provides a specific, valuable property: multi-party workflows where the routing coordinator is structurally blind to content and each participant sees only its designated fragment. This is a substantial improvement over the current model where every intermediary sees everything. It is not a solution to every privacy problem in multi-party coordination. The honest position is that it solves the intermediary content exposure problem while acknowledging that topology exposure, endpoint compromise, and availability trust remain as residual concerns that require their own mitigations.

Summary

The cryptogram and delegator architecture changes what it means to be an intermediary. In the current model, an intermediary is a party that facilitates coordination by seeing everything. In this model, an intermediary is a party that facilitates coordination while seeing nothing—or, more precisely, while seeing only the structural metadata necessary for routing and none of the content.

This is not a minor refinement. It is a structural change to the trust model. Under the current architecture, using a service requires trusting that service with your data. Under this architecture, using a service requires trusting that service only with its designated fragment. The delegator requires trust for availability and routing integrity, but not for confidentiality. The shift from "trust everyone with everything" to "trust each party with exactly what it needs" is the shift from policy-based protection to architectural protection.

The payment processor that previously accumulated cross-merchant spending profiles now sees individual authorization requests with no structural mechanism to link them across merchants, provided the payment section does not contain persistent identifiers that the processor can correlate. The store that previously accumulated customer purchase histories now sees individual orders with no persistent customer identity. The carrier that previously inferred package contents from shipping patterns now sees individual delivery instructions—though correlation through repeated delivery addresses remains possible, as the carrier must know where to deliver. Each party still performs its function. Each party is structurally prevented from performing surveillance.

The cryptographic primitives that enable this have existed for years. The engineering is not exotic. What has been missing is the composition—the deliberate architectural decision to fragment workflow information and enforce that fragmentation through encryption rather than through policy. The architecture does not ask intermediaries to be trustworthy. It makes their trustworthiness irrelevant to the confidentiality of the data they route. The delegator can be fully compromised, and the attacker obtains routing logs. The sections remain sealed. The content remains private.

The implications extend beyond individual workflows to the economics of intermediation. The previous chapter described three dynamics that define the SaaS model: data monetization, surveillance advertising, and vendor lock-in through data accumulation. All three depend on the intermediary's ability to read what it stores. Data monetization requires the platform to analyze client data. Surveillance advertising requires the platform to profile users. Lock-in through accumulation requires the data to be in a format that the platform controls and that the client cannot easily extract. The cryptogram architecture disrupts all three. Data monetization becomes impossible when the platform cannot read the data. Surveillance advertising collapses when the platform has no information to target with. Vendor lock-in weakens when the data is encrypted with client-held keys and can be transported to any platform that accepts opaque blobs.

The business model that remains is the honest one: charging for the coordination service itself. The platform routes workflows, manages availability, provides uptime guarantees. The platform is paid for what it does, not for what it sees. This is a smaller business than selling access to client data, but it is a sustainable one—and it is the only one that survives an architecture where the platform is structurally blind.

The next chapter addresses the distribution problem: how software and documents can propagate without centralized gatekeepers who control access and accumulate usage records. The coordination layer is now structurally blind. The distribution layer must be structurally ungoverned.

CHAPTER 12

The Distribution Problem

The most cryptographically secure application ever written provides no protection if users cannot install it.

The previous chapters addressed how data is stored, queried, communicated, and processed. Each chapter identified a structural vulnerability and proposed an architectural response. But none of that helps if the entity controlling the distribution channel decides the software should not be available. The architecture fails not at the cryptographic layer or the protocol layer but at the distribution layer—the mechanism by which code travels from developer to user. Software must be distributed. Distribution currently flows through gatekeepers. And gatekeepers can be pressured, compromised, or fail.

This chapter examines why the distribution layer is the least discussed and most consequential vulnerability in any privacy system. The analysis is structural, not political. The same architectural properties that make centralized distribution convenient also make it a single point of control. Control is the problem.

The Gatekeeper Stack

Software distribution involves multiple layers, each with its own controlling entity. These layers operate independently, but every one of them must function for software to reach users. A failure at any layer is sufficient to prevent distribution.

App stores are the most visible layer. Apple's App Store, Google Play, the Microsoft Store—each controls what software can be installed on devices within its ecosystem. The stores review submissions, enforce policies, and can remove applications unilaterally. The policies change over time. The enforcement is discretionary. The removal requires no judicial process. Software that exists in an app store exists at the pleasure of the store operator.

Certificate authorities are less visible but equally powerful. Code signing—the mechanism that tells operating systems that software is legitimate—requires certificates issued by trusted authorities. Those authorities can revoke certificates. A revoked certificate causes software to stop functioning. The certificate authority does not need to delete the software. It revokes the certificate, and the operating system refuses to run code that was previously trusted. The revocation propagates automatically through update mechanisms designed to protect users from compromised software. The same infrastructure that protects users from malware gives certificate authorities a kill switch over any signed application.

Content delivery networks and hosting providers sit between software and users. CDNs cache and distribute content globally. Hosting providers run the servers that store it. Both can be pressured to terminate relationships with customers whose content is deemed objectionable. When a CDN terminates service, the software becomes unavailable to anyone who depended on that CDN for delivery—which, for popular applications, is effectively everyone. The termination does not destroy the software. It destroys the infrastructure required to serve it at scale.

Domain registries and DNS providers translate human-readable addresses into the numerical identifiers that computers use. Domains can be seized by authorities, transferred by court order, or deleted from the global registry. A seized domain redirects to nothing or to a government notice. The seizure does not destroy the content. It destroys the map that users need to find it. Without the address, the content might as well not exist for users who do not know where else to look.

Package managers distribute libraries and dependencies for software development. npm, PyPI, Maven Central, crates.io—these central repositories hold the components that developers assemble into applications. A removed package breaks every project that depends on it. A compromised package injects vulnerabilities into every project that includes it. The centralization that makes package management convenient also makes it a single point of failure for entire software ecosystems.

The pattern across all these layers is consistent. A central party exists. The central party can be pressured by governments, compromised by attackers, or fail through ordinary operational causes. The effect propagates to everyone who depends on that party. The dependency is usually invisible until it fails. Developers build on package managers without contingency plans for package removal. Users install from app stores without considering what happens when applications disappear. The infrastructure is assumed until it is not available.

The VPN Removal: A Case Study

On July 29, 2017, Apple removed all major VPN applications from its App Store in China.[1] ExpressVPN, VyprVPN, StarVPN, and dozens of others disappeared overnight. These applications allowed users to bypass the government's internet controls, access websites blocked by the Great Firewall, and browse without their activity being visible to state surveillance. The applications were legal in most of the world. In China, they had become illegal without government authorization. Apple complied.

ExpressVPN responded publicly: "We're disappointed in this development, as it rep-

---

1   Apple Inc. removed VPN applications from the China App Store on July 29, 2017, following China's Ministry of Industry and Information Technology (MIIT) regulations requiring government authorization for VPN services. ExpressVPN published a statement the same day: "We're disappointed in this development, as it represents the most drastic measure the Chinese government has taken to block the use of VPNs to date." Apple CEO Tim Cook addressed the decision on Apple's Q3 FY2017 earnings call, August 1, 2017. Contemporary reporting: "Apple Removes VPN Apps From the App Store in China," *The New York Times*, July 29, 2017.

resents the most drastic measure the Chinese government has taken to block the use of VPNs to date, and we are troubled to see Apple aiding China's censorship efforts."

Tim Cook addressed the decision on an earnings call: "We would obviously rather not remove the apps. But like we do in other countries we follow the law wherever we do business."

The justification is familiar. Every company that operates internationally faces pressure to comply with local regulations. Following the law sounds reasonable. When the law requires censorship, following the law means being the instrument of censorship.

The architecture of iOS made the compliance total. Apple controls the only distribution channel for iOS applications. Unlike Android, which permits installation from sources outside the official store, iOS requires all applications to pass through Apple's App Store. Users cannot sideload applications. Users cannot install software from alternative markets. Users cannot bypass the gatekeeper because the operating system is designed to have exactly one gate, and Apple holds the key.

The contrast with Android is instructive. Google Play also removed VPN applications in China under the same regulatory pressure. But Android users had alternatives. They could download APK files directly from VPN providers. They could sideload the applications without Google's permission. The gatekeeper could be bypassed because the operating system permitted bypassing. The censorship was still present. The censorship was not architecturally enforced.

iOS users had no such option. When Apple removed the applications, the applications became unavailable. Users who had previously installed VPNs could continue using them until the applications needed updates that could not be delivered through the App Store. New users could not install them at all. The population of VPN users shrank with each new phone purchase, each factory reset, each migration to a new device. The censorship was not merely announced. It was progressively implemented through the normal operation of the platform.

This is the fact: the removal was not a one-time event. It became the ongoing condition of operating in that market. Apple's continued presence required continued compliance. The VPN ban was not hidden or reluctant. It was categorical policy.

Apple's decision was not malicious. Apple faced a choice between complying with Chinese law and exiting the Chinese market. Exiting would have harmed Apple's business and would not have helped Chinese users, who would simply have had no access to Apple devices rather than access to devices without VPNs. The decision was rational given the constraints. The problem is not the decision. The problem is the constraints—that the architecture creates a situation where a single entity's compliance determines what millions of users can access.

The Pattern Generalizes

The VPN removal is useful not because it is unique but because it is typical. The same pattern applies at every layer of the distribution stack, and the examples are numerous.

Certificate revocation kills running software. When a certificate authority revokes a code-signing certificate—whether under government pressure, legal process, or its own policy—every copy of the affected software becomes untrusted. Operating systems check revocation lists. Software that was running yesterday stops running today. The developer's code has not changed. The developer's infrastructure has not been compromised. A third party made a decision, and the software is dead.

Domain seizure destroys discoverability. The United States government has seized domains associated with software distribution, foreign media, and services it deems unlawful. The content continues to exist on servers somewhere. But users who typed the familiar address into their browsers find a government seizure notice instead of the software they were looking for. The seizure is technically trivial—a change in a DNS record—and operationally devastating.

CDN termination kills availability. When a CDN provider terminates service to a customer, the customer's content becomes unavailable to every user whose requests were routed through that CDN. For any service operating at scale, CDN termination is equivalent to going offline. The customer can, in theory, find another CDN or serve content directly. In practice, the migration takes days or weeks, and the reputational damage of extended unavailability may be permanent.

Package manager removal breaks dependencies. When npm removed the `left-pad` package in 2016—eleven lines of JavaScript—thousands of builds broke across the internet, including builds at Facebook and other major companies. The removal was not a government action. It was a dispute between a developer and npm's operators. Eleven lines of code, removed from one repository, cascaded into a global build failure. The package was restored within hours, but the lesson was clear: centralized package management creates centralized fragility.

Each of these failure modes operates independently. Each can be triggered by different actors for different reasons—government pressure, legal process, policy disputes, commercial disagreements, or simple operational failure. A privacy application that survives one failure mode may still be killed by another. An application that cannot be removed from the app store can still be killed by certificate revocation. An application that survives certificate revocation can still be rendered unfindable by domain seizure. The defense must address the entire stack, not any single layer.

Why Mirrors and Forks Are Insufficient

The obvious response to gatekeeper control is redundancy: mirror the software on multiple hosting providers, register backup domains, maintain relationships with alternative CDNs. This mitigates operational failures and makes censorship more expensive. It does not solve the structural problem.

Mirrors require maintenance. Someone must keep the mirrors updated, which requires infrastructure that can itself be pressured or compromised. Mirrors also require users to know about them. When the primary distribution channel is shut down, users who do not already know the mirror's address have no way to find it. The discovery problem is as significant as the availability problem.

Forking a project and hosting it under a different name faces similar difficulties. The fork must be discovered, trusted, and maintained. Users must determine whether the fork is legitimate or a malicious imitation. Without the original distribution channel's reputation and discoverability, the fork starts from zero in a market where trust is the primary barrier to adoption.

These approaches treat symptoms rather than causes. The cause is that distribution architectures route trust through channels rather than binding it to content. Users trust the app store, the certificate authority, the hosting provider, the domain name—all of which are properties of the channel, not properties of the software. When the channel is disrupted, the trust is disrupted, even though the software itself has not changed.

Trust Through Channels vs. Trust Through Content

Current distribution architectures assume that trust flows through channels. You trust the app store to vet applications. You trust the certificate authority to verify identities. You trust the hosting provider to maintain availability. You trust the domain registry to preserve mappings. Each trust relationship is reasonable in isolation. Each trust relationship is also a dependency on a third party that can fail, be pressured, or act against your interests.

The alternative is trust that flows from content itself. Self-validating content carries its own proof of integrity and provenance. The proof does not depend on the channel through which the content arrived. The proof depends on cryptographic properties that anyone can verify locally, without asking any authority, without trusting any intermediary, without depending on any service.

Self-validating content proves two properties.

The first is **provenance**: who published this content. The proof is a cryptographic signature from a key associated with the publisher. Anyone who knows the publisher's public key can verify that the signature is valid. The signature does not prove that the publisher is trustworthy. It proves that the content came from the entity that controls that key and has not been altered since signing.

The second is **integrity**: the content has not been tampered with. The proof is a hash chain or similar structure that links the current version to all previous versions. Any modification to any version breaks the chain. The chain can be verified by anyone with the content, using only the content itself.

These properties do not depend on third parties. A certificate authority might attest that a particular public key belongs to a particular entity, but the signature verification itself requires no authority. A hosting provider might distribute the content, but the integrity verification itself requires no provider. The content carries its proof with it. The verification happens wherever the content arrives, using whatever computing resources are locally available.

This distinction—between channel-mediated trust and content-inherent trust—is fundamental. It is the difference between "I trust this software because I got it from the App Store" and "I trust this software because I can verify the developer's signature and the integrity chain." The first statement depends on Apple. The second depends on mathematics.

Channel-mediated trust fails when the channel is compromised. Content-inherent trust survives channel compromise because it does not depend on the channel. The software can arrive via app store, direct download, USB drive, email attachment, QR code, peer-to-peer transfer, or carrier pigeon. The verification is identical regardless of transport. The channel becomes a transport mechanism, not an authority.

What Self-Validating Distribution Requires

The VPN applications removed from the Chinese App Store could not be self-validating. They were compiled binaries distributed through a controlled channel, signed with certificates that depended on Apple's approval, installed through mechanisms that required Apple's infrastructure. Every dependency on Apple was a point where Apple's compliance with government demands could block access.

A self-validating application would have no such dependencies. The requirements become clear when you examine what each gatekeeper controls and what it would mean to remove that control.

The software must carry its own logic. The executable code must be part of the distributed artifact, not fetched from a remote server at runtime. If the application depends on downloading components after installation, those downloads can be blocked. The artifact must be complete at the time of distribution.

The software must carry its own state. Configuration, user data, and operational state must be part of the artifact or derivable from it. If the application depends on a remote server for initialization, that server can be shut down. The artifact must be able to initialize and operate without phoning home.

The software must carry its own integrity proof. Cryptographic signatures and hash chains must be embedded in the artifact. The user must be able to verify the artifact's authenticity using only the artifact itself and the publisher's public key. No certificate authority, no OCSP responder, no online verification service should be necessary for the verification to succeed.

The software must be transport-agnostic. The artifact must function identically regardless of how it was delivered. App store, direct download, sneakernet, mesh network—the transport should not affect the software's integrity, authenticity, or functionality. This means the artifact cannot depend on transport-layer metadata for its security properties. The security must be intrinsic to the content.

The gatekeeper must be optional. A user who receives the artifact through a gatekeeper-controlled channel gets the same software as a user who receives it through an uncontrolled channel. The gatekeeper may add convenience—curated discovery, automated updates, malware scanning—but the gatekeeper's absence must not prevent the software from being verified and used. If the gatekeeper is removed from the equation, the software continues to function.

These five requirements—self-contained logic, self-contained state, self-contained integrity proof, transport agnosticism, and optional gatekeeping—define the minimum properties of software that can be distributed without depending on any single entity's continued cooperation.

The Scope of the Problem

Self-validating distribution solves specific problems and leaves others untouched.

Self-validating distribution solves the censorship problem. If software can be verified independently of the channel that delivered it, then blocking the channel does not block the software. Users who obtain the artifact through any means can verify that it is genuine and use it.

Self-validating distribution solves the certificate revocation problem. If the software's integrity proof is intrinsic rather than dependent on a revocable certificate, then certificate revocation does not kill the software. The software validates itself.

Self-validating distribution solves the availability problem. If the software is a complete, self-contained artifact, it can be hosted anywhere, mirrored trivially, and distributed through any channel. Killing one hosting provider does not kill the software because the software does not depend on any particular hosting provider.

Self-validating distribution does not solve the discovery problem completely. Users still need to learn that the software exists and where to find it. This is a real limitation, but it is a different category of problem. Discovery can happen through multiple channels—word of mouth, social media, search engines, link sharing—none of which need to be the same channel that distributes the software. Separating discovery from distribution reduces the gatekeeper's power because controlling one does not automatically control the other.

Self-validating distribution does not solve the trust bootstrapping problem. A user who receives a self-validating artifact must still trust the publisher's public key. The first time a user encounters a publisher, they must establish that the public key they have actually belongs to the entity they think it belongs to. This is the same key distribution problem that has existed since public-key cryptography was invented. It is a real problem, but it is a problem that can be solved incrementally—through web-of-trust models, key transparency logs, out-of-band verification, or social proof—without requiring a centralized authority.

Self-validating distribution does not solve the update problem automatically. If the app store is the update mechanism and the app store has been bypassed, updates must flow through whatever alternative channel distributed the original software. This is operationally harder than automatic app store updates. It is the cost of independence from the gatekeeper.

Requirements for a Solution

The analysis produces a specific architectural challenge. The privacy system described in this book must be distributable without depending on any gatekeeper. The system must satisfy the five requirements identified above: self-contained logic, self-contained state, self-contained integrity proof, transport agnosticism, and optional gatekeeping.

These requirements constrain the implementation architecture. The software cannot be a traditional compiled binary distributed through a traditional app store. It cannot depend on certificate authorities for its integrity. It cannot depend on a specific hosting provider for its availability. It cannot depend on a domain name for its discoverability. It must carry everything it needs within itself.

The next chapter presents an architecture that satisfies these constraints. The architecture treats software not as a binary that runs on a specific platform but as a self-validating artifact that carries its own logic, its own state, and its own proof of integrity—an artifact that can be transported through any channel, verified by any recipient, and executed without any gatekeeper's permission. The distribution problem does not disappear. It is restructured so that no single point of control can prevent the software from reaching users who want it.

CHAPTER 13

Chess Architecture

What if software carried its own proof of integrity—verifiable by any device, deliverable through any channel, requiring no gatekeeper's permission to run?

The previous chapter identified the distribution problem: privacy software that cannot reach users provides no privacy. Every layer of the current distribution stack—app stores, certificate authorities, hosting providers, domain registries—routes through a gatekeeper who can be pressured, compromised, or fail. The chapter concluded with five requirements for software that can be distributed without depending on any single entity's continued cooperation: self-contained logic, self-contained state, self-contained integrity proof, transport agnosticism, and optional gatekeeping.

This chapter presents an architecture that satisfies those requirements. The architecture is called Chess. It is not a game. It is a document format in which applications are represented as structured, self-validating artifacts. The document carries its own code, its own state, and its own cryptographic proof of integrity. It can be transported through any channel, verified by any recipient, and executed without any gatekeeper's permission.

The architecture has three structural components: a genesis block that establishes the application's initial state and logic, a chain of moves that records every state transition, and a sandboxed interpreter that executes the embedded code. Each component addresses a specific requirement from the previous chapter. Together, they produce an application format in which the document is the application and the channel is irrelevant.

Document Structure

A Chess document is a JSON structure containing three sections: a genesis block, a sequence of moves, and the current state. The genesis block is the foundation. It contains the application's code, its initial state, the author's public key, and the author's signature over the code and state. The genesis block is the root of trust for the entire document. Everything that follows is verified against it.

The move chain is a sequence of state transitions. Each move records what changed, who authorized the change, and cryptographic proof that the change was applied correctly to the previous state. The chain is ordered. Each move references the previous state by hash. The sequence from genesis through the final move constitutes the complete, verifiable history of the application.

The current state is a convenience. It represents the application's state after all moves have been applied. Any recipient can reconstruct the current state by replaying all moves from the genesis block. The included current state saves the recipient from having to perform that computation on every load, but the recipient never needs to trust it. The replay is the verification.

The schema, in JSON-like pseudocode:

```
{
  "chess_version": "1.0",

  "genesis": {
    "code": "(define (apply-move state operation) ...)",
    "state": { /* initial application state */ },
    "author": "ed25519_public_key",
    "signature": "ed25519_sign(author_key, hash(code || state))",
    "timestamp": 1703880000
  },

  "moves": [
    {
      "prev_state_hash": "sha256(serialize(state_before_move))",
      "operation": "(apply-move state input)",
      "new_state_hash": "sha256(serialize(state_after_move))",
      "actor": "ed25519_public_key",
      "signature": "ed25519_sign(actor_key,
                    prev_state_hash || operation ||
                    new_state_hash || timestamp)",
      "timestamp": 1703880100
    }
  ],

  "current_state": { /* state after all moves applied */ }
}
```

The genesis block contains three things that, in conventional software distribution, live in separate systems. The code is the application logic, embedded as source in a minimal Lisp dialect rather than living in a compiled binary downloaded from an app store. The initial state is the application's starting configuration, part of the document rather than fetched from a remote server. The author's signature binds the code and state together, attesting that this specific code operating on this specific initial state constitutes the application as the author intended it. No certificate authority participates. No app store review is required. The signature is verifiable by anyone who knows the author's public key.

The move chain is the application's history. Each entry records what the state was before the move (identified by hash), what operation was applied, what the state became after (identified by hash), who authorized the move (identified by public key), and a signature proving that the identified actor authorized exactly this transition. The chain is append-only. Previous moves cannot be altered without breaking the hash chain, because each move's prev_state_hash must match the hash of the state produced by the preceding move. Altering any move in the middle invalidates every subsequent move.

This is similar in structure to Git, which also uses content-addressed hashing to provide an immutable history of changes. The difference is that Chess includes the execution logic within the document itself. Git stores changes to files. Chess stores changes to application state, along with the code that defines what valid changes look like.

Why Lisp-in-JSON

The code embedded in a Chess document is written in a minimal Lisp dialect, serialized within the JSON structure. This choice is not aesthetic. It follows from four properties that the architecture requires, and Lisp satisfies all four simultaneously.

Homoiconicity. Lisp is homoiconic: code and data share the same representation. A Lisp program is a list. A list is a data structure. The program (define (increment x) (+ x 1)) is syntactically identical to a list containing the symbols define, a sublist (increment x), and a sublist (+ x 1). This means that storing code in a data structure—which is exactly what Chess requires, since the code must be embedded in a JSON document—requires no special encoding, no separate compilation step, no format conversion. The code is data. The data is code. They serialize the same way, transport the same way, and hash the same way.

This property is not merely convenient. It is structurally important for integrity verification. When the genesis block is signed, the signature covers both the code and the state. If the code required a separate representation—compiled bytecode, for instance, or a syntax that cannot be directly embedded in JSON—the signing process would need to handle two different formats. With homoiconic code, the signing process hashes one uniform structure. The verification process hashes the same uniform structure. There is no format conversion that could introduce ambiguity.

Minimal core. A conformant Lisp interpreter can be built from a small number of primitives. The recommended set for Chess is:

- **Binding and abstraction:** define, lambda, let
- **Conditionals:** if, cond
- **List operations:** car, cdr, cons, list
- **Arithmetic and comparison:** +, -, , /, =, <, >
- **Higher-order functions:** map, filter, fold
- **Cryptographic operations:** hash, verify-signature

This is a complete set. From these primitives, any computation the application requires can be constructed. The set is small enough that a competent programmer can read the entire interpreter implementation in an afternoon. This matters for auditability. The interpreter is the trust boundary—it is the component that executes potentially untrusted code. If the interpreter is thousands of lines long with complex features, auditing it for security vulnerabilities is expensive and error-prone. If the interpreter is a few hundred lines implementing roughly twenty well-understood primitives, the audit is tractable.

The inclusion of hash and verify-signature as primitives allows the application logic itself to perform cryptographic operations. An application can verify that a move was authorized by checking a signature within the Lisp code, not just at the chain verification level. This enables fine-grained authorization policies: the code can define which actors are permitted to perform which operations, and the authorization check is part of the application logic rather than an external policy.

Determinism. Given the same code and the same inputs, a Lisp interpreter produces the same outputs. This property is essential. When a recipient verifies a Chess document, the recipient replays every move—executing the code against each previous state to produce each subsequent state, and comparing the computed state hashes against the declared state hashes. If two interpreters could produce different results from the same code and inputs, verification would be unreliable. Two honest verifiers might disagree about whether a document is valid.

Determinism requires excluding non-deterministic features from the language. Random number generation is excluded. System time access is excluded. Filesystem access is excluded. Network access is excluded. Any operation whose output depends on something outside the document is excluded. If the application needs a timestamp, the timestamp is provided as a parameter in the move, not read from the system clock. If the application needs randomness, the random seed is provided as a parameter, making the output reproducible. The interpreter is a pure function: inputs determine outputs completely.

This is a restriction, not a limitation. Applications that need timestamps get them from the move data. Applications that need randomness get seeds from the move data. The restriction ensures that verification is possible. Every recipient who replays the chain from genesis will arrive at the same final state, because the computation is deterministic and all inputs are recorded in the chain.

Auditability. The combination of minimal core and homoiconic representation means that a Chess application can be audited in its entirety. The code is visible in the document. The interpreter is small enough to verify. There is no compiled bytecode to reverse-engineer, no obfuscated binary to disassemble, no server-side logic that executes invisibly. Most users will not read the Lisp code, just as most users do not read source code today. But security researchers, journalists, and concerned users can audit without decompilation or reverse engineering. The barrier to audit is the lowest it can be for any executable format.

Other languages satisfy some of these properties. JavaScript has a massive runtime that resists auditing. Python depends on a large standard library and is not straightforwardly deterministic. WebAssembly is deterministic and sandboxable but is a compilation target, not a source language—designed to be generated by compilers, not read by humans. Lisp is the intersection of all four requirements.

Move Validation

When a recipient receives a Chess document containing a new move, the move must be validated before the recipient accepts the state transition as legitimate. Validation is a sequence of checks, each of which must pass. If any check fails, the move is rejected.

The validation sequence, in pseudocode:

```
function validate_move(previous_state, move, genesis_code):

    // Step 1: Verify the actor's signature
    // The signature must cover the move's critical fields
    signed_data = move.prev_state_hash
                  || move.operation
                  || move.new_state_hash
                  || move.timestamp
    if not verify_signature(move.actor, move.signature, signed_
data):
        return REJECT("Invalid signature")

    // Step 2: Verify the previous state hash
    // The declared prev_state_hash must match the actual hash
    // of the state before this move
    computed_prev_hash = sha256(canonical_serialize(previous_state))
    if computed_prev_hash != move.prev_state_hash:
        return REJECT("Previous state hash mismatch")

    // Step 3: Execute the operation
    // Run the move's operation against the previous state
    // using the code defined in the genesis block
    new_state = execute_in_sandbox(genesis_code,
                                   previous_state,
                                   move.operation)

    // Step 4: Verify the new state hash
    // The declared new_state_hash must match the hash of
    // the state that the operation actually produced
    computed_new_hash = sha256(canonical_serialize(new_state))
    if computed_new_hash != move.new_state_hash:
        return REJECT("New state hash mismatch")

    // Step 5: Verify actor authorization
    // The genesis code defines who can perform which operations
    // This check is application-specific
    if not is_authorized(genesis_code, previous_state,
                         move.actor, move.operation):
        return REJECT("Actor not authorized for this operation")

    return ACCEPT(new_state)
```

Each step addresses a distinct integrity property.

Step 1 verifies provenance. The signature proves that the entity controlling the actor's private key authorized this exact combination of previous state hash, operation, new state hash, and timestamp. If any field were altered after signing, the signature would not verify.

Step 2 verifies chain continuity. The validator independently computes the hash of the actual previous state and compares it against the declared hash. A mismatch means the chain is broken.

Step 3 performs the computation. The validator does not trust the declared outcome. It executes the operation against the previous state using the sandboxed Lisp interpreter and computes the outcome independently.

Step 4 verifies computational integrity. The independently computed new state is hashed and compared against the declared new state hash. A mismatch means the mover either computed incorrectly or lied about the outcome.

Step 5 verifies authorization. Different Chess applications will have different authorization rules—single-author documents, collaborative groups, voting applications where each voter casts exactly one vote. The authorization logic is defined in the genesis code, and the validator executes that logic to determine whether the actor was permitted to perform the operation.

The order matters for efficiency. Signature verification and hash comparison are cheap and come first. Code execution is the most expensive step and is performed only after the cheaper checks pass.

Chain Verification

Validating a single move is necessary but not sufficient. A recipient who receives a complete Chess document must verify the entire chain, from genesis to the current state. This ensures that the document has not been tampered with at any point in its history.

Chess: Document Verification Chain

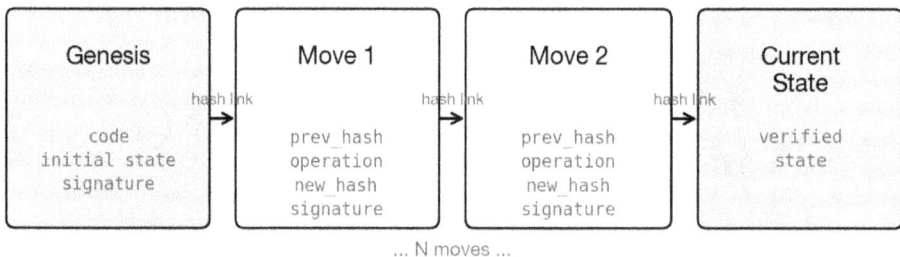

... N moves ...

Verifier replays all moves from genesis, checking each hash and signature.

Figure 13.1: Chess Document Lifecycle. The flow from creation through move chain extension and verification.

The verification algorithm is a straightforward replay:

```
function verify_chain(document):

    // Verify the genesis block
    if not verify_signature(document.genesis.author,
                            document.genesis.signature,
                            hash(document.genesis.code
                                 || document.genesis.state)):
        return REJECT("Invalid genesis signature")

    // Start from the genesis state
    state = document.genesis.state

    // Replay every move in sequence
    for move in document.moves:

        // Verify this move against the current state
        result = validate_move(state, move, document.genesis.code)

        if result is REJECT:
            return REJECT("Chain invalid at move " + index)

        // Advance to the new state
        state = result.new_state

    // After replaying all moves, the computed state
    // must match the declared current state
    if state != document.current_state:
        return REJECT("Final state mismatch")

    return ACCEPT
```

The algorithm starts at the genesis block. It verifies the author's signature over the initial code and state. Then it replays every move in sequence, validating each one against the state produced by the previous move. At the end, it compares the state produced by the final replay against the declared current state in the document.

If the chain is valid, the recipient knows several things with high cryptographic confidence.[1] The code in the genesis block was signed by the author. The initial state was signed by the author. Every state transition was authorized by a party whose signature is in the chain. Every state transition was computed correctly—the declared outcomes match the actual outcomes of executing the operations. The current state is the genuine result of applying every move in sequence to the initial state.

---

[1]   SHA-256 collision resistance provides 128-bit security against birthday attacks. No collision has been found for SHA-256 as of this writing. The chain's integrity guarantee rests on this: finding two different states that produce the same hash would require roughly 2^{128} operations, which is beyond any known or projected computational capability. See NIST FIPS 180-4 for the SHA-256 specification and Rogaway & Shrimpton (2004), "Cryptographic Hash-Function Basics," for formal treatment of collision resistance properties.

If any move has been altered—if an operation was changed, if a state was modified, if a signature was forged—the chain breaks. The hash mismatch propagates forward. Every move after the altered one will fail validation because its prev_state_hash will not match the hash of the state actually produced by the altered move. The chain is tamper-propagating: any modification cascades forward, making localized tampering detectable.[2] Any modification to any part of the history invalidates the remainder of the history.

The computational cost of full chain verification is proportional to the number of moves. For long-lived applications with thousands of moves, this cost is nontrivial. Optimizations are possible—checkpoint hashes at regular intervals, for instance, allow verification to start from a trusted checkpoint rather than from genesis. But the fundamental capability remains: any recipient can verify the entire history from scratch, using nothing but the document itself and a conformant interpreter. No external service is required. No network connection is required. The document is self-validating.

Transport Agnosticism

A Chess document is data. Specifically, it is a JSON structure of a known schema. Any channel that can transport data can transport a Chess document. The integrity of the document does not depend on the integrity of the channel, because the document carries its own integrity proof. A document that arrives corrupted will fail chain verification. A document that arrives intact will pass chain verification. The channel's trustworthiness is irrelevant.

This means Chess documents can travel through any of the following, with identical security properties:

HTTP. A web server hosts the document at a URL. A client downloads it. This is the most conventional transport and works exactly as file downloads work today. The server does not need to be trusted. The document verifies itself.

Email. The document is attached to an email message. The recipient downloads the attachment and verifies it. The email provider does not need to be trusted. The email could be intercepted, read, forwarded—none of these affect the document's integrity, because the integrity is intrinsic to the content, not the envelope.

Messaging applications. The document is shared through Signal, WhatsApp, Telegram, or any other messaging platform. The messaging provider does not need to be trusted for the document's integrity (though end-to-end encryption in the messaging layer provides confidentiality for the transfer itself).

Peer-to-peer networks. The document propagates through a decentralized network with no central server. Nodes relay the document without being able to alter it undetect-

---

2   The tamper-propagation property follows from SHA-256's second-preimage resistance. Given a state S and its hash H(S), finding a different state S' such that H(S') = H(S) requires roughly 2256 operations. Each move's prev_state_hash binds it to the exact output of the preceding move. Altering any move produces a different state, a different hash, and a mismatch with the next move's prev_state_hash. This makes tampering detectable, not impossible—an attacker who possesses all signing keys could construct a new valid chain, but cannot alter an existing one without detection.

ably. This is particularly relevant for censorship resistance: there is no central point to shut down.

Physical media. The document is copied to a USB drive, an SD card, or any other storage medium and handed to the recipient. The transfer happens offline. No network is involved. The recipient plugs in the media, reads the document, and verifies it.

QR codes. For small Chess documents—applications with minimal code and state— the entire document can be encoded as a QR code. The recipient scans the code with a camera, reconstructing the document from the visual encoding. The document is verified as usual. The transport medium is a printed image.

Not all channels are equally practical for all applications. A complex application with megabytes of state will not fit in a QR code. A real-time collaborative application will not work well over email. The point is that none of these channels are architecturally excluded. The security properties do not change when the channel changes.

This is the property that defeats gatekeeper censorship. An app store removes the application. The application continues to exist as a document that can travel through any channel the gatekeeper does not control. The gatekeeper must control every possible transport mechanism to prevent distribution. Controlling every mechanism is, for practical purposes, impossible. The document is the application. The channel is the transport. Separating these two concerns is the structural change that makes censorship-resistant distribution possible.

What Chess Is Not: The Blockchain Distinction

Chess uses hash chains and cryptographic signatures. So do blockchains. The superficial resemblance invites confusion. The distinction is fundamental, and getting it wrong leads to misunderstanding what Chess provides, what it costs, and what problems it solves.

A blockchain solves the problem of establishing consensus among parties who do not trust each other about a shared global ledger. The Bitcoin blockchain, for example, maintains a single authoritative record of every transaction that has ever occurred, agreed upon by thousands of nodes that have no reason to trust each other. Achieving this consensus is expensive by design. Proof of work requires energy expenditure. Proof of stake requires capital lockup. The expense is the security mechanism—making it costly to falsify history deters falsification.

Chess solves a different problem. Chess establishes the integrity and provenance of a specific document. There is no global ledger. There is no need for consensus among untrusted parties. There is only a chain of state transitions for one application, signed by the parties who made those transitions. The properties that matter—integrity, provenance, ordering—come from different mechanisms than blockchains use.

Integrity in a blockchain comes from consensus: the majority of nodes agree on the state. Integrity in Chess comes from the hash chain: any modification to any move breaks every subsequent hash. No consensus is required because the verification is deterministic. Any single verifier who replays the chain will arrive at the same conclusion as any other verifier.

Provenance in a blockchain comes from mining or staking: the entity that created a block demonstrated expenditure of resources. Provenance in Chess comes from signatures: the entity that created a move signed it with a private key. The signature proves authorship without requiring resource expenditure.

Ordering in a blockchain comes from block timestamps and consensus about which block came first. Ordering in Chess comes from the chain sequence: each move references the previous state by hash, establishing an unambiguous order. No timestamp consensus is necessary.

Cost in a blockchain is high by design. Transactions incur fees. Validation requires significant computation. The entire history must be maintained by every full node. Cost in Chess is minimal. Creating a move requires computing a hash and a signature—both are computationally trivial. Validation requires replaying the chain, which is proportional to the chain's length. There are no fees, no mining, no staking, no resource expenditure beyond what any consumer device can provide.

The practical consequences are significant. Blockchains are slow—Bitcoin processes roughly seven transactions per second. Chess has no throughput limitation beyond interpreter speed. Blockchains require network connectivity for consensus. Chess requires no network connectivity at all. Blockchains grow indefinitely as the global ledger accumulates transactions. Chess documents grow only as the specific application accumulates moves.

The distinction matters because blockchain's costs buy properties that Chess does not need. Blockchain consensus prevents double-spending in a global currency. Chess has no global currency. Blockchain mining prevents history rewriting by making it computationally infeasible. Chess prevents history rewriting by making it cryptographically detectable—sufficient when the goal is integrity verification rather than financial consensus. Applying blockchain overhead to Chess would make it slow, expensive, and dependent on network infrastructure, destroying the transport agnosticism that is the entire point.

Sandboxing: Safety Through Incapacity

A Chess document contains executable code. The code runs on the recipient's device. This is the same basic situation as downloading and running any software, with the same fundamental risk: the code might be malicious. Chess addresses this risk through sandboxing—restricting what the code can do, regardless of what it tries to do.

The sandbox is the execution environment provided by the Lisp interpreter. The interpreter defines what operations are available to the code. The recommended primitives—define, lambda, let, if, cond, car, cdr, cons, list, arithmetic, map, filter, fold, hash, verify-signature—are the complete set of capabilities. Nothing else is available. The interpreter does not provide:

- **Filesystem access.** No reading files, writing files, or interacting with local storage. The code cannot access the user's documents, photos, or any data on the device.

- **Network access.** No connections, HTTP requests, or DNS resolution. The code cannot phone home, exfiltrate data, or download additional code.

- **Process control.** No spawning processes, executing shell commands, or interacting with the operating system.

- **Device access.** No camera, microphone, GPS, accelerometer, clipboard, or access to other applications' data.

- **System information.** No access to the current time, device identity, user identity, or network configuration unless explicitly provided as a parameter in a move.

The security model is not "the code is checked for malicious behavior and allowed to run." The security model is "the code cannot do anything harmful because the environment does not provide the capability." This is safety through incapacity. The distinction matters. Checking code for malicious behavior is an arms race—new evasion techniques defeat new detection techniques in an endless cycle. Restricting available capabilities is a stronger defense than behavioral detection, though it is not absolute—the guarantee is only as strong as the interpreter implementation.3 The code cannot access the filesystem because the interpreter provides no filesystem primitive. No technique within the language can conjure a capability from an environment that does not provide it, but bugs in the interpreter itself could, in principle, provide an escape path.

The sandbox boundary is the interpreter itself. The interpreter is the only software that directly executes the Chess code. If the interpreter is correct—if it faithfully implements only the specified primitives and nothing more—then the sandbox should hold. "Should" rather than "will" because sandbox escapes are a real and ongoing concern in computing; even carefully audited interpreters have had vulnerabilities.4 The interpreter's small size (a few hundred lines for a minimal Lisp) makes auditing tractable and reduces the attack surface, but it does not eliminate it. The interpreter is the single component that must be verified for the security model to hold, which is why keeping it small matters so much.

This is a meaningful constraint. Chess is not a general-purpose application platform. It is a format for self-validating, self-contained applications whose computation is limited to transforming their internal state. Within that constraint, applications can be surprisingly capable—document editors, games, voting systems, form processors, data

---

3   The sandbox guarantee is a property of the interpreter implementation, not a mathematical invariant. A formally verified interpreter would provide stronger assurance. In practice, the small size of a minimal Lisp interpreter (a few hundred lines) makes thorough auditing feasible and reduces the probability of exploitable bugs, but does not eliminate it. Defense in depth—running the interpreter inside an OS-level sandbox as well—is advisable for any production deployment.

4   Historical examples include JavaScript engine vulnerabilities in web browsers (which are, in effect, sandbox escapes from the browser's execution environment), Java applet sandbox bypasses in the 2010s, and Lua interpreter vulnerabilities in game engines. The common factor is that the interpreter itself, written in a lower-level language, can contain memory safety bugs that allow escape from the interpreted language's constraints. Chess's minimal interpreter reduces but does not eliminate this attack surface.

analysis tools—but the constraint is real and deliberate. The constraint is the security property. Removing it would make Chess more capable and less safe in the same measure.

Composition with the Privacy Stack

Chess does not exist in isolation. The privacy architecture described in this book includes identity (Chapter 3), storage (Chapter 5), accountability (Chapter 7), communication (Chapter 9), and workflow coordination (Chapter 11). Chess is the distribution layer. It composes with the other layers.

Authors can sign Chess documents using Anonymous Identity keys from Chapter 3. The author's public key in the genesis block can be an anonymous identity key—one that is verifiable but unlinkable to the author's real-world identity. This means authorship is cryptographically verifiable (the document was signed by the entity controlling that key) but pseudonymous (the key does not reveal who that entity is). A developer can publish privacy tools without revealing their identity to governments or corporations that might target them for doing so.

Distribution through HermesP2P (Chapter 9) provides censorship-resistant transport. When Chess documents propagate through a peer-to-peer network with no central server, there is no hosting provider to pressure, no domain to seize, no CDN to terminate. The document travels through the network as any other message travels—relayed between nodes, each node verifying the document's integrity, no node controlling the document's availability.

These compositions are not required. A Chess document can be signed with a conventional identity key and distributed through a conventional web server. The compositions are available when the threat model demands them. An author facing government pressure can use Anonymous Identity and peer-to-peer distribution. An author facing no particular threat can use their real name and a web server. The architecture accommodates both without structural modification.

Recommended Cryptographic Primitives

Function	Primitive
State hashing	SHA-256
Document signatures	Ed25519
Serialization	JSON (canonical form for hashing)

The primitives are deliberately minimal. Chess documents must be verifiable on any device, including resource-constrained ones. SHA-256 and Ed25519 are available in every major cryptographic library and run efficiently on mobile hardware. Canonical JSON serialization ensures that all implementations produce identical hashes from identical state—a requirement for deterministic chain verification.

Prior Art and Design Rationale

Urbit is the most ambitious attempt at self-contained computing. It is an entire operating system built from scratch: deterministic execution, identity bound to computation, persistent state as a first-class concept. Urbit treats the computer as a single function that maps its event history to its current state—which is remarkably close to what a Chess document does. The difference is scope and opacity. Urbit replaces everything: the OS, the network stack, the programming language, the identity system. The result is powerful but opaque. Understanding Urbit requires learning Hoon (its language), Nock (its virtual machine), and Arvo (its kernel). The barrier to independent verification is high. Chess takes one narrow slice of that vision—deterministic state evolution with a verifiable history—and implements it simply enough that anyone can write a verifier in an afternoon.

IPFS and content-addressing solve the integrity half of the problem cleanly. In a content-addressed system, the address of a piece of data is the hash of its contents. If the data changes, the address changes. You cannot be tricked into accepting modified data, because the modification would change the hash, and the hash is the identifier. Chess uses content-addressing for the same reason: each move references the previous state by hash, and any alteration breaks the reference. But content-addressing alone gives you integrity without execution. IPFS can store a file and guarantee you received the right one. It cannot store a program and guarantee that the program's state transitions are valid. Chess adds the execution and verification layers that content-addressing lacks.

Nix demonstrates that reproducible builds are achievable in practice. Given the same inputs, Nix produces the same outputs, every time. This is the build-level equivalent of what Chess requires at the document level: deterministic computation with verifiable results. Nix proves that determinism is not merely a theoretical property but a practical one that real systems can enforce across complex dependency chains. Chess operates at a different granularity—individual state transitions rather than build processes—but the underlying insight is the same. If the computation is deterministic and the inputs are known, anyone can reproduce the output and check it.

Smalltalk's image-based persistence is, historically, the closest precedent for what Chess does at the document level. In Smalltalk, the entire running system—code, data, execution state—lives in a single image file. The image is the program. You do not install Smalltalk applications; you open a Smalltalk image that contains both the application and the environment it runs in. Chess documents have the same structure: code and state in one artifact, the document is the application. The Lisp-in-JSON representation even echoes Smalltalk's heritage—both Lisp and Smalltalk descend from the tradition of systems where code and data are made of the same material. The difference is that Smalltalk images are opaque binary blobs. Chess documents are readable JSON with a cryptographic history. You can inspect a Chess document with a text editor. A Smalltalk image requires a Smalltalk runtime to examine.

Blockchain-based document attestation is worth addressing directly because the surface similarity causes confusion. Systems like Ethereum-based notarization services, Proof of Existence, and OpenTimestamps store document hashes on a distributed ledger.

The ledger provides a timestamp and a consensus that the document existed at a particular time. This is useful for proving priority. But it is not what Chess does. Chess does not need a distributed ledger because it does not need consensus. A Chess document is self-validating—any single verifier can check the entire chain independently. There is no dispute to resolve between untrusted parties about which state is canonical. The document carries its own canonical state. Adding a blockchain would add cost, latency, and network dependency while providing a property—distributed consensus—that the architecture does not require.

Chess combines ideas from content-addressing (integrity through hashing), reproducible builds (deterministic computation), and image-based persistence (code and state in one artifact) into a single self-validating document format. No individual piece is novel. Content-addressing predates IPFS. Hash chains predate Bitcoin. Lisp predates most of computing. The contribution is the specific combination: a document that carries its own code, its own state, its own history, and its own proof of correctness, in a format simple enough that independent verification is cheap. The Lisp-in-JSON representation is deliberately minimal—the execution model is simple enough that multiple independent implementations can verify the same chain, which is the property that makes the format trustworthy without requiring trust in any single implementation.

What This Does Not Protect Against

Endpoint compromise. If the device running the Chess interpreter is compromised—if malware has root access, if the operating system is backdoored, if the hardware is tampered with—no software running on that device is safe. Chess code runs on the device. If the device cannot be trusted, the Chess interpreter cannot be trusted, the sandbox cannot be trusted, and the verification results cannot be trusted. This is not a limitation specific to Chess. It is a limitation of all software. No application can defend itself against a compromised host.

Malicious authors. A valid signature proves that the document was signed by the entity controlling the corresponding private key. It does not prove that the entity is benign. A malicious author can sign a Chess document that, within the sandbox constraints, does something the user did not intend—misrepresents data, implements unfair rules in a voting application, or manipulates state in a way that benefits the author. The sandbox prevents the malicious code from escaping its container, but it does not prevent the code from behaving badly within its container. The signature proves authorship, not benevolence. Trust in the author remains necessary, just as it is with any software distribution model.

Users who do not verify. The architecture provides verification mechanisms. It cannot force users to use them. A user who ignores a verification failure and runs a tampered document anyway will get exactly the experience the tampered document provides. A user who accepts documents without checking signatures will not benefit from the signature infrastructure. The tools exist. The user must use them. This is the same limitation that applies to HTTPS certificate warnings, GPG signature verification, and every other security mechanism that depends on user action.

Ecosystem immaturity. Chess, as described in this chapter, is an architecture, not a deployed system. The interpreters for minimal Lisp dialects exist but are not widely deployed in the sandboxed configuration Chess requires. The developer tools for creating Chess documents—editors, debuggers, signing utilities, chain management tools—are not mature. The browsers and operating systems that would execute Chess documents do not yet provide native support for the format. User expectations around software distribution assume app stores and the institutional structures Chess bypasses.

This is a practical limitation, not a theoretical one. The previous chapters presented architectures deployable today with existing tools. Chess requires ecosystem development: the interpreter must be implemented, audited, and deployed; the sandbox must be verified; the toolchain must be built; the user experience must be designed so that verification happens automatically, as transparently as app store signature checking happens today.

The distinction is between what is architecturally sound and what is production-ready. Chess is architecturally sound—the hash chain provides integrity, the signatures provide provenance, the deterministic interpreter provides verifiable computation, the sandbox provides safety. The integrity and provenance properties hold as a matter of mathematical structure. The verifiable computation and safety properties hold as a matter of interpreter design—they depend on the interpreter faithfully implementing a deterministic, capability-restricted specification. But sound architecture is necessary and not sufficient. The implementation, the tooling, and the ecosystem must exist before Chess can protect actual users.

The privacy stack described in this book could function without Chess, using traditional distribution channels for as long as those channels remain open. Chess is the contingency—the architectural path that remains available when gatekeepers close other paths. Building that path before it is needed is more valuable than building it after, because the circumstances that make it necessary are the same circumstances that make building it difficult.

A Concrete Example

Consider a simple Chess document: a counter application that allows authorized users to increment a value.

The genesis block:

```
{
  "chess_version": "1.0",
  "genesis": {
    "code": "(define (apply-move state op)
             (cond
               ((= (car op) 'increment)
                (+ state 1))
               ((= (car op) 'decrement)
                (- state 1))
```

```
                    (else state)))",
        "state": 0,
        "author": "ed25519_pub_abc123...",
        "signature": "ed25519_sig_...",
        "timestamp": 1703880000
    },
    "moves": [],
    "current_state": 0
}
```

The application starts with a state of 0. The code defines two operations: increment and decrement. Any other operation leaves the state unchanged.

A user increments the counter:

```
{
    "prev_state_hash": "sha256(0) = 5feceb...",
    "operation": "(apply-move state '(increment))",
    "new_state_hash": "sha256(1) = 6b86b2...",
    "actor": "ed25519_pub_def456...",
    "signature": "ed25519_sig_...",
    "timestamp": 1703880100
}
```

The move is appended. The current state becomes 1. A verifier replays the chain: start with state 0, execute the increment operation, get state 1, confirm the hash matches. The chain is valid.

Another user decrements:

```
{
    "prev_state_hash": "sha256(1) = 6b86b2...",
    "operation": "(apply-move state '(decrement))",
    "new_state_hash": "sha256(0) = 5feceb...",
    "actor": "ed25519_pub_ghi789...",
    "signature": "ed25519_sig_...",
    "timestamp": 1703880200
}
```

The state returns to 0. The verifier replays both moves: 0 to 1 to 0. Both hashes match. Both signatures verify. The chain is valid.

Now suppose an attacker modifies the first move, changing the operation from increment to decrement. The first move would claim to produce a new state of 1 from state 0 using a decrement operation. But executing a decrement on 0 produces -1, not 1. The computed hash of -1 does not match the declared new state hash. The verification fails. The tampering is detected.

Alternatively, suppose the attacker modifies the declared new state hash to match -1. Now the first move is internally consistent. But the second move's prev_state_hash was computed from state 1, not state -1. The second move's prev_state_hash does not match the hash of -1. The chain breaks at the second move. The tampering is detected.

The attacker would need to modify every subsequent move in the chain and re-sign each one with the original actors' private keys. Without those private keys, this is computationally infeasible. The chain's integrity depends on the secrecy of the signing keys, not on the security of any transport channel.

This example is trivial by design. The same structure supports applications of arbitrary complexity. A document editor where the state is the document content and the operations are insertions, deletions, and formatting changes. A voting system where the state is the tally and the operations are votes. A configuration manager where the state is the system configuration and the operations are policy changes. The pattern is identical: genesis defines the rules, moves record the transitions, the chain proves the history.

There is a useful asymmetry here. Creating a valid Chess document requires possession of the signing keys and correct computation of all state transitions. Verifying a Chess document requires only the document itself and a conformant interpreter. The cost of forgery is high—forging Ed25519 signatures requires solving the elliptic curve discrete logarithm problem, which remains computationally infeasible with current and near-term technology;[5] creating a new document with attacker keys is possible but the document will bear the attacker's key, not the original author's. The cost of verification is low. This asymmetry favors defenders over attackers, which is the correct orientation for a security system.

Design Constraints and Future Work

The Chess architecture as described in this chapter is deliberately minimal. It specifies a document format, a verification algorithm, and a sandboxed execution model. It does not specify a complete application platform.

Several problems remain open.

State size. As a Chess document accumulates moves, it grows. The complete history must be retained for full chain verification. For long-lived applications with many moves, the document may become large. Checkpoint mechanisms—where the state at a particular point is signed and verified, allowing future verifiers to start from the checkpoint rather than from genesis—can mitigate this, but the design of a secure checkpoint mechanism requires care to ensure that the checkpoint itself is trustworthy.

Concurrent moves. The move chain as described is linear: each move references exactly one previous state. If two users make moves concurrently, one move must come first. Conflict resolution—deciding how to order concurrent moves and how to handle operations that conflict—is an application-level concern that the architecture does not prescribe. Some applications may use last-writer-wins. Others may require explicit merge operations. The architecture supports any resolution strategy that can be expressed in the genesis code.

---

5   Ed25519 provides approximately 128 bits of security against known attacks. The best known algorithms for the elliptic curve discrete logarithm problem on Curve25519 require roughly 2128 operations. This security level is considered sufficient through at least 2030 by NIST guidelines, though advances in quantum computing could change this calculus. See Bernstein et al. (2012), "High-speed high-security signatures," for the Ed25519 specification and security analysis.

Update distribution. When an author publishes a new version of a Chess application, users who have the old version need to receive the new one. In the app store model, updates are pushed automatically. In the Chess model, updates are additional moves appended to the chain (or, for major revisions, new documents that reference the old). The distribution of updates through non-gatekeeper channels is operationally harder than automatic app store updates. This is a genuine cost of gatekeeper independence.

Interpreter standardization. For verification to be reliable, all conformant interpreters must produce identical results from identical inputs. This requires a precise specification of the Lisp dialect—how arithmetic overflow is handled, how floating-point computation works (or whether floating-point is excluded in favor of exact arithmetic), how canonical serialization is defined. Without such a specification, two correct interpreters might produce different results, causing one to accept a chain that the other rejects. The specification must be written, published, and tested against reference implementations.

These are engineering problems, not architectural problems. The architecture is sound: hash chains provide integrity, signatures provide provenance, deterministic execution provides verifiable computation, sandboxing provides safety. The engineering work is to build the implementations, standardize the specification, develop the tooling, and create the ecosystem that makes Chess practical for real users.

Summary

Chess is a document format for self-validating applications. A Chess document contains the application's code (in a minimal Lisp dialect), its current state, and a cryptographically signed chain of every state transition from the initial state to the current one. Any recipient can verify the entire history of the document by replaying the chain and checking every hash and signature. No external service is required. No network connection is needed. The document is the application.

The architecture satisfies the five requirements from Chapter 12. The code in the genesis block is the self-contained logic. The state field is the self-contained state. The hash chain and signatures are the self-contained integrity proof. The JSON-based document format provides transport agnosticism—any channel that can carry data can carry a Chess document. And gatekeepers are optional—the document can be distributed through app stores for convenience, but the document's integrity does not depend on the app store's participation.

The Lisp-in-JSON approach provides four properties simultaneously: homoiconicity (code and data share representation), minimal core (few primitives, auditable interpreter), determinism (same inputs produce same outputs), and auditability (source code is visible in the document). The sandbox ensures safety through incapacity—the code cannot access the filesystem, network, or any external resource because the interpreter does not provide those capabilities.

Chess is not a blockchain. It has no global ledger, no consensus mechanism, no mining, no proof of work, no proof of stake, no transaction fees. It uses hash chains for integrity and signatures for provenance—tools that predate blockchains and serve a different purpose.

Chess is not production-ready. The interpreter, sandbox, toolchain, and ecosystem require development. The architecture is sound, but architecture is not implementation. The previous chapters described systems deployable with current tools. Chess describes where the architecture leads when gatekeeper-free distribution becomes necessary.

The next chapter examines how the layers compose—how Anonymous Identity, Blind Database, Proof of Human, peer-to-peer communication, cryptogram workflows, and Chess distribution combine into an architecture where each layer addresses a failure mode and the full stack provides protection that no individual layer can achieve alone.

CHAPTER 14

The Architecture Composed

The previous chapters presented six components. Anonymous Identity eliminates cross-site correlation. Blind Database eliminates server-side data exposure. Proof of Human eliminates cheap abuse. HermesP2P eliminates metadata accumulation. Cryptogram and Delegator eliminate intermediary surveillance. Chess eliminates gatekeeper control over software distribution. Each component works alone. Each component, working alone, has a gap.

This chapter is about the gaps, and about what happens when the components close them for each other.

The Gap-Closure Problem

Every security architecture has seams. A door lock does not protect windows. A fence does not protect the airspace above it. The question is not whether individual components have limitations—they always do—but whether the limitations of one component fall within the protection of another. An architecture that composes well is one where the gaps do not overlap.

The six components of this architecture were designed independently, each to solve a specific problem. The composition was not an afterthought, but the gaps are real and deserve explicit examination. The following table maps each component's primary gap and identifies which other component closes it.

Component	What It Provides	Gap When Used Alone	What Closes the Gap
Anonymous Identity	Unlinkable site-specific tokens; no cross-site correlation	The User Service stores identity mappings. A breach or subpoena of the User Service exposes which users have accounts on which sites.	Blind Database. Identity mappings are stored encrypted with client-derived keys. The User Service operator cannot read what it stores.

Blind Database	Client-side encryption; server stores ciphertext it cannot read	The client must authenticate to store and retrieve records. If authentication uses conventional identifiers, the operator knows which user owns which encrypted blobs—who stores how much, when they access it, how frequently. Content is private; attribution is not.	Anonymous Identity. The client authenticates with a site-specific token. The storage operator cannot link the token to a civil identity or correlate it with tokens used on other services. Access patterns exist but cannot be attributed to identified individuals.
Proof of Human	Bot resistance through accumulated humanness score; economic disincentive for abuse at scale	The score itself becomes a tracking vector. If the same score is visible across sites, it creates a new correlation channel—not as precise as an email address, but sufficient for probabilistic linking.	Anonymous Identity. The humanness score binds to site-specific pseudonyms, not to a global identity. Each site sees a score attached to an unlinkable token. The scores cannot be correlated across contexts because the identities cannot be correlated.
HermesP2P	No metadata accumulation; no central server logging communication patterns	Without identity stake, the network is open to spam, bots, and Sybil attacks. Any peer can flood public channels. The absence of gatekeepers becomes the absence of any defense.	Proof of Human. Public channels require a minimum humanness score to post. Spam becomes expensive because each posting identity must accumulate genuine credential value before it can broadcast. The economic floor eliminates abuse at scale.

Cryptogram / Delegator	Intermediaries see only their fragment; no party accumulates the complete workflow picture	Workflow state must sometimes persist across steps that do not execute simultaneously. Persistent state is readable state—unless it is stored somewhere the storage operator cannot read it.	Blind Database. The delegator stores encrypted workflow state indexed by opaque identifiers derived from the workflow ID. The storage operator holds ciphertext it cannot decrypt. Persistence does not require exposure.
Chess	Self-validating documents; no app store or gatekeeper required for distribution	The author who signs a Chess document may be identifiable. Signatures are public. If the signing key is linked to a civil identity, the distribution is uncensorable but the author is not protected.	Anonymous Identity. Authors sign Chess documents with keys derived from anonymous identities. The signature is verifiable—readers can confirm that this version came from the same author as the previous version—but the signing key is unlinkable to any civil identity. Distribution is uncensorable and authorship is private.

The table reveals a pattern. Anonymous Identity appears three times as the gap-closer. Blind Database appears twice. This is not an accident. Identity correlation is the most pervasive structural vulnerability in any privacy system, and server-side data exposure is the second most pervasive. The components that address these two problems do the most gap-closing work because these two problems create the most gaps.

The pattern also reveals which components are load-bearing in the composition. Anonymous Identity and Blind Database are foundational. Without Anonymous Identity, Proof of Human scores become tracking vectors, Chess authorship becomes identifiable, and the entire architecture leaks correlation data through the identity layer. Without Blind Database, the User Service is a single point of breach exposure, and workflow state creates a readable record of every multi-party transaction. The other components—Proof of Human, HermesP2P, Cryptogram, Chess—address specific threat surfaces. The foundational components close the privacy gaps that would otherwise limit the specific components' protections. Figure 14.1 maps these data flows and trust boundaries across all six components.

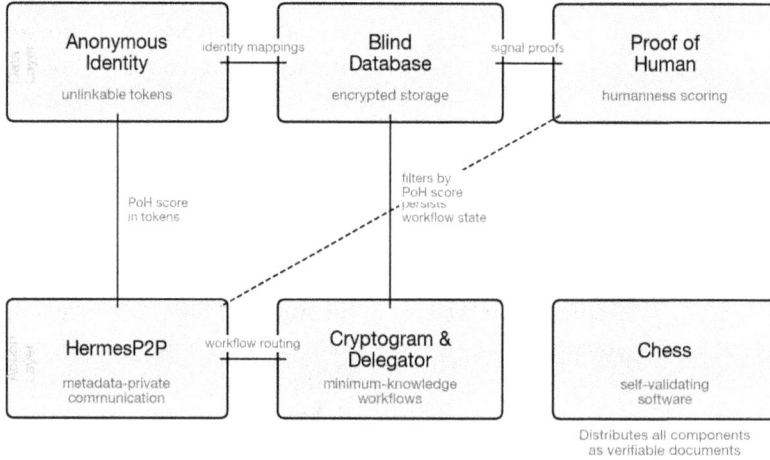

The Six Components: Composed

Figure 14.1: Composed Architecture Overview. The following diagram shows all six components, their trust boundaries, and how they compose. Arrows indicate data flow; labels indicate what crosses each trust boundary.

Composition Patterns

The gap-closure table describes what composes. The composition patterns describe how. Each pairing has a specific integration point where one component's output becomes another component's input. The integration is not conceptual. It is a data flow with a defined protocol.

Anonymous Identity + Blind Database

The User Service must store identity mappings: which credential hash maps to which user ID, which user ID maps to which site-specific tokens. In a conventional deployment, this data lives in a database the operator can query. The operator can enumerate all users, determine which sites they visit, and reconstruct the complete authentication graph. A breach exposes the same.

When the User Service stores its mappings in a Blind Database, the data flow changes.

The client derives the record identifier and encryption key from its own secrets, encrypts the mapping, and sends the encrypted result to the server. The server stores an opaque blob indexed by an opaque key.

```
function store_identity_mapping(master_secret, site_id, user_id,
user_salt, token_hash):
    // Client derives the record identifier
    record_id = HASH(master_secret || "identity_mapping" || site_
id)

    // Client derives the encryption key
    key = KDF(master_secret, record_id, "encrypt")

    // Client encrypts the identity mapping
    plaintext = serialize(user_id, user_salt, token_hash)
    nonce = random_bytes(24)
    ciphertext = AEAD_encrypt(key, nonce, plaintext, associated_
data = record_id)

    // Server stores opaque blob at opaque index
    server.store(record_id, nonce || ciphertext)
```

The recovery path works in reverse. When the client authenticates to a new site, it derives the record identifier from its master secret and the site identifier, requests the blob from the server, decrypts locally, and uses the stored mapping to derive the site-specific token.

```
function recover_identity_mapping(master_secret, site_id):
    // Reconstruct the record identifier
    record_id = HASH(master_secret || "identity_mapping" || site_
id)

    // Request the encrypted blob
    stored_value = server.retrieve(record_id)

    // Derive the key and decrypt
    key = KDF(master_secret, record_id, "encrypt")
    nonce = stored_value[0:24]
    ciphertext = stored_value[24:]
    plaintext = AEAD_decrypt(key, nonce, ciphertext, associated_
data = record_id)

    return deserialize(plaintext)  // (user_id, user_salt, token_
hash)
```

The operator sees a collection of opaque key-value pairs. An attacker who breaches the server sees the same. A subpoena demands data the operator cannot read. The identity mappings exist, they persist, they are recoverable by the user—and they are invisible to everyone else.

The composition is clean because both components use the same cryptographic substrate. The Blind Database does not need to know that it is storing identity mappings. It stores opaque blobs. The Anonymous Identity system does not need to know that its storage layer is blind. It stores and retrieves mappings. The integration happens at the client, which holds the secrets necessary for both systems.

Proof of Human + HermesP2P

HermesP2P public channels face the spam problem that every open communication system faces. Without some mechanism for filtering, the cost of posting is zero and the network degrades into noise. Traditional systems solve this with centralized moderation—a server operator who can delete posts and ban users. HermesP2P has no server operator. The solution must be structural.

Proof of Human provides the structure. The integration point is the message header. Every message posted to a public channel carries a PoH attestation: the sender's current score and a signature from the PoH verifier confirming that score.

```
function post_to_public_channel(message, sender_identity, poh_
credential):
    // Construct the message with PoH attestation
    msg = {
        "channel_id":  target_channel,
        "content":     encrypt_for_channel(message),
        "sender":      sender_identity.pseudonym,
        "timestamp":   current_time(),
        "poh_attestation": {
            "score":              poh_credential.current_score,
            "verifier_signature": poh_credential.signature,
            "issued_at":          poh_credential.timestamp
        },
        "sender_signature": sign(sender_identity.key, message ||
timestamp)
    }

    // Send to network
    gossip_broadcast(msg)
```

Receiving nodes validate the attestation before forwarding:

```
function receive_public_message(msg, channel):
    // Verify the PoH attestation signature
    if not verify_signature(poh_verifier_key, msg.poh_
attestation):
        reject("invalid PoH attestation")

    // Check the score against channel threshold
    if msg.poh_attestation.score < channel.minimum_poh_score:
        reject("score below channel threshold")
```

```
    // Check attestation freshness
    if current_time() - msg.poh_attestation.issued_at > MAX_
ATTESTATION_AGE:
        reject("stale attestation")

    // Verify sender signature
    if not verify_signature(msg.sender, msg.content || msg.
timestamp):
        reject("invalid sender signature")

    // Accept and forward
    store_in_buffer(msg, ttl = channel.message_ttl)
    forward_to_peers(msg)
```

The threshold is set per channel. A channel for casual discussion might require a score of 0.15—roughly tens of dollars of forging cost per identity. A channel for coordinating sensitive investigations might require 0.5—roughly a hundred thousand dollars per identity. The channel creator sets the threshold. The network enforces it. No moderator is required.

The critical detail is that the PoH score binds to the sender's pseudonym on this channel, which is derived through Anonymous Identity. The score attests that the underlying identity has accumulated genuine credential value. It does not reveal which underlying identity. The spam protection works without deanonymization.

Blind Database + Cryptogram

Cryptogram workflows often span time. A purchase workflow that begins with payment authorization may not complete shipping for days. A document review workflow that begins with submission may not complete approval for weeks. Between steps, the workflow state must persist somewhere.

The delegator is the natural custodian of workflow state—it routes the workflow and tracks which step is current. But if the delegator stores state in readable form, it accumulates a surveillance record of every transaction it coordinates. The delegator's structural blindness to section contents is undermined by its structural access to workflow metadata and state.

Blind Database closes this gap. The delegator stores workflow state as encrypted blobs it cannot read.

```
function persist_workflow_state(workflow_id, step_number, state_
data, workflow_key):
    // Derive a storage identifier from the workflow ID and step
    state_id = HASH(workflow_id || "state" || step_number)

    // Derive an encryption key for this state record
    key = KDF(workflow_key, state_id, "workflow_state")

    // Encrypt the state
    nonce = random_bytes(24)
```

```
ciphertext = AEAD_encrypt(key, nonce, serialize(state_data),
                          associated_data = state_id)

// Store in blind database
blind_store(state_id, nonce || ciphertext)


function resume_workflow(workflow_id, step_number, workflow_key):
    // Reconstruct the storage identifier
    state_id = HASH(workflow_id || "state" || step_number)

    // Retrieve and decrypt
    stored = blind_retrieve(state_id)
    key = KDF(workflow_key, state_id, "workflow_state")
    nonce = stored[0:24]
    ciphertext = stored[24:]
    state_data = AEAD_decrypt(key, nonce, ciphertext,
                             associated_data = state_id)

    return deserialize(state_data)
```

The workflow_key is held by the workflow participants, not by the delegator. The delegator can store and retrieve the encrypted state—it knows the state_id because it derives that from the workflow ID and step number, both of which it needs for routing. But it cannot decrypt the state because it does not hold the workflow key. The delegator is a blind courier for workflow state just as it is a blind courier for workflow sections.

This pattern extends naturally. If a workflow spans days, the encrypted state persists in the Blind Database for days. If a workflow is abandoned, the state remains as unreadable ciphertext until it is either retrieved or crypto-erased by discarding the workflow key. The persistence introduces no new exposure because the persistent data is opaque.

Where Trust Concentrates

The composed architecture is not trustless. No useful system is. The composition does not eliminate trust. It narrows trust, distributes it, and makes it explicit.

The User Service must be trusted for availability—for being present when a user needs to authenticate—and for the integrity of the client code it serves. It need not be trusted for confidentiality because the Blind Database ensures it cannot read the identity mappings it stores. The trust assumption narrows from "trust the operator with your complete authentication history" to "trust the operator to stay online and serve unmodified client code." If the operator fails the availability assumption, users cannot authenticate. If the operator is compromised, users' identity mappings remain encrypted. The failure mode is downtime or client code tampering, not bulk data exposure.

The delegator must be trusted for routing—for delivering cryptogram fragments to the correct participants in the correct order. It need not be trusted for content because every fragment is encrypted for someone else. The delegator is a blind courier. The trust assumption is that the courier delivers rather than discards, not that the courier keeps secrets. A compromised delegator can disrupt workflows by dropping fragments. It cannot read them.

The PoH verifier must be trusted for score computation—for honestly accumulating signals and producing accurate scores. It need not be trusted with behavioral profiles because signals are converted to cryptographic proofs that attest to effort without revealing activity. The trust assumption is that the score reflects genuine humanness, not that the verifier knows everything about the user's behavior.

HermesP2P relay nodes must be trusted for message passing—for forwarding messages rather than dropping them. They need not be trusted for content or identity because messages are onion-encrypted and routing addresses are ephemeral. The trust assumption is availability, not confidentiality.

In every case, the pattern is the same: trust an operator for liveness, not for secrecy. An operator who fails the liveness assumption causes a service disruption. An operator who is compromised, subpoenaed, or malicious causes a service disruption. Neither causes data exposure. In most cases, the worst an adversary can do by compromising any single operator is deny service—though a compromised User Service could serve modified client code, and a compromised PoH verifier could issue fraudulent scores. Even these attacks do not expose stored data. The worst they can do in today's systems is expose everything.

The Full Threat Model

The composed architecture creates a defense surface that no individual component provides. The composition is not merely additive—closing one component's gap eliminates attack paths that would otherwise undermine multiple components simultaneously. A breach of the User Service, for example, would compromise not just identity mappings but also PoH score correlation and Chess author identification—all of which are closed by the same Blind Database integration.

What the Composed Architecture Defeats

Database breaches. The Blind Database ensures that server-side data is encrypted with keys the server never holds. A breach yields ciphertext with no content-derived structural leakage—no frequency distributions, no ordering relationships, no co-occurrence patterns. The inference attacks that succeed against property-preserving encryption fail because no content-derived properties are preserved. The attacker gets noise, though the number and sizes of encrypted records remain visible.

Subpoenas and compelled disclosure. An operator served with a legal demand for user data can comply truthfully and completely: here is everything we store. The production consists of opaque blobs indexed by opaque identifiers. The operator cannot decrypt the data because the operator never possessed the keys. This is not obstruction. This is architecture. The operator cannot produce what it does not have, and the content of each record is computationally indistinguishable from random data under the encryption scheme used (see Chapter 5).

Gatekeeper censorship. Chess documents are self-validating. They carry their own code, their own state, their own proof of integrity. They do not require an app store for distribution or a hosting provider for availability. A court order in one jurisdiction can remove a document from one server. The document continues to circulate through every other channel. The gatekeeper cannot prevent distribution because no gatekeeper is architecturally required.

Bot abuse and Sybil attacks. Proof of Human makes large-scale abuse economically irrational. The logarithmic relationship between score and forging cost (Chapter 7) means that a single fake identity with a score of 0.3 costs approximately a thousand dollars in forging effort. A thousand fake identities at the same threshold cost approximately a million dollars, because each must independently accumulate the required signals. Bot networks depend on near-zero marginal cost per identity. Against any meaningful PoH threshold, that assumption fails.

Intermediary surveillance. Cryptograms fragment workflow information so that each intermediary sees only its section. The payment processor sees payment details but not the shipping address. The store sees the order but not the payment details. The carrier sees the delivery address but not what was ordered. No intermediary accumulates the complete picture because no intermediary can decrypt sections encrypted for other parties.

Identity correlation across services. Anonymous Identity produces site-specific tokens that are cryptographically unlinkable. The token you present to one service cannot be derived from the token you present to another. An advertising network that collects tokens from a thousand sites gets a thousand unrelated identifiers. The correlation that currently enables behavioral profiling across the web becomes computationally infeasible, assuming the token derivation scheme described in Chapter 3 is a secure pseudorandom function.

Communication metadata analysis. HermesP2P eliminates the central server that would accumulate metadata. Messages flow through onion-routed paths where no single node knows both the sender and the recipient. Relationship graphs cannot be constructed because no entity possesses the edges. A government that demands communication records receives a truthful answer: there are no records.

What the Composed Architecture Does Not Defeat

Honest engineering requires explicit boundaries. The architecture has them.

Endpoint compromise. If your device is compromised—by malware, by physical seizure, by a vulnerability in the operating system—then everything you do on that device is visible to the attacker. The attacker sees plaintext before encryption and after decryption. No cryptographic architecture can protect against an adversary who controls the endpoint. This limitation is shared by every system ever built or proposed. The architecture protects data in transit and at rest. It cannot protect data in use on a compromised device.

Global passive adversaries. An adversary capable of monitoring all network traffic simultaneously can perform traffic analysis: correlating the timing, volume, and pattern of encrypted communications to infer who is communicating with whom. HermesP2P's onion routing makes this harder—the adversary must correlate across multiple hops with injected latency and cover traffic—but a sufficiently powerful global observer can, in theory, defeat traffic analysis countermeasures. This is a theoretical limitation that applies to all known anonymity networks, including Tor and Signal.

Malicious authors. Chess ensures that documents are self-validating and uncensorable. It does not ensure that documents are benign. A malicious author can distribute harmful software through Chess exactly as a malicious author can distribute harmful software through any other channel. The architecture makes trust explicit—you must verify the signature and trust the signer—but it does not eliminate the need for trust. If you execute code signed by an adversary, the architecture will faithfully verify that the adversary signed it. The harm follows from the trust decision, not from the distribution mechanism.

Targeted active surveillance. A nation-state that decides to surveil a specific individual can compromise their devices through zero-day exploits, intercept their communications through active network attacks, conduct physical surveillance, and apply resources that no cryptographic system can withstand. The architecture makes mass surveillance computationally infeasible—no operator holds the data needed to conduct it—and raises the cost of targeted surveillance substantially. It does not make targeted surveillance impossible. No system does. The distinction between mass and targeted surveillance is the operationally relevant one: mass surveillance affects millions of people at near-zero marginal cost; targeted surveillance requires significant per-target investment and therefore cannot scale.

Multi-operator collusion. The composed architecture distributes trust across independent operators, and no single operator can read data, correlate identities, or reconstruct communication patterns. But operators who collude can potentially combine their partial views. A User Service operator who colludes with a site operator could attempt to correlate identity mappings with site-specific activity. A PoH verifier who colludes with a site operator could attempt to link humanness scores with behavioral data. The architecture limits what any single operator sees. It does not prevent multiple operators from pooling what they individually possess. The mitigation is operational: distribute infrastructure across organizations in different jurisdictions with different incentive structures. The mitigation is imperfect.

User error. If a user copies their decrypted data into an email and sends it to the wrong person, the architecture cannot help. If a user shares their master secret with a phishing site, the architecture cannot help. If a user announces their pseudonymous identity on social media, the architecture cannot help. The architecture protects against structural vulnerabilities—the kind built into the system's design. It does not protect against voluntary disclosure, whether through carelessness or deception.

The Panama Papers: A Case Study in Structural Protection

In early 2015, an anonymous source contacted Bastian Obermayer of Süddeutsche Zeitung through an encrypted channel. Over the following months, the source transferred 2.6 terabytes of data—11.5 million documents from Mossack Fonseca, a Panamanian law firm that specialized in creating offshore shell companies. The International Consortium of Investigative Journalists coordinated more than 400 journalists across more than 80 countries. They worked in secret for more than a year. The story broke simultaneously worldwide on April 3, 2016. The source, who used the name John Doe, remains anonymous.

The operation was a triumph of human discipline. It was also a case study in the fragility of discipline-dependent security.

What the Operation Required

Custom infrastructure. The ICIJ built Blacklight, a search system based on Apache Solr, to allow journalists to query the 11.5 million documents without distributing copies. They built Global iHub, a secure forum, for cross-border coordination. Both systems were purpose-built, maintained by the ICIJ's technical team, and required continuous security monitoring.

PGP training. All email between participants required PGP encryption. Nearly half of the 400+ journalists had never used PGP before. The consortium had to train them. PGP's notorious usability problems meant that the training was not optional—incorrect use would expose communications in plaintext.

Behavioral discipline across 400+ participants. Every journalist had to maintain operational security for the duration of the investigation. No premature leaks. No careless communications. No use of cloud translation services (uploading a Russian contract to Google Translate would create a trace on Google's servers). No discussion of the investigation outside secure channels. One lapse by one journalist in one country could have compromised the entire operation.

Secrecy maintained for more than a year. The investigation ran from early 2015 through April 2016. Every additional month increased the probability that someone would make a mistake, that a server would be breached, that a government would discover the operation through signals intelligence.

Trust concentrated in the ICIJ. The consortium's servers held the documents. The consortium's forum held the coordination. Every journalist trusted the ICIJ to maintain server security, to vet other journalists, and to enforce operational discipline. The ICIJ justified that trust—their execution was exemplary. But the trust was required because the architecture demanded it.

It is an unreplicable model. Consider the failure modes that did not materialize but easily could have. A single journalist, under legal pressure from a government investigating their sources, could have been compelled to reveal their PGP keys and decrypt archived communications. A single breach of the ICIJ's servers—which held the documents in searchable, queryable form—would have exposed the entire corpus plus the search logs revealing which journalist was investigating which entity. A single operational lapse—a journalist discussing their story on an unsecured channel, or forwarding a document to a colleague at a publication not yet vetted by the consortium—would have created a trace outside the secured perimeter.

None of these happened. But probability does not favor discipline at this scale. Four hundred people maintaining perfect operational security for fourteen months is not a reproducible engineering outcome. It is an extraordinary achievement by extraordinary people. The next investigation may not have the ICIJ's resources. The next group of 400 journalists may include one who makes a mistake. The next year-long operation may face a server breach in month three. The question is not whether the ICIJ's model was effective—it was—but whether the protection should depend on human perfection at all.

What the Composed Architecture Would Provide

Consider the same operation with the architecture described in this book.

Source communication occurs over HermesP2P. No server logs the conversation. No metadata accumulates about when the source was online, how often they communicated, or the volume of their messages. The journalist cannot be compelled to produce communication records because no records exist. The source's anonymity is structural, not behavioral—there is nothing to reveal even under compulsion.

Document storage uses a Blind Database. The consortium's servers hold encrypted fragments. The consortium cannot read the documents it hosts. Each journalist has access to documents relevant to their investigation, but the access is cryptographically bounded. A breach of the consortium's infrastructure yields encrypted fragments that reveal nothing without keys the attackers do not have.

Journalist identity is managed through Anonymous Identity. The consortium knows that a certain pseudonym has authorization to access certain documents. It does not know which journalist corresponds to which pseudonym. A government demanding the identity of the journalist investigating a particular politician receives a truthful answer: the consortium does not know.

Coordination uses cryptograms. A journalist querying the document set submits encrypted queries that the consortium routes without reading. The collaboration graph—who is working with whom on which stories—is fragmented across participants who each see only their piece. The consortium cannot reconstruct the graph even if compelled to try.

Publication uses Chess. The stories exist as self-validating documents carrying their own proof of integrity. A court injunction in one jurisdiction orders removal from one server. The document continues to circulate through every other channel. No gatekeeper can prevent publication because no gatekeeper is architecturally required.

PGP training becomes unnecessary. The communication channel handles encryption transparently. The journalist does not need to understand key exchange, trust models, or the difference between signing and encrypting. The security is in the architecture, not in the journalist's technical competence.

Behavioral discipline becomes structurally enforced rather than individually maintained. A journalist cannot accidentally expose coordination metadata because coordination metadata does not exist in readable form. A journalist cannot leak the collaboration graph because no journalist possesses the collaboration graph. The architecture eliminates the need for the discipline that the Panama Papers required.

The contrast is not between a system that worked and a system that would work better. The Panama Papers worked brilliantly. The contrast is between protection that depends on 400 people maintaining perfect discipline for a year and protection that depends on mathematics. The mathematics does not get tired, does not make mistakes at 2 AM, and does not crack under legal pressure.

The Perfection Fallacy

The threat model section was explicit about what this architecture does not defeat. Critics will read that section and conclude that the architecture is insufficient. Endpoint compromise, global adversaries, malicious authors, targeted active surveillance—these are real limitations. The criticism writes itself: "This system cannot protect against a nation-state adversary, so what is the point?"

The criticism is a perfection fallacy. It compares the proposed architecture to an imagined ideal rather than to the actual alternative. The actual alternative is not a system without limitations. The actual alternative is today's infrastructure.

Consider the comparison systematically.

Threat	This Architecture	Today's Infrastructure
Database breach	Yields only ciphertext with no structural leakage	Yields plaintext, or encrypted data with structural properties that enable inference
Legal compulsion (subpoena)	Operator produces data it cannot read	Operator produces plaintext records, complete metadata, full relationship graphs
Gatekeeper censorship	No gatekeeper required; documents self-validate	Single-point removal through app stores, hosting providers, DNS seizure
Bot abuse / Sybil attacks	Economically prohibitive through PoH thresholds	CAPTCHAs solved by AI; phone verification costs cents per number; bot farms operate at industrial scale
Intermediary surveillance	Each intermediary sees only its fragment	Intermediaries hold complete transaction records as a structural byproduct
Cross-site identity correlation	Computationally infeasible without client secrets	Trivial through email addresses, cookies, device fingerprinting, SSO logs
Communication metadata	No metadata accumulates; no logs exist	Complete relationship graphs stored indefinitely by service operators

Endpoint compromise	**No protection**—plaintext visible on compromised device	**No protection**—plaintext visible on compromised device
Global passive adversary	**Resistant but not immune**—traffic analysis theoretically possible	**Defeated trivially**—adversary can simply request logs from operators
Malicious authors	**No protection**—trust decisions remain necessary	**No protection**—app store review is security theater; malware passes regularly
Targeted active surveillance	**No protection**—sufficient resources overcome any defense	**No protection**—sufficient resources overcome any defense

The bottom four rows—the limitations critics will cite—apply equally to the status quo. The top seven represent failures this architecture eliminates and the status quo does not.

The honest comparison is not "this architecture versus perfection." The honest comparison is "this architecture versus what people actually use today." Rejecting improvement because it falls short of perfection is not an argument for something better. It is an argument for the status quo.

The framing matters because the incentive structure predicts it. Parties whose business models depend on data accumulation have a rational interest in comparing privacy alternatives against an unachievable ideal rather than against current practice. The comparison against perfection always fails—no system defeats all threats. The comparison against the status quo reveals that the proposed architecture eliminates seven categories of failure while inheriting only the four that are physically unavoidable. The perfection fallacy is not merely an intellectual error. It is a predictable consequence of concentrated interests defending valuable capabilities—the same dynamic analyzed in Chapter 16's discussion of political economy.

The correct standard is improvement over the status quo. By that standard, the architecture is not merely adequate. It represents a categorical shift in what privacy means: from a policy promise that depends on the goodwill of operators to a structural property that holds regardless of their intentions.

The Consortium Model

The full architecture described in this chapter—Anonymous Identity, Blind Database, Proof of Human, HermesP2P, Cryptogram, Chess, all composing into a unified privacy stack—is not something any individual reader needs to build. It is not something any individual organization is likely to deploy in full. The architecture is aspirational in the engineering sense: it defines what complete structural privacy looks like so that partial implementations can be evaluated against a known standard.

In practice, the full stack is what a consortium provides. A consortium is a group of organizations that collectively operate the infrastructure: some run User Service nodes, some run Blind Database storage, some run PoH verification, some maintain relay nodes for HermesP2P, some operate delegator services for cryptogram routing. The infrastructure is distributed across organizations in different jurisdictions, under different legal regimes, with different threat models. No single organization holds all the pieces. No single government has jurisdiction over the complete system.

This is not a new organizational model. The Internet itself is a consortium product—the infrastructure is operated by thousands of independent organizations coordinating through shared protocols. Certificate authorities, DNS root servers, BGP routing—all are consortium-operated infrastructure that individual users consume without operating. The privacy stack described here follows the same pattern: shared infrastructure, shared protocols, independent operation, collective benefit.

The reader who is building a single application does not need to deploy the full stack. The reader who integrates Anonymous Identity into their authentication flow gets cross-site unlinkability. The reader who stores user data in a Blind Database gets breach resistance and subpoena immunity. The reader who adds PoH to their platform gets bot resistance. Each component provides value independently. The full composition provides comprehensive protection.

The consortium model has its own failure modes. Governance is contentious—who decides protocol changes, who arbitrates disputes between operators, who sets the rules for admission and expulsion. Incentive alignment is uncertain—the organizations best positioned to operate privacy infrastructure are often the ones whose current business models depend on the data access that privacy infrastructure eliminates. The bootstrap problem is real—a privacy network with few users provides little privacy, and users have limited incentive to join until the network reaches critical mass. These are organizational and economic challenges, not cryptographic ones. The architecture cannot solve them. It can only define what the infrastructure looks like if the coordination succeeds.

The aspiration is not that every developer becomes a privacy infrastructure operator. The aspiration is that privacy infrastructure exists as a shared resource—like HTTPS, like DNS, like email transport—that developers integrate rather than build. The architecture described in this chapter defines what that shared resource looks like when it is complete.

The components compose because they were designed to compose. Each addresses a different layer of the privacy problem. Identity, storage, accountability, communication, coordination, distribution—each layer has its vulnerability and each vulnerability has its architectural response. The responses are independent but complementary. Independence means that partial adoption provides partial protection. Complementarity means that full adoption closes every gap.

The architecture is complete in the sense that it addresses the structural failures of current infrastructure. It is incomplete in the sense that deployment requires implementation, implementation requires coordination, and coordination requires will. The mathematical foundations are sound. The cryptographic primitives are standard. The composition patterns are clean. What remains is the engineering—and the political economy of building systems that protect users at the expense of the business models that exploit them.

CHAPTER 15

Implementation Roadmap

The preceding chapters describe six components: Anonymous Identity, Blind Database, Proof of Human, HermesP2P, Cryptogram/Delegator, and Chess. Each chapter presents the component's design, its security properties, and its role in the composed architecture. This chapter answers the engineering question: what do you actually build, in what order, and with what tools?

The answer is not "build everything at once." The architecture is deliberately decomposable. Each component provides independent value. The adoption path is incremental, each step closing a specific gap in the threat model. An organization that deploys only Anonymous Identity has improved its privacy posture. An organization that adds Blind Database has improved it further. At no point does the architecture require a commitment to the full stack before delivering value.

This matters because the history of privacy engineering is littered with ambitious architectures that failed because they required wholesale adoption. A system that demands everything-at-once competes not with the current system's weaknesses but with the current system's inertia. Inertia wins. The architecture described here is designed to be adopted in pieces, each piece justifying its own deployment cost.

Component Readiness

Not all components are equally ready for production deployment. Some can be built today with off-the-shelf cryptographic libraries. Others require research, ecosystem development, or sustained engineering effort before they can meet production reliability standards. Acknowledging this is part of getting the engineering right.

The following table summarizes the current state:

Component	Maturity	What Works Today	What Requires Further Work
Anonymous Identity	Implementable now	Hash construction, token derivation, verification protocol. Standard crypto libraries provide all necessary primitives.	Token refresh flows, account recovery UX, integration with existing OAuth ecosystems.

Blind Database	Implementable now; scale research needed	Client-side encryption, opaque blob storage, key derivation, crypto-erasure.	Performance at scale. Querying patterns over large encrypted datasets. Index structures for encrypted record enumeration.
Proof of Human	Core implementable; accuracy/accessibility need research	Signal accumulation, proof storage, score computation, token attachment.	Weight calibration against real forgery economics. Accessibility for users who cannot provide certain signals. Governance for weight adjustment.
HermesP2P	Prototype achievable; production reliability requires engineering	Onion routing, gossip protocols, ephemeral storage. All protocol patterns exist in current systems.	Offline message delivery. Consistency across network partitions. Bootstrap for new participants. Performance matching centralized messaging expectations.
Cryptogram/Delegator	Implementable now; developer tooling needed	Encrypted sections, blind routing, stateless coordination. Standard web services patterns with cryptographic wrappers.	Developer libraries that make cryptogram creation as simple as API calls. Debugging tools for encrypted workflows. Error handling when intermediate services fail.
Chess	Requires ecosystem development	Lisp interpreters, JSON serialization, hash chains, cryptographic signatures all exist independently.	Sandboxing environments for safe execution. Browser integration for seamless use. Developer tools for authoring. The ecosystem surrounding execution, not the execution itself, is immature.

The readiness gap between components is deliberate in the ordering. Anonymous Identity, which is fully implementable today, is also the foundation on which everything else builds. Blind Database, the next most ready component, closes the most critical gap that Anonymous Identity leaves open. The components that require the most development—HermesP2P for production reliability, Chess for ecosystem maturity—are also the components that address threats further down most organizations' priority lists.

This is not a coincidence. The architecture was designed so that the most urgent protections are the most implementable, and the components requiring the most investment address threats that become relevant only after the foundational protections are in place.

The Incremental Adoption Path

The adoption sequence is not arbitrary. Each step builds on the previous one, and each step provides independent value that justifies its deployment cost before the next step is considered.

Step 1: Anonymous Identity

Start here. Authentication is the foundation. Every interaction between a user and a service begins with identity, and if identity leaks correlation data, nothing built on top of it can compensate.

Anonymous Identity replaces stable cross-site identifiers with derived, site-specific tokens. The cryptographic construction uses standard hash functions. The integration point is the authentication layer—a single, well-defined component in most service architectures.

What you gain: Cross-site tracking stops. A breach at Service A does not reveal which users also have accounts at Service B. Advertising networks lose the ability to correlate behavior across sites through identity tokens.

What gap remains: The User Service—the entity that issues tokens—still holds the mapping between the user's master identity and their site-specific tokens. A compromise of the User Service exposes the correlation table. For many applications, this gap is acceptable. The User Service is a single, hardened system under the operator's control, not the open internet. But the gap exists.

When this step alone is sufficient: When the primary threat is cross-site correlation by third parties (advertising networks, data brokers, breached services), and the operator of the User Service is trusted or is the user themselves.

Step 2: Blind Database

Adding Blind Database storage closes the gap that Anonymous Identity leaves open. The User Service's identity mappings are encrypted with keys the server never holds. A compromise of the User Service yields ciphertext that is computationally indistinguishable from random noise.

More broadly, Blind Database protects all stored data, not just identity mappings. Application data, user preferences, transaction records—everything stored through the blind database protocol is opaque to the server operator.

What you gain: Operational blindness for all stored data. Server compromise yields nothing usable. Subpoenas directed at the operator produce ciphertext the operator cannot decrypt. Crypto-erasure becomes possible: deleting a user's keys permanently destroys their data without requiring the operator to locate every copy.

What gap remains: The system has identity and storage privacy, but no mechanism for accountability. Any entity that can create an account can abuse the service. Bot networks can create unlimited identities. Without a humanness signal, the system provides perfect privacy for both legitimate users and automated abuse.

When these two steps are sufficient: When the threat model centers on data breaches and operator-side privacy (medical records, financial data, legal documents), and the service has alternative means of abuse prevention (rate limiting, payment requirements, invitation-only access).

Step 3: Proof of Human

Adding Proof of Human provides accountability without surveillance. The system can now distinguish, with calibrated confidence, between human users and automated accounts. The distinction is probabilistic—a score rather than a binary—and the score is attached to the anonymous identity token without revealing any identifying information about the human behind it.

What you gain: Bot filtering. Spam resistance. The ability to set minimum humanness thresholds for actions (posting in public forums, creating accounts, initiating transactions) without requiring identity disclosure. Services can require that a user demonstrate $1,000 worth of forgery-resistance effort without knowing who the user is.

What gap remains: Identity is private. Storage is blind. Accountability exists. But multi-party workflows still expose data to intermediaries. A purchase that routes through a payment processor, a fulfillment service, and a shipping carrier exposes transaction details to each intermediary, and each intermediary aggregates data across transactions.

When these three steps are sufficient: When the service operates primarily as a bilateral relationship between users and a single operator, and multi-party data exposure is not a significant threat. Most user-facing applications fall into this category.

Step 4: Cryptogram/Delegator

Adding Cryptogram workflows addresses intermediary exposure. Multi-party coordination happens through encrypted documents where each party can read only its designated section. The delegator routes sections to services without possessing decryption keys.

What you gain: No intermediary sees more data than it needs for its specific role. A payment processor sees payment details but not shipping addresses. A shipping carrier sees the destination but not what was purchased or what it cost. The delegator that coordinates the workflow sees encrypted blobs it cannot read.

What gap remains: Communication metadata. The fact that Alice communicated with Bob, the timing of the communication, the volume of traffic—this metadata is still visible to network infrastructure. For many applications, this is acceptable. For applications where communication patterns themselves are sensitive (journalism, legal consultation, political organizing), this gap matters.

When these four steps are sufficient: When the threat model includes multi-party workflows with sensitive data (e-commerce, healthcare referrals, legal proceedings), but communication metadata is not a primary concern.

Step 5: HermesP2P

Adding HermesP2P removes metadata logging from communications. Messages route through a peer-to-peer network using onion routing. No single node knows both the sender and the recipient. Messages are ephemeral—stored only long enough for delivery, then discarded.

What you gain: Communication privacy that survives network-level surveillance. No server logs recording who talked to whom. No metadata available for subpoena. Combined with PoH for spam resistance, the system provides private, accountable communication.

What gap remains: The application itself. If the application is distributed through a gatekeeper (an app store, a browser extension marketplace), the gatekeeper can remove it. The privacy architecture is complete, but access to it depends on distribution channels controlled by parties who may not share the user's interests.

When these five steps are sufficient: When communication metadata is a significant threat, but application distribution is not at risk. Most applications in democratic jurisdictions with functioning rule of law fall into this category.

Step 6: Chess

Adding Chess removes gatekeeper control over application distribution. Applications are self-contained documents—code, state, and integrity proofs bundled together—that can be distributed through any channel: email, USB drives, peer-to-peer networks, printed QR codes. No app store approval required. No hosting infrastructure to be taken down.

What you gain: Censorship resistance for application distribution. The application cannot be removed from users who already have it, and it can be transmitted through any medium that carries data.

When to consider this step: When gatekeeper censorship is a realistic threat. This is not a theoretical concern in many jurisdictions, but it is a concern that applies to specific categories of applications (privacy tools, dissident communication, whistleblowing platforms) rather than to applications generally. Chess requires the most ecosystem investment of any component. Deploy it when the threat justifies the cost.

The Stop-Anywhere Principle

The correct deployment depth is determined by the threat model, not by architectural completeness. A medical records system may need steps 1 through 3 and nothing else. An e-commerce platform may need steps 1 through 4. A messaging platform for journalists may need steps 1 through 5. A dissident communication tool may need all six. Deploying more than the threat model requires wastes engineering resources and adds operational complexity without corresponding security benefit.

Recommended Cryptographic Primitives

The components described in this book use a small set of cryptographic primitives. The following table lists the recommended choices:

Function	Recommended Primitive	Notes
Hash	SHA-256 or SHA-3-256	SHA-256 for compatibility; SHA-3 if regulatory requirements favor it. Both are suitable.
Symmetric Encryption	AES-256-GCM or ChaCha20-Poly1305	AES-256-GCM where hardware acceleration (AES-NI) is available. ChaCha20-Poly1305 for software implementations or platforms without AES hardware. Both provide authenticated encryption.
Asymmetric Encryption	X25519 + XSalsa20-Poly1305	X25519 for key agreement, XSalsa20-Poly1305 for the symmetric layer. This is libsodium's `crypto_box` construction. For AEAD operations, use `crypto_aead_xchacha20poly1305_ietf`, which provides ChaCha20-Poly1305 with extended nonces.
Digital Signatures	Ed25519	Fast, small signatures, well-analyzed security properties.
Key Derivation	HKDF-SHA256	Extracts and expands key material. Used to derive record-specific encryption keys from a master secret.
Password Hashing	Argon2id	For any operation that derives key material from a human-chosen password. Argon2id provides resistance to both GPU and side-channel attacks.

Why libsodium

The recommended implementation library for all of these primitives is libsodium. The reasons are specific and practical:

Consistent API. libsodium provides a single, coherent API across all primitives. The same library handles hashing, symmetric encryption, asymmetric encryption, signatures, and key derivation. This eliminates the integration complexity of combining libraries from different sources with different conventions, different error handling patterns, and different assumptions about memory management.

Audited. libsodium has been subjected to multiple independent security audits. The audit reports are public. The issues found have been addressed. This does not guarantee the absence of vulnerabilities—no audit can provide that guarantee—but it provides a level of confidence that the implementation matches the specification and that common implementation errors (buffer overflows, timing leaks, insufficient randomness) have been checked by people whose job is finding them.

Cross-platform. libsodium compiles and runs on every major platform: Linux, macOS, Windows, iOS, Android, WebAssembly. Language bindings exist for Python, JavaScript, Go, Rust, C#, Java, Ruby, PHP, and others. A choice made in one language or on one platform carries over to others without re-evaluating the cryptographic library selection.

Misuse-resistant. libsodium's API is designed to make correct use easy and incorrect use difficult. Nonces are generated automatically where possible. Key sizes are enforced by the type system. Authenticated encryption is the default—there is no way to accidentally use unauthenticated encryption. The library does not offer ECB mode, does not allow users to choose their own IVs for modes that require random IVs, and does not provide access to raw block cipher operations that are easy to misuse.

No algorithm negotiation. libsodium does not support algorithm negotiation. The function crypto_box uses X25519 + XSalsa20 + Poly1305. There is no option to downgrade to a weaker algorithm. This eliminates an entire class of downgrade attacks that have plagued protocols like TLS, where the flexibility to negotiate algorithms became a vulnerability when attackers could force negotiation toward weak options.

libsodium is not the only acceptable choice. OpenSSL, BoringSSL, and platform-native cryptographic libraries (CommonCrypto on Apple platforms, the Web Crypto API in browsers) are all capable implementations. But they require more careful use. OpenSSL exposes low-level primitives that are easy to misuse. Platform-native libraries vary across platforms. libsodium is the recommendation because it minimizes the distance between "a developer who understands the architecture" and "a correct implementation."

Algorithm Selection

The specific algorithms recommended here—SHA-256, AES-256-GCM, ChaCha20-Poly1305, X25519, Ed25519—are conservative choices with extensive analysis behind them. They are not the newest algorithms available. They are the algorithms with the longest track record of resisting both cryptanalysis and implementation attacks.

There is a temptation in cryptographic engineering to adopt the newest construction, the one with the strongest theoretical security proof, the one presented at last year's conference. Resist this temptation. A primitive with twenty years of scrutiny and no practical attacks is a better engineering choice than a primitive with a tighter security reduction and two years of analysis. The former has survived sustained attention from the world's best cryptanalysts. The latter has not yet faced it.

If and when quantum computing threatens the security of X25519 and Ed25519 (both rely on the hardness of the elliptic curve discrete logarithm problem, which Shor's algorithm would break), post-quantum replacements will be necessary. NIST has standardized post-quantum algorithms (ML-KEM for key encapsulation, ML-DSA for signatures). The architecture described here can migrate to post-quantum primitives by replacing the asymmetric layer while leaving the symmetric layer unchanged—AES-256 and ChaCha20 are already quantum-resistant at their current key sizes. That migration is a future concern, not a present one. Build with the well-analyzed primitives now. Migrate when the threat materializes.

Security Checklist

Correct choice of primitives is necessary but not sufficient. The following security practices are required for any implementation of this architecture. Each addresses a class of vulnerability that is independent of the cryptographic algorithms chosen.

Constant-Time Comparisons

When comparing hashes, signatures, or authentication tokens, the comparison must execute in constant time—the same number of CPU cycles regardless of where the inputs differ. A naive byte-by-byte comparison that returns early on the first mismatched byte leaks information through timing: an attacker who can measure response time can determine how many leading bytes of a hash match the expected value and iterate toward the correct value one byte at a time.

```
// WRONG: early-return comparison
function compare(a, b):
    for i in range(length(a)):
        if a[i] != b[i]:
            return false
    return true

// RIGHT: constant-time comparison
function constant_time_compare(a, b):
    if length(a) != length(b):
        return false
    result = 0
    for i in range(length(a)):
        result = result | (a[i] ^ b[i])
    return result == 0
```

libsodium provides `sodium_memcmp` for this purpose. Use it. Do not implement your own unless you have verified, through measurement, that your implementation does not branch on secret-dependent values.

Key Management

Client-side keys are the root of trust in this architecture. If the keys are compromised, the cryptographic properties are meaningless. Key storage must use the strongest mechanism available on the platform:

- **macOS/iOS:** Keychain Services, backed by the Secure Enclave on devices that have one. Keys stored in the Secure Enclave never leave the hardware; cryptographic operations are performed on the chip.

- **Android:** Android Keystore with hardware backing (StrongBox or TEE). Similar to the Secure Enclave: keys are generated and used inside the hardware module.

- **Windows:** DPAPI (Data Protection API) for per-user key storage, or TPM-backed key storage for hardware-level protection.

- **Linux/Server:** Hardware Security Modules (HSMs) for production deployments. For development, encrypted key files with passphrase-derived keys are acceptable but not sufficient for production.

- **Browser:** The Web Crypto API provides `CryptoKey` objects that can be made non-extractable—the key exists in the browser's memory but cannot be read by JavaScript. This is a software protection, not a hardware one, but it raises the bar above plaintext storage in localStorage.

The general principle: keys should be stored in the most isolated storage available, and ideally should never exist in application memory in a form that could be extracted by a memory dump. Where hardware-backed storage is available, use it. Where it is not, encrypt keys at rest with a passphrase-derived key using Argon2id, and accept the limitation.

Replay Protection

Any signed message that can be replayed—re-submitted at a later time and accepted as valid—is a vulnerability. An attacker who captures a valid authentication token and replays it later gains the access the token grants.

Protection requires two mechanisms used together:

Timestamps. Every signed message includes a timestamp. Recipients reject messages whose timestamps are outside an acceptable window (typically seconds to minutes, depending on the protocol). This prevents replay of old messages.

Nonces. Every signed message includes a nonce—a unique, non-repeating value. Recipients track recently seen nonces and reject duplicates. This prevents replay of messages within the valid time window.

Timestamps alone are insufficient because an attacker can replay a message within the valid window. Nonces alone are insufficient because the recipient must store nonces indefinitely (or risk accepting a replay of a very old message after the nonce cache is cleared). Together, they provide complete protection: the timestamp limits the window, and the nonce prevents replay within that window.

```
message = {
    payload: ...,
    timestamp: current_time(),
    nonce: random_bytes(16),
    signature: sign(key, payload || timestamp || nonce)
}
```

```
function validate(message):
    if abs(current_time() - message.timestamp) > MAX_CLOCK_SKEW:
        reject("timestamp outside valid window")
    if nonce_cache.contains(message.nonce):
        reject("duplicate nonce")
    if not verify_signature(message):
        reject("invalid signature")
    nonce_cache.add(message.nonce, expires_at = message.timestamp
+ MAX_CLOCK_SKEW)
    accept()
```

Forward Secrecy

Forward secrecy means that compromise of current key material does not retroactively compromise past communications. If an attacker obtains today's keys, messages encrypted with last month's keys remain secure—because last month's keys no longer exist.

Achieving forward secrecy requires two practices:

Key rotation. Encryption keys are rotated on a regular schedule. New messages use new keys. The rotation frequency depends on the threat model—daily for high-sensitivity applications, weekly or monthly for lower sensitivity.

Key destruction. Old keys are securely destroyed after rotation. This is the critical step. Rotation without destruction provides no forward secrecy—an attacker who obtains the system's key storage gets all historical keys. Destruction means overwriting the key material in memory and in persistent storage, not just deleting the file (file deletion typically leaves the data recoverable until the storage is overwritten).

For the Blind Database component, forward secrecy interacts with data access. If encryption keys are rotated and old keys destroyed, data encrypted with old keys becomes permanently unreadable. This is exactly the crypto-erasure property—but it means that data the user still wants to access must be re-encrypted with the new key before the old key is destroyed. The re-encryption operation is the cost of forward secrecy for stored data.

For HermesP2P, forward secrecy is more natural. Messaging protocols routinely rotate keys per-message or per-session using ratcheting constructions (the Signal Protocol's Double Ratchet is the canonical example). Each message is encrypted with a key derived from the previous key, and the previous key is discarded. Compromise of the current key reveals only the current and future messages, not past ones.

First Milestones

Engineering confidence comes from concrete demonstrations, not architectural documents. For each component, the following milestones define the minimum demonstration that confirms the implementation is working correctly. These are not production readiness criteria. They are "you know it works when..." checkpoints.

Anonymous Identity

> **Production note.** *For the authentication exchange in Step 1, production deployments should use OPAQUE (RFC 9807) or another standardized PAKE protocol rather than transmitting password-derived hashes directly. OPAQUE ensures the server never learns the password, even transiently, providing stronger protection during the authentication handshake. The privacy properties of the architecture—cross-site unlinkability, breach resistance, mutual impersonation resistance—are independent of the authentication exchange protocol and hold equally with OPAQUE or with the hash construction described in Chapter 3.*

Milestone: A single user authenticates to two different sites and receives two different tokens. The tokens are verified as valid by their respective sites. No party other than the user can determine that both tokens belong to the same person.

Verification procedure:

1. Client computes `client_hash` and authenticates with the User Service.

2. Client derives `token_A` for Site A and `token_B` for Site B.

3. Site A verifies `token_A` through the User Service. Verification succeeds.

4. Site B verifies `token_B` through the User Service. Verification succeeds.

5. Given `token_A` and `token_B`, confirm that no mathematical operation on the tokens alone produces a linkage. (Formal verification: the tokens are outputs of a hash function with distinct inputs; preimage resistance prevents deriving the shared input.)

What this proves: The core unlinkability property works. The hash construction produces site-specific tokens that resist correlation.

Blind Database

Milestone: A client stores an encrypted record, retrieves it, and decrypts it successfully. A separate process with full database access examines the stored record and cannot determine its contents, its type, or any structural property of the plaintext.

Verification procedure:

1. Client derives `record_id` and `encryption_key` from a master secret.

2. Client encrypts plaintext, uploads (`record_id, ciphertext`).

3. Client retrieves by `record_id`, decrypts, confirms plaintext matches.

4. An examiner with direct database access reads the stored (`record_id, cipher-text`) pair. The examiner cannot determine whether the plaintext is a name, a number, an image, or any other data type. The `record_id` is opaque. The ciphertext is indistinguishable from random bytes.

What this proves: Operational blindness. The server genuinely cannot read what it stores.

Proof of Human

Milestone: A user verifies an email address. The system stores a proof that verification occurred (not the email address). The humanness score increases. The score is attached to an identity token.

Verification procedure:

1. User triggers email verification. System sends verification challenge.

2. User completes verification. System stores attestation: (`signal_type`, `timestamp`, `cryptographic_proof`).

3. Score before verification: 0.0. Score after verification: 0.02 (the weight for email verification).

4. System issues an identity token. The token includes `poh_score: 0.02`.

5. Confirm that the stored attestation does not contain the email address. The proof confirms that *an* email was verified, not *which* email.

What this proves: The core accumulation mechanism works. Proofs attest to facts without containing the underlying data. Scores increase monotonically with signal collection.

HermesP2P

Milestone: Alice sends a message to Bob through three intermediate relay nodes. Bob receives the original message. No relay node can determine both the sender and the recipient.

Verification procedure:

1. Alice constructs a three-layer onion-encrypted message.

2. Node 1 decrypts layer 1. Node 1 learns the address of Node 2 and nothing else.

3. Node 2 decrypts layer 2. Node 2 learns the address of Node 3. Node 2 does not know Node 1 was the previous hop (the message does not carry path history).

4. Node 3 decrypts layer 3. Node 3 learns Bob's address.

5. Bob decrypts the final payload. The message matches what Alice sent.

6. Confirm: Node 1 knows Alice's address and Node 2's address. Node 2 knows Node 1's address and Node 3's address. Node 3 knows Node 2's address and Bob's address. No single node knows both Alice and Bob.

What this proves: Onion routing works. Path information is compartmentalized. The message arrives intact.

Cryptogram/Delegator

Milestone: A cryptogram with three sections is created, routed through a delegator, and delivered to three services. Each service decrypts only its designated section. The delegator processes the entire workflow without reading any section's contents.

Verification procedure:

1. Client creates a cryptogram with sections encrypted for Service A, Service B, and Service C.

2. Delegator receives the cryptogram. Delegator reads routing metadata (unencrypted). Delegator forwards each section to its designated service.

3. Service A decrypts its section. Service A cannot decrypt sections for B or C.

4. Services B and C likewise decrypt only their own sections.

5. Delegator logs are examined. The logs contain routing metadata and encrypted blobs. No plaintext from any section appears in the delegator's logs, memory dumps, or error outputs.

What this proves: Compartmentalization works. The delegator coordinates without seeing. Each service sees only what it needs.

Chess

Milestone: A Chess document is created with an initial state, a code definition, and an author signature. A move is appended. The chain is verified. A tampered move is detected and rejected.

Verification procedure:

1. Author creates a genesis block: code, initial state, signature.

2. An actor appends a move: operation, resulting state hash, signature.

3. Verification function walks the chain: for each move, it recomputes the state transition and verifies the hash and signature. Verification succeeds.

4. A single byte of the move's operation field is altered. Verification is re-run. Verification fails—the state hash no longer matches the recomputed state.

What this proves: Integrity. The hash chain detects any modification. The chain of signatures establishes provenance. The code is deterministic—the same inputs always produce the same state.

Migration Patterns

Most implementations will not be greenfield. They will be migrations of existing systems toward this architecture. Every migration pattern described here rejects "flag days"—single cutover moments—in favor of incremental transitions where old and new systems run simultaneously and rollback is possible at every step.

Authentication: Parallel Token Types

The migration from conventional authentication to Anonymous Identity runs parallel token types simultaneously.

Phase 1: Dual issuance. The User Service issues both legacy tokens (conventional session tokens, JWTs with user identifiers) and anonymous identity tokens. Both are valid. Both grant access. The application accepts either type.

Phase 2: New users default to anonymous. New account registrations receive anonymous identity tokens by default. Existing users continue with legacy tokens. The system's anonymous token population grows with new signups while legacy users experience no change.

Phase 3: Migration offers. Existing users are offered migration to anonymous tokens. The migration is a client-side operation: the client computes its site-specific tokens, the User Service stores the verification hashes, and the client begins presenting anonymous tokens instead of legacy ones. The legacy token remains valid as a fallback.

Phase 4: Legacy deprecation. Once the anonymous token population is sufficiently large and the system has been verified, legacy token issuance is deprecated. Existing legacy tokens continue to work until they expire. No legacy tokens are renewed.

At no point does the system stop working. At no point is a user unable to authenticate. The migration is invisible to users who do not opt in and seamless for users who do.

Storage: Encrypt New, Leave Old

The migration from conventional database storage to Blind Database follows an encrypt-new-leave-old pattern.

Phase 1: New records encrypted. All newly created records are stored through the Blind Database protocol: client-side encryption, opaque blob storage. Existing records remain in their current form (plaintext or server-side encrypted). The application's read path checks both: if a record is in the blind store, decrypt client-side; if a record is in the legacy store, read as before.

Phase 2: Background migration. A background process reads legacy records, encrypts them client-side, writes them to the blind store, and marks the legacy record as migrated. The process runs at a controlled rate to avoid disrupting production traffic. Records are migrated in priority order: the most sensitive data first.

Phase 3: Legacy read-only. Once all records are migrated, the legacy store is set to read-only. The application still checks the legacy store on cache misses (in case the background migration missed a record), but all writes go to the blind store.

Phase 4: Legacy removal. Once sufficient time has passed with no legacy reads, the legacy store is decommissioned. The data in it—if it was encrypted server-side—can be crypto-erased by destroying the server-side keys. If it was plaintext, it must be securely wiped.

The critical property: at no point does the application fail to serve a request because data is mid-migration. Both stores are accessible throughout the process.

Communication: Bridging

The migration from conventional messaging to HermesP2P uses bridges that connect the two networks.

Phase 1: Bridge deployment. A bridge node participates in both the conventional messaging system and the HermesP2P network. Messages from HermesP2P users to conventional users pass through the bridge: the bridge receives the HermesP2P message, strips the onion routing (the bridge is necessarily a metadata exposure point), and delivers through the conventional system.

Phase 2: Prefer-HermesP2P routing. When both sender and recipient are on HermesP2P, messages route entirely through the peer-to-peer network. When either party is on the conventional system, the bridge handles translation. The system prefers the private path when available and falls back to the bridged path when necessary.

Phase 3: Bridge as legacy compatibility. As HermesP2P adoption grows, the proportion of bridged traffic decreases. The bridge handles an ever-smaller fraction of messages. Eventually, the bridge exists only for the long tail of users who have not migrated.

Phase 4: Bridge retirement. When bridged traffic drops below a threshold, the bridge is retired. Users still on the conventional system lose the ability to communicate with HermesP2P users. This is the only step in any migration that involves functionality loss for non-migrated users, and it should be deferred as long as practically possible.

The bridge is a deliberate compromise. It is a point of metadata leakage—the bridge knows the HermesP2P identity of the sender and the conventional identity of the recipient. This is an accepted cost of interoperability during migration. The alternative—requiring all users to migrate simultaneously—is not a real alternative. It is a wish.

Workflow Coordination: Gradual Encryption

The migration from conventional API integrations to Cryptogram/Delegator workflows is the most gradual of the four patterns.

Phase 1: Single-section cryptograms. Begin by encrypting a single section of a multi-party workflow. The payment section is encrypted for the payment processor; the order and shipping sections remain in conventional plaintext API calls. This protects the most sensitive data first while leaving the rest of the workflow unchanged.

Phase 2: Section-by-section encryption. Additional sections are encrypted as the corresponding services add support for receiving and decrypting cryptogram sections. Each service migrates independently. The delegator handles a mix of encrypted and unencrypted sections in the same workflow.

Phase 3: Full cryptogram workflows. Once all services support encrypted sections, the entire workflow is a cryptogram. The delegator sees only routing metadata and encrypted blobs.

This migration is particularly forgiving because it does not require coordinated deployment across organizations. Service A can add cryptogram support in Q1. Service B can add it in Q3. The delegator adapts to whatever mix of encrypted and unencrypted sections it encounters. No flag day. No coordinated release. Each party migrates on its own schedule.

The Never-a-Flag-Day Principle

The common thread across all migration patterns is the rejection of flag days. A flag day—a single moment when the old system is turned off and the new system is turned on—is the enemy of production deployment. Flag days require:

- Complete confidence that the new system works (never justified for a system that has not run in production)
- A rollback plan that accounts for all state changes during the transition (often impossible)
- Organizational coordination across all teams simultaneously (rarely achievable)
- User communication that reaches every affected user (never complete)

Incremental migration requires none of these. The new system proves itself in production alongside the old system. Rollback is trivial because the old system never stopped running. Teams migrate on their own schedules. Users migrate at their own pace or are migrated transparently.

The cost of incremental migration is carrying two systems simultaneously. This is a real cost—operational complexity, additional testing, dual code paths. But it is a cost measured in engineering effort, not in production outages or user impact. Engineering effort is recoverable. A botched flag day is not.

Putting It Together

The implementation roadmap, summarized:

1. Choose your primitives. SHA-256, AES-256-GCM or ChaCha20-Poly1305, X25519, Ed25519, HKDF-SHA256, libsodium. These choices are correct for the vast majority of implementations. Do not spend time evaluating alternatives unless you have a specific, articulable reason that these choices are insufficient for your requirements.

2. Implement security fundamentals. Constant-time comparisons, hardware-backed key storage, replay protection, forward secrecy through key rotation and destruction. These are non-negotiable regardless of which components you deploy.

3. Start with Anonymous Identity. Get unlinkable authentication working. Verify with the milestone test. Run in parallel with legacy authentication.

4. Add Blind Database. Encrypt new data. Migrate old data in the background. Verify with the milestone test.

5. Add Proof of Human when accountability is needed. Start with simple signals (email, phone, payment instrument). Verify with the milestone test. Tune weights over time.

6. Add Cryptogram/Delegator when multi-party workflows require compartmentalization. Migrate section by section. Verify with the milestone test.

7. Add HermesP2P when communication metadata is a threat. Deploy bridges for interoperability. Verify with the milestone test.

8. Consider Chess when gatekeeper censorship threatens application availability. This requires ecosystem investment beyond what a single team can provide.

9. Stop when your threat model is satisfied. Not every application needs every component. The architecture provides independent value at every step. Deploy what you need. Leave the rest for when you need it.

The architecture is designed to be built incrementally, deployed incrementally, and adopted incrementally. No component requires faith in the whole. No step requires commitment to the next. Each step stands on its own, delivers its own value, and creates the foundation for the step that follows—if and when that step becomes necessary.

The cryptographic primitives are mature. The protocol patterns are established. The integration work is real but bounded. The hardest part is not the cryptography. It is the decision to start.

CHAPTER 16

The Political Economy of Privacy

The architecture described in this book is not neutral. It redistributes power. Some parties lose capabilities they currently possess. Others gain protections they currently lack. Understanding who wins and who loses explains why adoption will be contested and why the contest is worth engaging.

Who Loses Power

Surveillance Capitalists

The advertising industry depends on knowing what you do online. Browsing history, purchase patterns, communication graphs, location data—these feed algorithms that predict which advertisements will capture your attention. The predictions have value because they are accurate. The accuracy depends on access to behavioral data. When blind databases make stored data unreadable and anonymous identities make cross-site tracking impossible, the predictions degrade.

The largest technology companies built their market positions on this data. Google's search advertising depends on knowing what you search for. Meta's social advertising depends on knowing your relationships and interests. Amazon's product recommendations depend on knowing your purchase history. Each company's competitive advantage is its data accumulation. The architecture described in this book makes that accumulation architecturally impossible.

These companies will not welcome architectures that eliminate surveillance. They will fund research emphasizing the dangers of anonymity. They will lobby for regulations requiring identity verification and data retention. They will frame privacy as a threat to security, to child safety, to economic growth. The arguments will sound reasonable. The arguments will serve their interests.

Engagement Platforms

The attention economy depends on knowing what holds your attention and for how long. When anonymous identity prevents cross-session profiling, when blind databases prevent content analysis, when ephemeral communication prevents engagement tracking, the feedback loop that drives algorithmic amplification breaks. The platform can still serve content. It cannot measure which content maximizes time-on-site for each individual user and adjust accordingly. Platforms that cannot optimize for engagement cannot exploit the dynamics that currently drive their growth.

Platform Gatekeepers

Apple and Google control what software runs on most mobile devices. Amazon Web Services and Microsoft Azure host a majority of cloud infrastructure. Cloudflare and Akamai sit between users and most web content. Each gatekeeper extracts value from its position at the chokepoint. The value depends on being necessary.

When Chess (Chapter 13) enables distribution without app stores, the app stores become optional. When HermesP2P (Chapter 9) enables communication without cloud infrastructure, the cloud becomes optional for messaging. Optional parties cannot extract the same rents as necessary parties. The thirty percent commission that app stores charge exists because developers have no alternative distribution channel for mobile software. Remove the necessity and the commission becomes a choice rather than a tax.

The gatekeeper problem extends beyond economics. Apple removed VPN applications from its Chinese App Store at the request of the Chinese government. A single decision by a single company eliminated privacy tools for an entire country's mobile users. The architectural dependency that requires app store distribution creates a censorship surface that any government with sufficient leverage can exploit. Chess eliminates this surface by making the distribution channel irrelevant to the document's integrity.

Data Brokers

The market for personal information depends on collecting, aggregating, and selling data about individuals. Credit bureaus, advertising networks, people-search services, and thousands of smaller operations trade in personal data. The trade depends on the information existing in readable form somewhere in the chain.

When information is encrypted before it leaves the user's device, when identities are unlinkable across contexts, when communications leave no persistent records, the brokers' inventory evaporates. Their business model assumes a world where personal data is accessible. The architecture creates a world where it is not.

The scale of this market is not commonly understood. Data brokers hold profiles on hundreds of millions of individuals, with thousands of data points per profile—inferred income, health conditions, political leanings, purchase propensities, relationship status. The profiles are assembled from public records, purchase data, location tracking, and cross-referencing across sources. The cross-referencing depends on stable identifiers—names, email addresses, device fingerprints—that enable linking a person's activity at one source to their activity at another. Anonymous identity eliminates the stable identifiers. Without them, the cross-referencing fails. Without the cross-referencing, the profiles cannot be assembled. The entire supply chain of personal data collapses at its foundation.

Authoritarian Governments

The ability to monitor dissidents, track journalists, and identify protest participants depends on infrastructure that logs and retains. Centralized services with readable databases make surveillance operationally simple. A request to a service provider yields the target's activity history. A breach of a database yields everyone's.

When the infrastructure is ephemeral, when the databases are blind, when the identities are unlinkable, the easy surveillance disappears. Targeted surveillance remains possible through endpoint compromise—installing malware on a specific person's device still works and requires a warrant or its authoritarian equivalent. Mass surveillance becomes architecturally infeasible.

The distinction matters. Mass surveillance is the tool of authoritarian control. Targeted investigation is the tool of legitimate law enforcement. The architecture preserves the latter while eliminating the former. A government that wants to investigate a specific suspect can still obtain a warrant, seize a device, and examine its contents. A government that wants to identify every citizen who searched for a particular phrase, visited a particular website, or communicated with a particular person cannot do so when the infrastructure retains nothing to query.

Democratic governments will argue that they need mass surveillance capabilities for legitimate purposes—counterterrorism, counterintelligence, organized crime. The argument assumes that the capabilities will be used responsibly and within legal constraints. The historical record of every democracy that has possessed mass surveillance capabilities contradicts this assumption. The capabilities have been consistently abused, expanded beyond their original mandate, and applied to domestic political opponents, journalists, and activists. The architecture described here resolves the dilemma by making the capability structurally unavailable to any government, democratic or otherwise.

Who Gains Power

The parties who gain power are diffuse while the parties who lose power are concentrated. This asymmetry—concentrated losses, diffuse gains—is a standard pattern in political economy and explains why adoption faces structural resistance.

Individuals

Users currently have no architectural choice but to trust every service they use. A health application can read medical records. A bank can track spending patterns. A communication platform can log conversations. The trust is compelled by the architecture—the service must be able to read the data to function, or so the assumption goes.

When the architecture changes, the compelled trust becomes unnecessary. Users can employ services that cannot read what they store. They can communicate through channels that leave no traces. The control shifts from service providers to users. This is not abstract. It is the difference between a health record that can be breached and one that is computationally unreadable to the operator.

The gain is not merely theoretical protection against breaches. It is the elimination of compelled disclosure. A health service operating on a blind database cannot comply with a subpoena for a user's medical records—not because it refuses to comply, but because it cannot read the records it stores. A communication service operating on HermesP2P cannot produce metadata about who communicated with whom—not because it destroys the logs, but because no logs were ever created. The protection comes from architecture, not from the operator's willingness to resist legal pressure. Architecture does not negotiate with court orders. It simply cannot comply with requests for data it does not possess.

Small Creators and Developers

An independent developer who wants to distribute software currently needs app store approval. A musician reaching listeners needs platform placement. A journalist publishing needs hosting that might be pressured. The gatekeepers take their cut, enforce their policies, and can revoke access unilaterally.

When distribution becomes self-validating—when Chess applications travel through any channel—the gatekeeper's permission becomes unnecessary. The creator who has an audience can reach that audience directly. The thirty percent commission disappears for developers willing to use alternative distribution. The editorial control disappears for content that gatekeepers would prefer to suppress.

Privacy-First Services

Currently, services that take privacy seriously face a competitive disadvantage. They cannot monetize user data like surveillance-based competitors. They carry the engineering costs of encryption without capturing equivalent advertising revenue.

When the architecture makes surveillance impossible for everyone, the playing field levels. The privacy-first service that already knows how to operate without user data faces no new constraints. The surveillance-based service that depended on user data must find new business models. First-mover advantage shifts to those who built for privacy from the start.

The competitive dynamics are already visible. Signal demonstrated that an encrypted messaging application can compete with surveillance-based alternatives on functionality and user experience. ProtonMail demonstrated that encrypted email can serve ordinary users, not just security specialists. Each successful privacy-first service disproves the claim that surveillance is required for viability and creates competitive pressure on incumbents who rely on user data as a revenue source.

Journalists and Activists

The Panama Papers required extraordinary operational security from hundreds of people for more than a year. Not every investigation has access to such resources. Not every source can maintain such discipline.

When source protection is architectural—when HermesP2P ensures no metadata exists to subpoena, when anonymous identity ensures the journalist cannot identify the source even under compulsion—the protection extends to everyone. Small newsrooms gain the capabilities that currently require large security teams. Whistleblowers gain protection that does not depend on the competence or courage of every person in the chain.

Democratic Institutions

The information asymmetry described in this chapter is not merely an economic problem. It is a democratic problem. Democratic governance assumes an informed electorate making decisions about power. When corporations and governments know everything about citizens while citizens know almost nothing about corporations and governments, the informational prerequisites of democratic self-governance are absent.

The architecture does not solve this problem directly—it does not make governments transparent. What it does is remove the structural information advantage that allows institutions to manipulate, coerce, and pre-empt civic action. A citizen whose communications cannot be monitored, whose associations cannot be mapped, and whose browsing history cannot be analyzed is a citizen who can organize, dissent, and vote without fear of retaliation.

Law Enforcement and Good Police Work

The most substantive objection to privacy architecture comes from law enforcement. The argument is direct: if you eliminate the data that investigators use, you make investigation harder. Crimes that would have been solved will go unsolved. The argument deserves a direct answer.

The answer is not that privacy makes investigation impossible. The answer is that this architecture preserves legitimate investigation while preventing mass surveillance.

A specific suspect can still be targeted. Endpoints can be compromised with legal authorization. Devices can be seized with warrants. Suspects can be compelled to provide testimony (subject to constitutional protections against self-incrimination). The investigative tools that require a prior hypothesis about a specific person remain available.

What becomes impossible is the fishing expedition. The mass query that identifies everyone who visited a particular website. The bulk metadata request that maps every person who communicated with a particular phone number. The database trawl that searches every user's records for a pattern that might indicate criminal activity.

The architecture enforces what legal process is supposed to enforce: investigation requires a hypothesis before it begins. The suspect must be identified before they can be surveilled. This is the Fourth Amendment principle—no unreasonable searches—implemented at the architectural level rather than the policy level.

The policy level has demonstrably failed. The legal constraints on mass surveillance have been circumvented, reinterpreted, secretly modified, and openly violated by agencies that face minimal consequences for overreach. An architectural constraint cannot be circumvented by a secret legal interpretation. The server that does not hold the data cannot produce it regardless of what a court orders or a secret memo authorizes.

Consider two investigative scenarios. In the first, investigators suspect a specific individual of financial fraud. They obtain a warrant, seize the suspect's devices, and examine the locally stored data. The blind database that stored the suspect's records cannot be queried by the operator—but the data on the suspect's own device, decrypted with the suspect's own keys, is available through standard forensic procedures. The investigation proceeds. The architectural change is irrelevant to this case.

In the second scenario, investigators have no specific suspect. They want to identify everyone in a metropolitan area who purchased a particular chemical in the past six months. Under the surveillance paradigm, they query retail databases, cross-reference with identity records, and generate a list of names. Under the privacy paradigm, the retail database contains encrypted records that the operator cannot read, and the purchase identities are unlinkable tokens that cannot be correlated across stores. The mass query is impossible. The fishing expedition fails.

The first scenario is targeted investigation—the foundation of legitimate policing. The second scenario is mass surveillance—the foundation of authoritarian control. The architecture preserves the first and eliminates the second. The policy level is supposed to make the same distinction. The architecture enforces it.

The architecture makes investigation more expensive and more targeted. Some investigations that would have succeeded through mass data collection will fail. This is a cost. The question is whether the cost is justified by the benefit—the elimination of mass surveillance as a structural capability of both governments and corporations. The answer depends on values, not technology. The architecture creates the choice. The politics determines which choice is made.

Why Resistance Is Predictable

The pattern of resistance to privacy-enhancing technology is well-established and follows the logic of concentrated versus diffuse interests.

The parties who lose from privacy enhancement are few, wealthy, and organized. Technology companies, data brokers, and government surveillance agencies have lobbyists, legal teams, and public relations operations. They can coordinate their opposition. They have access to policymakers. They can frame the debate in terms that serve their interests.

The parties who gain from privacy enhancement are numerous, dispersed, and unorganized. Individual users, small developers, journalists, and activists have no coordinating body and no unified political voice. Each individual's gain from privacy is real but small relative to the concentrated losses of the opposing parties. The classic collective action problem applies.

This asymmetry predicts the form that opposition will take:

Security framing. Privacy will be characterized as enabling crime, terrorism, and child exploitation. The most extreme cases will be emphasized. The routine benefits of privacy—protection from stalkers, protection from discrimination, protection from corporate manipulation—will be minimized. The argument that "if you have nothing to hide, you have nothing to fear" will persist—despite the obvious rejoinder that the definition of "something to hide" is set by whoever holds the surveillance capability, not by the person being observed.

Economic framing. Privacy will be characterized as destroying the free internet. The advertising model that funds most online services will be presented as the only viable model. The existence of subscription services, transaction-based services, and other non-surveillance business models will be ignored.

Technical framing. Privacy will be characterized as impractical. Performance costs will be exaggerated. Implementation complexity will be emphasized. The decades of successful deployment of encryption, anonymization, and decentralization technologies will be discounted.

Governmental framing. Governments will argue that privacy enables crime. Law enforcement agencies will describe cases solved through access to communication records, location histories, and identity databases. They will present the successes of surveillance. They will not present the abuses—the warrantless wiretapping programs, the bulk metadata collection, the location tracking of protesters, the chilling effects on journalistic sources. They will demand backdoors and exceptional access. The demands will sound necessary. The demands will undermine the architecture, because a backdoor that law enforcement can use is a backdoor that anyone who compromises or coerces law enforcement can use.

Each framing contains a kernel of truth wrapped in motivated reasoning. Privacy does make some investigations harder. Privacy does disrupt some business models. Privacy does impose engineering costs. Privacy does complicate certain governmental functions. The kernel of truth makes each argument credible. The motivated reasoning makes each argument misleading. The appropriate response is not to deny the kernel of truth but to weigh it against the harms of the status quo—harms that the same parties rarely acknowledge.

Transition Forces

Despite the structural resistance, several forces push toward privacy-enhancing architecture.

Regulatory pressure. The European Union's GDPR imposes significant costs on data collection. California's CCPA creates compliance burdens. More jurisdictions are considering privacy legislation. Each regulation makes the surveillance model more expensive to operate. At some point, the costs of compliance with ever-tightening regulations exceed the costs of adopting privacy-preserving architecture. The rational response to regulatory pressure is to stop collecting the data that the regulations constrain.

Security disasters. Breaches expose hundreds of millions of records. Identity theft affects a growing fraction of the population. Each breach demonstrates that centralized data collection creates centralized risk. The harms become personal when your own medical records, financial data, or Social Security number appears in a breach notification. Public tolerance for the status quo erodes with each incident.

Competitive dynamics. Privacy-focused alternatives are emerging and gaining users. Signal competes with WhatsApp. DuckDuckGo competes with Google Search. ProtonMail competes with Gmail. Each successful privacy-preserving service demonstrates that surveillance is not required for functionality. The existence of alternatives normalizes the expectation of privacy and creates competitive pressure on incumbents.

Generational shift. Survey data suggests that younger users who grew up with social media report greater awareness of its privacy costs, though evidence on generational privacy attitudes is mixed. The backlash against constant surveillance, algorithmic manipulation, and permanent digital records is stronger among people who never consented to the arrangement. Demographic change shifts the demand curve toward privacy.

Geopolitical competition. Nations that adopt privacy-preserving infrastructure gain advantages in attracting businesses and individuals who value data protection. The competition between jurisdictions for talent, capital, and economic activity creates incentives for governments to support rather than oppose privacy-enhancing technology. The European Union's positioning as a privacy-forward jurisdiction is partly a competitive strategy—attracting data-sensitive industries that cannot operate under the surveillance norms of other jurisdictions.

Technical maturation. The cryptographic primitives underlying this architecture are no longer experimental. AES-256-GCM, X25519, Ed25519, and SHA-256 are standard, audited, and available in production-quality libraries. Searchable encryption, while slower than plaintext queries, has improved by orders of magnitude. Peer-to-peer networking libraries handle NAT traversal, relay selection, and connection management without requiring bespoke implementations. Each year, the engineering cost of privacy-preserving architecture decreases while the regulatory cost of surveillance-based architecture increases. The crossover point—where privacy-first is cheaper than surveillance-first—approaches at different rates for different components, but the direction of the trend is uniform.

None of these forces is individually sufficient to overcome the structural resistance. Collectively, they create pressure that the status quo will increasingly struggle to contain. The outcome is not predetermined. The architecture creates possibility. The politics determines whether the possibility is realized.

The Honest Assessment

The political economy of privacy is unfavorable to rapid change. The losers are powerful, organized, and motivated. The winners are dispersed, unorganized, and individually underinvested. The transition will be slow, contested, and incomplete in most jurisdictions for the foreseeable future.

The assessment does not argue for resignation. It argues for realism about what the technical architecture can and cannot accomplish. The architecture creates options that do not currently exist. It does not guarantee that those options will be exercised. Building the architecture is necessary. Building the architecture is not sufficient.

The history of encryption provides a useful precedent. In the 1990s, the United States government classified strong encryption as a munition and restricted its export. The Clipper Chip proposal would have required government-accessible backdoors in all encryption hardware. The opposition came from technologists, civil liberties organizations, and businesses that needed secure communications. The government's position was that unbreakable encryption would make law enforcement impossible. The opposition's position was that compromised encryption would make security impossible. The opposition won. Strong encryption became ubiquitous. Law enforcement adapted. The predicted catastrophe did not materialize.

The parallel is imperfect—the privacy architecture described here is more comprehensive than encryption alone. But the political dynamics are similar. Concentrated interests will argue that the capability makes their work harder. They will be correct. The question is whether the difficulty justifies maintaining a surveillance infrastructure that threatens everyone's privacy. The encryption precedent suggests that when the technical community builds the tools and the market demands them, the political opposition eventually yields.

The encryption wars also demonstrate something else: the government did not abandon its position after losing the Clipper Chip debate. It adapted its arguments, pursuing exceptional access through different legal and technical mechanisms for decades. The same persistence should be expected in opposition to the broader privacy architecture. The contest is ongoing, not a single battle with a decisive outcome.

The non-technical user does not need to understand political economy. That user needs applications that implement these patterns without requiring them to understand the underlying architecture. The work of building falls on engineers and architects. The work of adoption falls on organizations and their users. The work of creating a political environment where privacy-enhancing technology can be built and deployed without obstruction falls on everyone who believes that the current arrangement—where mass surveillance is architecturally trivial and privacy is a policy fiction—is unacceptable.

Most organizations will adopt one or two components based on their specific threat model and regulatory environment. Each successful deployment demonstrates feasibility to others considering the same step. The aggregate of individual adoptions creates the conditions under which further adoption becomes easier—each privacy-preserving service that succeeds makes the next one less risky to build.

The architecture is ready. The political conditions are imperfect. The economics are shifting. The question is not whether the transition will happen, but how long it takes, how contested it is, and how much unnecessary harm accumulates while the status quo persists.

CHAPTER 17

Remembering Why Forgetting Matters

The Default That Changed

For most of human history, forgetting was the default. A conversation in a market square left no record. A transaction at a store was forgotten once the receipt was discarded. A letter could be burned after reading. Remembering required deliberate effort—writing things down, filing documents, maintaining archives. The expense and effort of remembering meant that most interactions were ephemeral. This was not a failure. This was the normal condition under which civilization developed, commerce operated, and private life existed.

The digital age inverted this default. Every click creates a log entry. Every transaction enters a database. Every communication passes through servers that retain metadata indefinitely. Every search query is recorded. Every location ping is stored. The effort now lies in forgetting—in deleting data, in configuring retention policies, in navigating privacy settings designed to be confusing. Memory has become the default because it is technically easier. Storing everything is cheaper than deciding what to store. Logging is simpler than not logging.

The inversion happened not through deliberate social choice but through the path of least resistance. No legislature voted to end the presumption of privacy in daily life. No public referendum endorsed permanent surveillance as the cost of digital convenience. The change was a side effect of engineering decisions made by people optimizing for functionality, for debugging capability, for business intelligence, for advertising revenue. Each decision was locally rational. The aggregate was a world where forgetting became expensive and difficult while remembering became free and automatic.

The economics reinforced the inversion. Storage costs fell by orders of magnitude every decade. A database administrator deciding whether to implement a retention policy or simply store everything faced an obvious calculation: the engineering cost of selective retention exceeded the storage cost of keeping everything indefinitely. The decision to retain was not a decision at all—it was the absence of a decision, the default path when no one chose otherwise. The accumulated defaults of millions of engineering decisions created an infrastructure of permanent memory that no one designed and no one voted for.

The Assumption That Memory Is Necessary

The ease of digital memory created an assumption that memory is necessary. Services depend on historical data for personalization. Advertising depends on behavioral profiles built over years. Security teams depend on logs for post-incident analysis. Machine learning depends on training data accumulated at scale. Each dependency treats historical data as essential infrastructure.

But the dependency was created by the availability of data, not by inherent necessity. Commerce existed for millennia before customer profiles. Services personalized before they had decades of user history. Security existed before comprehensive logging—it was different security, based on different assumptions, but it functioned. The argument that modern digital services cannot function without comprehensive data retention confuses what is convenient with what is necessary.

Consider what each component of this book demonstrates about the necessity assumption:

The identity problem seemed to require stable identifiers that could be tracked across contexts. The solution was site-specific identifiers that serve the same verification function without enabling correlation. The storage problem seemed to require databases that operators could query and inspect. The solution was databases where operators provide availability without reading content. The communication problem seemed to require servers that relay and retain. The solution was networks where relays are blind and nothing persists beyond delivery.

Each component refutes a specific instance of the necessity assumption. The engineering is harder. The architecture is different. The result is a system that works because it forgets, not despite forgetting.

Not every interaction requires a durable record. The purchase of a gift does not need to be logged in a marketing database. The conversation between a patient and a doctor does not need to be stored on a communication platform's servers. The websites visited during ordinary browsing do not need to be tracked and aggregated into behavioral profiles. These records exist because systems are designed to create them, not because the interactions require them. The confusion between system behavior and interaction requirements is the core error that the necessity assumption perpetuates.

The Cost of Never Forgetting

The argument for permanent memory emphasizes what is gained: personalization, convenience, security analytics, business intelligence. The argument rarely accounts for what is lost.

The permanence of mistakes. In a world that forgets, a youthful indiscretion fades from social memory. In a world that remembers, a social media post from fifteen years ago resurfaces during a job interview. A search query made during a health scare becomes a permanent data point in an insurance risk model. A purchase made during a difficult period becomes evidence in a custody proceeding. The inability to move beyond past actions—to grow, to change, to be judged by who you are rather than who you were—is a cost of permanent memory that no personalization algorithm compensates for.

The chilling effect on expression. When every communication is logged, people communicate differently. They self-censor. They avoid topics that might be misinterpreted. They use euphemisms and indirection. The knowledge that words might be retrieved years later and read in a context the speaker never intended changes what people are willing to say. The chilling effect is real, measurable, and corrosive to the open discourse that democratic societies depend on.

The power asymmetry. The entities that accumulate data are not the entities whose data is accumulated. Corporations know their users' behavior in detail; users know almost nothing about corporate behavior. Governments know their citizens' communications; citizens know almost nothing about government communications. The asymmetry is structural, growing, and incompatible with the power relationships that democratic governance requires.

The breach inevitability. Data that is retained is data that can be stolen. The question is not whether a sufficiently large database will be breached but when. Each breach exposes records that were retained because forgetting was not the default. Medical records from a decade ago. Financial transactions from five years ago. Communication metadata from last month. The harm from each breach is proportional to the data retained. An architecture that forgets by default limits breach exposure to data that was deliberately chosen for retention.

The function creep. Data collected for one purpose migrates to other purposes. Location data collected for navigation becomes evidence in a criminal investigation. Communication metadata collected for billing becomes input to a social network analysis. Purchase history collected for inventory management becomes a behavioral profile sold to advertisers. Each migration was not consented to by the person whose data was collected, because the original collection was justified by a different purpose. In a system that forgets, function creep is architecturally impossible—the data does not exist to be repurposed.

The aggregation problem. Individual data points that seem harmless in isolation become revealing when combined. A coffee shop visit is trivial. A coffee shop visit at 6 AM every Tuesday near a therapist's office is a pattern. A pattern combined with pharmacy purchases and browsing history becomes a medical profile that was never explicitly disclosed. The aggregation happens because the data exists in readable, linkable form across systems. Each system collects only what it needs. The aggregation across systems reveals what no individual system intended to expose. The privacy architecture prevents the aggregation by ensuring that identities are unlinkable across contexts—the coffee shop token and the pharmacy token and the browser token cannot be connected because they share no common identifier.

The Paradigm Shift

The architecture in this book represents a shift in default assumptions—not merely new technology applied to the existing model, but a different starting point about what systems should record and what they should forget.

The surveillance paradigm assumes data availability. Systems are designed with the expectation that operators can read what they store, that logs can be queried for debugging, that databases can be inspected for anomalies. The availability seems natural because it has been the default for three decades of digital infrastructure development.

The privacy paradigm assumes data opacity. Systems are designed with the expectation that operators cannot read what they store, that debugging happens through structured outputs rather than data inspection, that anomalies are detected through patterns rather than content. The opacity is not a limitation. It is the security property.

The shift affects every layer of system design:

Layer	Surveillance Paradigm	Privacy Paradigm
Authentication	Stable identifiers enabling correlation	Site-specific tokens preventing correlation
Storage	Readable records with access controls	Encrypted fragments with client-held keys
Communication	Central servers logging metadata	Distributed relays retaining nothing
Coordination	Intermediaries seeing complete picture	Fragments encrypted per recipient
Distribution	Gatekeepers controlling access	Self-validating documents via any channel

The shift is not incremental improvement within the existing paradigm. Encrypting a surveillance-paradigm database is not the same as building a privacy-paradigm system. Adding anonymization to a logging architecture is not the same as building an architecture that does not log. The distinction matters because incremental improvements preserve the assumptions that create the vulnerability, while the paradigm shift replaces them.

The shift affects how systems are designed from the beginning. A surveillance-paradigm system asks what data to collect and how to protect it. A privacy-paradigm system asks what data is necessary and how to avoid collecting everything else. The question changes from protection to minimization. Protection can fail—access controls can be bypassed through breaches, insider access, or legal compulsion. Minimization cannot expose what was never collected. The most secure data is data that does not exist.

The Honest Assessment

Building the privacy paradigm is harder than building the surveillance paradigm. This is not a minor point. It is a structural fact that will determine adoption timelines.

Client-side encryption requires key management that users are not accustomed to. Searchable encryption is slower than plaintext queries. Peer-to-peer networks are harder to debug than client-server architectures. Fragmented workflows require more careful design than monolithic ones. Self-validating distribution requires tooling that does not yet exist at production quality.

The difficulty is the cost of privacy. The surveillance paradigm is easier because it externalizes costs onto users. Users bear the burden of breaches, tracking, profiling, and permanent records. Operators bear none of these costs. The privacy paradigm internalizes costs that were previously externalized. Operators bear the engineering complexity. Users receive the protection. The redistribution of costs is the redistribution of power.

The components are independently adoptable, as Chapter 15's implementation roadmap details. The full architecture is aspirational for most organizations. A single component is achievable for most engineering teams.

The Architecture of Judgment

Systems that remember everything substitute storage for judgment. Remembering everything is the cheap alternative to deciding what matters. Judgment requires attention, and attention is expensive—someone must decide what to retain and what to discard. Storage costs approach zero. Judgment costs remain constant. The economic logic drives the default toward total retention.

The privacy paradigm applies judgment at the architectural level. By defaulting to forgetting, by requiring explicit action to remember, the architecture reverses the cost structure. Retention becomes the expensive choice—it requires deliberate key management, explicit storage decisions, conscious acts of preservation. Forgetting becomes free—it is what the system does when no one intervenes. The result is that records exist only when someone chose to create them, not because systems accumulated them automatically.

This is not the elimination of memory. It is the restoration of intentional memory. The pre-digital world had extensive record-keeping—birth certificates, property deeds, financial ledgers, historical archives. What it did not have was incidental recording of every mundane interaction as a side effect of using infrastructure. The privacy paradigm preserves deliberate record-keeping while eliminating incidental surveillance.

Forgetting as a Feature

The technology to forget exists. The cryptographic primitives are standard. The protocol patterns are established. The integration work is tractable.

The harder question is cultural. Three decades of digital infrastructure have normalized the assumption that systems should remember everything. Developers reach for logging as a first instinct. Product managers assume behavioral analytics as a given. Executives treat accumulated data as a strategic asset. Reversing that assumption requires recognizing what the pre-digital world understood implicitly: most interactions do not need to be recorded. The conversation that serves its purpose and is forgotten is not a failure of record-keeping. It is the normal condition of human interaction.

The original internet was closer to this understanding than the current one. Early email was designed to be deleted after reading. Web browsing was designed to be ephemeral. The accumulation came later, layered on by services whose business models required retention, enabled by storage costs that fell until deleting data was more expensive than keeping it. Reclaiming ephemerality requires deliberate architectural choice.

The challenges are real—migration, business model disruption, regulatory adjustment. But the person who wants ordinary privacy should not need to understand cryptographic primitives or configure anonymizing proxies. That person needs applications built on this architecture, applications that protect by default, applications whose operators cannot surveil even if they wanted to. The cultural shift—the recognition that forgetting is the healthy default and remembering is the exception requiring justification—takes longer than any technical migration.

Forgetting was the default condition under which private life developed, commerce operated, and democratic governance emerged. The architecture described in this book restores that default through engineering rather than policy. The question is whether we remember why forgetting matters enough to build systems that make it possible again.

Appendix

Appendix A: Status Quo vs. This Architecture

The following table compares outcomes under current infrastructure against outcomes under the architecture described in this book. The comparison is not to an ideal system but to what actually exists today.

• • •

Identity and Tracking

Scenario	Status Quo	This Architecture
You log into multiple websites	Each site receives the same identifier or correlatable tokens. Ad networks, data brokers, and platforms build a unified profile of your activity across the web.	Each site receives a different, unlinkable token. No party can correlate your activity across sites without secrets only your device holds.
The identity provider is breached	Attackers obtain your credentials and the complete map of every site you've visited. Your identity is compromised everywhere simultaneously.	Attackers obtain encrypted fragments they cannot read. Your site-specific tokens remain underivable without your client-side secrets.
A government demands your browsing history	The identity provider hands over complete logs showing every site you authenticated to, with timestamps.	The identity provider cannot comply. The blind database contains encrypted mappings unreadable without keys the provider never possessed.

• • •

Data Storage

Scenario	Status Quo	This Architecture
A service storing your data is breached	Attackers obtain your records in plaintext: health data, financial records, messages, photos. Everything is exposed.	Attackers obtain ciphertext. Without your encryption keys, the data is computationally indistinguishable from random noise.
An insider at the service wants to snoop	The insider queries the database and reads your records. Access controls may slow them; nothing prevents a determined insider with credentials.	The insider sees encrypted blobs. No credential within the organization provides decryption capability. The keys exist only on user devices.
The service receives a subpoena for your data	The service produces your records in readable form. You may or may not be notified.	The service produces ciphertext. The legal demand is satisfied; the data remains private.
The service changes its privacy policy	Your existing data, stored in readable form, becomes subject to new uses you never consented to.	Your existing data remains encrypted. Policy changes cannot retroactively grant the service reading capability it never had.
You want to delete your data permanently	You request deletion. The service may or may not comply fully. Backups persist. Deletion is unverifiable.	You discard your encryption keys. The ciphertext becomes permanently unreadable. Deletion is cryptographic and certain.

• • •

Bot Abuse and Accountability

Scenario	Status Quo	This Architecture
You block a harasser	They create a new account in seconds and continue. Account creation is free; blocking is meaningless.	Their new account starts with zero humanness score. Accumulating enough score to interact with you again costs time and money. Blocking has teeth.

A botnet floods a platform with spam	Each bot creates free accounts. The platform plays whack-a-mole, banning accounts faster than bots create them. The bots win through volume.	Each bot identity requires costly signal accumulation. Spam at scale becomes economically prohibitive. The bots lose to economics.
A scammer builds trust, then exploits it	The scammer burns their established persona, extracts value, and starts fresh with a new account. No consequence persists.	The scammer loses accumulated humanness stake. Starting over means re-accumulating signals from zero. Reputation has weight.

· · ·

Communication Metadata

Scenario	Status Quo	This Architecture
You message someone	The messaging service logs sender, recipient, timestamp, frequency, and duration. Content may be encrypted; the relationship graph is not.	Messages route through peer-to-peer nodes. No central server accumulates logs. The relationship exists only in the participants' clients.
A government demands communication records	The service produces complete metadata: who you talked to, when, how often. Patterns reveal relationships, habits, and vulnerabilities.	No service possesses the records. The demand cannot be satisfied because the data does not exist in any subpoenable location.
The service is breached	Attackers obtain the complete social graph: every relationship, every communication timestamp, every pattern.	Attackers find no central repository. Metadata is distributed across ephemeral nodes that retain nothing.

· · ·

Multi-Party Workflows

Scenario	Status Quo	This Architecture

| You buy a gift online | The payment processor sees what you bought and where it ships. The store sees your payment details. The shipper sees the contents and the recipient. No single party sees everything, but each sees more than it needs, and the union of what all parties see is everything. | The payment processor sees payment details only. The store sees the order only. The shipper sees the address only. No party sees more than necessary for its function. |
| One service in the chain is breached | Attackers obtain everything that service saw—which under current architecture is often everything about the transaction. | Attackers obtain only the encrypted fragment that service was authorized to see. Other fragments remain protected. |

• • •

Software Distribution

Scenario	Status Quo	This Architecture
An app store removes your privacy tool	Users cannot install it. The app store's decision is final. You have no recourse except persuading the gatekeeper.	Users obtain the application through any channel: web download, peer-to-peer, physical media. The app store's decision does not prevent distribution, though it may reduce discoverability.
A government pressures platforms to ban software	Platforms comply. Users in that jurisdiction lose access. The software effectively ceases to exist for them.	The software is a self-validating document. It travels through channels no government controls. Pressure on one channel leaves others open.
You want to verify software hasn't been tampered with	You trust that the app store verified it. The app store's review is opaque. Malicious apps regularly pass review.	You verify the cryptographic signature yourself. The hash chain confirms integrity. Verification requires no trust in intermediaries.

• • •

The Limitations Both Share

Scenario	Status Quo	This Architecture
Your device is compromised	Everything you do is visible to the attacker.	Everything you do is visible to the attacker.
You trust a malicious author	You run malicious software.	You run malicious software.
A nation-state targets you specifically	Sophisticated attacks can surveil you despite technical protections.	Sophisticated attacks can surveil you despite technical protections.

The difference: the status quo fails in all the ways listed above *plus* these shared fundamental limitations. This architecture fails only in the limitations that no system can prevent.

Appendix B: Technical Specifications

Formal schemas, protocols, and recommended primitives for each component. Use alongside the architecture chapters (3, 5, 7, 9, 11, 13) for implementation guidance.

• • •

B.1 Anonymous Identity

Hash Construction

```
Step 1:  h = hash(username, password)                  //
client-side
Step 2:  h → (user_id, user_salt)                      // SSO
lookup
Step 3:  t = hash(username, site_id, user_id, user_salt) //
client-side
Step 4:  SSO stores: hash(user_id, site_id) → (hash(t, salt),
salt)
Step 5:  Token T = { hash(t, salt), salt, PoH_score, site_id,
signature }
Step 6:  Site uses: hash(t, salt) as persistent user identifier
```

Security Properties

- **Cross-site unlinkability**: Different `site_id` ⧫ different tokens. No correlation without username.

- **Breach resistance**: Database stores `hash(user_id, site_id)` → (`hash(t, salt)`, `salt`). Attacker cannot determine which users visit which sites without brute-forcing usernames.

- **Impersonation resistance**: Sites receive `hash(t, salt)`, not t. Cannot impersonate users to the SSO.

Recommended Primitives

Function	Primitive
Hash	SHA-256 or SHA-3-256
Credential hash	Argon2id (or bcrypt/scrypt)

Signature	Ed25519
Salt	CSPRNG, minimum 128 bits
Authentication exchange	OPAQUE (RFC 9807) or SRP for production deployments

Note on OPAQUE. *The pseudocode in Chapter 3 transmits a password-derived hash for clarity. For production implementations, the authentication exchange in Step 1 should use OPAQUE, a standardized asymmetric PAKE protocol that ensures the server never learns the password, even transiently. OPAQUE provides protection against pre-computation attacks and server compromise during the authentication handshake. The architecture's privacy properties (cross-site unlinkability, breach resistance, mutual impersonation resistance) hold regardless of whether the authentication exchange uses OPAQUE or the simpler hash construction. See Jarecki, Krawczyk, and Xu, "OPAQUE: An Asymmetric PAKE Protocol Secure Against Pre-Computation Attacks," EUROCRYPT 2018; standardized as RFC 9807.*

• • •

B.2 Blind Database

Key Derivation

```
record_id = hash(master_secret, record_type, record_discriminator)
key       = HKDF(master_secret, record_id, "encrypt")
```

Storage Schema

```
Server stores: record_id → ciphertext
```

Security Levels

Level	Key Derivation Inputs	Recoverability
Recoverable	hash(purpose, username, server_salt)	Survives password change
Session-bound	Includes password-derived value	Lost on password change
Unrecoverable	Includes device-specific secret	Never recoverable

Write Protocol

```
1. record_id = hash(master_secret, type, discriminator)
```

```
2. key        = HKDF(master_secret, record_id, "encrypt")
3. ciphertext = Encrypt(key, plaintext)
4. Send: (record_id, ciphertext)
5. Server stores: record_id → ciphertext
```

Read Protocol

```
1. record_id  = hash(master_secret, type, discriminator)
2. Send: record_id
3. Receive: ciphertext
4. key        = HKDF(master_secret, record_id, "encrypt")
5. plaintext  = Decrypt(key, ciphertext)
```

Crypto-Erasure

```
1. Discard: master_secret (or relevant derivation inputs)
2. Server retains: record_id → ciphertext (permanently unreadable)
```

Recommended Primitives

Function	Primitive
KDF	HKDF-SHA256
Encryption	AES-256-GCM or ChaCha20-Poly1305
Record ID hash	SHA-256

• • •

B.3 Proof of Human

Score Computation

```
score = min(0.99, sum(signal_weight[i] * signal_present[i] *
decay[i]))
```

Effort Scale

Score	Effort to Forge
0.0	Free
0.1	~$10
0.2	~$100
0.3	~$1,000
0.4	~$10,000
0.5	~$100,000

Signal Taxonomy

Signal Type	Weight	Decay
Email verification	0.02	None
Phone verification	0.03	None
Payment instrument	0.05	None
Postal mail verification	0.05	None
Device attestation	0.04	6-month half-life
Typing patterns (30 days)	0.08	Continuous refresh
Activity patterns (1 year)	0.15	Continuous refresh
Human-in-loop verification	0.10	1-year half-life
Government ID (optional)	0.20	None

Signal Storage Schema

```
{
  "signal_type": "string",
  "proof": "cryptographic_proof",
  "weight": 0.05,
  "timestamp": 1703880000,
  "decay_params": { "half_life_seconds": 15768000 }
}
```

Proofs attest that signals were validated without containing the signals themselves.

Retrieval Protocol

```
1. Server challenges: key_identifier, nonce
2. Client computes: key = hash(client_secret, key_identifier,
nonce)
3. Client responds: HMAC(key, challenge)
4. Server verifies: response matches expected HMAC
5. Server returns: signal proofs for this identity
6. Client discards: key (ephemeral)
```

Recommended Primitives

Function	Primitive
Proofs	Hash-based commitments (or SNARKs for stronger guarantees)
HMAC	HMAC-SHA256

• • •

B.4 HermesP2P

Channel Types

Public Channels

```
{
  "channel_id": "hash(channel_name)",
  "poh_threshold": 0.3,
  "messages": []
}
```

Private Channels

```
{
  "channel_id": "random_id",
  "symmetric_key": "shared_secret",
  "members": ["public_key_1", "public_key_2"]
}
```

Direct Messages

```
{
  "recipient_address": "derived_ephemeral_address",
  "ciphertext": "encrypted_for_recipient_public_key",
  "sender_proof": "optional_signature"
}
```

Message Structure

```
{
  "envelope": {
    "recipient": "ephemeral_address",
    "sender_proof": "optional"
  },
  "layers": [
    {
      "next_hop": "node_address",
      "encrypted_inner": "..."
    }
  ],
  "payload": {
    "content": "encrypted_message",
    "ttl": 3600,
    "timestamp": 1703880000
  }
}
```

Onion Routing

```
Layer_3 = Encrypt(key_3, (next_hop_2, Layer_2))
Layer_2 = Encrypt(key_2, (next_hop_1, Layer_1))
Layer_1 = Encrypt(key_1, (recipient, payload))
```

Gossip Protocol

1. Node receives message
2. Node validates signature and PoH
3. Node stores in short-term buffer (TTL-limited)
4. Node forwards to k random peers not in message's path

Recommended Primitives

Function	Primitive
Identity keys	Ed25519
Key agreement	X25519
Symmetric encryption	ChaCha20-Poly1305
Onion encryption	Sphinx or similar

• • •

B.5 Cryptogram and Delegator

Cryptogram Structure

```
{
  "workflow_id": "uuid",
  "created": "timestamp",
  "routing": {
    "steps": [
      {
        "service": "payment_processor",
        "encrypted_for": "payment_processor_public_key"
      },
      {
        "service": "fulfillment",
        "encrypted_for": "store_public_key"
      },
      {
        "service": "shipping",
        "encrypted_for": "carrier_public_key"
      }
    ]
  },
```

```
  "sections": {
    "payment": "encrypted_blob_for_payment_processor",
    "order": "encrypted_blob_for_store",
    "shipping": "encrypted_blob_for_carrier"
  }
}
```

Section Encryption

```
section_ciphertext = Encrypt(
  recipient_public_key,
  plaintext_section,
  associated_data = workflow_id
)
```

Delegator Protocol

```
1. Receive cryptogram
2. Read routing.steps[current_step]
3. Extract sections[current_service]
4. Forward to service endpoint
5. Service decrypts its section, processes, encrypts response
6. Receive encrypted response
7. Advance to next step
8. Repeat until workflow complete
```

Ephemeral Worker Schema

```
{
  "worker_id": "uuid",
  "limits": {
    "max_operations": 10,
    "max_duration_seconds": 3600,
    "trigger_on_complete": "next_workflow_step"
  },
  "state": "encrypted_for_worker",
  "created": "timestamp"
}
```

Recommended Primitives

Function	Primitive
Asymmetric encryption	X25519 + ChaCha20-Poly1305 (libsodium sealed boxes)
Workflow signatures	Ed25519

• • •

B.6 Chess

Document Structure

```
{
  "chess_version": "1.0",
  "genesis": {
    "code": "(define initial-state ...)",
    "state": {},
    "author": "public_key",
    "signature": "...",
    "timestamp": 1703880000
  },
  "moves": [
    {
      "prev_state_hash": "sha256_of_previous_state",
      "operation": "(apply-operation state input)",
      "new_state_hash": "sha256_of_resulting_state",
      "actor": "public_key",
      "signature": "ed25519_signature",
      "timestamp": 1703880100
    }
  ],
  "current_state": {}
}
```

Move Validation

1. Verify actor signature over (`prev_state_hash`, `operation`, `new_state_hash`, `timestamp`)

2. Verify `prev_state_hash` matches hash of state before move

3. Execute operation on previous state

4. Verify computed state hash matches `new_state_hash`

5. Verify actor is authorized (defined by application logic)

Chain Verification

```
function verify_chain(document):
  state = document.genesis.state
  for move in document.moves:
    assert hash(state) == move.prev_state_hash
    assert verify_signature(move)
    state = execute(document.genesis.code, state, move.operation)
    assert hash(state) == move.new_state_hash
  assert state == document.current_state
  return true
```

Lisp Subset Primitives

- define, lambda, let
- if, cond
- car, cdr, cons, list
- +, -, , /, =, <, >
- map, filter, fold
- hash, verify-signature

The interpreter must be deterministic. No I/O, no randomness, no time access except via explicitly provided parameters.

Recommended Primitives

Function	Primitive
State hashing	SHA-256
Signatures	Ed25519
Serialization	JSON (canonical form for hashing)

•   •   •

B.7 Composition Patterns

Anonymous Identity + Blind Database

```
record_id  = hash(master_secret, "identity_mapping", site_id)
key        = HKDF(master_secret, record_id, "encrypt")
ciphertext = Encrypt(key, (user_id, user_salt, site_token_hash))
Server stores: record_id → ciphertext
```

Proof of Human + HermesP2P

```
{
  "message": "...",
  "sender": "pseudonymous_id",
  "poh_attestation": {
    "score": 0.45,
    "verifier_signature": "...",
    "timestamp": 1703880000
  }
}
```

Nodes reject messages below channel threshold.

Blind Database + Cryptogram

```
state_id = hash(workflow_id, step_number)
Server stores: state_id → Encrypt(workflow_key, partial_state)
```

$$\bullet \quad \bullet \quad \bullet$$

B.8 Implementation Notes

Library Recommendations

Function	Recommended
Hashing	libsodium (crypto_generichash)
Symmetric encryption	libsodium (secretbox)
Asymmetric encryption	libsodium (box, sealed_box)
Signatures	libsodium (sign)
Key derivation	libsodium (kdf) or HKDF
Password hashing	Argon2id (libsodium crypto_pwhash)

Security Checklist

1. **Constant-time comparisons**: All hash and signature comparisons must be constant-time.

2. **Key storage**: Client-side keys stored in keychain or secure enclave where available.

3. **Replay protection**: Timestamps and nonces in all signed messages.

4. **Forward secrecy**: Regular key rotation; old keys discarded to enable crypto-erasure.

5. **Test vectors**: Validate against published test vectors for all chosen primitives.

Appendix C: Formal Security Analysis

This appendix provides formal adversary models, game-based security definitions, proof sketches, and per-component attack surface documentation. It is designed to be skipped entirely without losing the book's argument. Readers who want the mathematical grounding for the security claims made in the architecture chapters will find it here.

• • •

C.1 Adversary Models and Capability Bounds

The architecture chapters use informal threat descriptions. This section formalizes the adversary models that underpin the security claims.

Honest-but-Curious Operator (HbC)

The adversary controls the server. It follows the protocol faithfully—responding to queries, storing data, routing messages as specified. It simultaneously attempts to learn everything it can from what it observes.

Formally: The HbC adversary A_hbc receives a transcript T of all interactions with the server: every request, every response, every stored value, every timing observation. A_hbc runs in probabilistic polynomial time (PPT). The security claim is that A_hbc cannot extract information I (defined per component) from T with probability better than negligible in the security parameter λ.

Capability bounds:

- Observes all ciphertext and access patterns on the server

- Knows the protocol specification

- Can enumerate public parameters (site identifiers, public keys)

- Cannot deviate from the protocol (does not return wrong values, does not inject messages)

- Cannot access client-side state

Active Adversary (Act)

The adversary controls the server and may deviate from the protocol. Formally: A_act receives the same transcript as A_hbc and additionally may:

- Return incorrect values in response to queries

- Delay or drop messages selectively

- Inject messages not generated by legitimate clients
- Modify stored data
- Serve modified client code (in browser-based deployments)

This appendix formalizes the active adversary scenarios that each component's "What This Does Not Protect Against" section describes informally.

Multi-Operator Collusion Adversary (Col)

The adversary controls multiple operators simultaneously—for example, the identity provider and one or more receiving sites, or the delegator and one or more workflow participants.

Formally: `A_col` receives the combined transcripts of all colluding operators. The security question is whether the combined view reveals information that no individual view contains.

Capability bounds:

- Observes all ciphertext and metadata at every colluding operator
- Can correlate timing, identifiers, and access patterns across operators
- Cannot access client-side state
- Cannot access transcripts of non-colluding operators

• • •

C.2 Anonymous Identity: Unlinkability Proof Sketch

Definition: Cross-Site Unlinkability Game

```
Game Unlink(A, λ):
  Setup:
    1. Challenger generates user credentials (username, password)
       where |username| ≥ λ bits of entropy
    2. Challenger computes:
       h = H(username || password)
       (user_id, user_salt) ← SSO.Lookup(h)
    3. Challenger selects two sites: site_0, site_1

  Challenge:
    4. Challenger computes:
       t_0 = H(username || site_0 || user_id || user_salt)
       t_1 = H(username || site_1 || user_id || user_salt)
    5. Challenger flips bit b ⊠ {0, 1}
    6. If b = 0: give A the pair (t_0, t_1)
       If b = 1: give A the pair (t_0, t_random)
       where t_random ← {0,1}^|H|
```

```
Response:
  7. A outputs bit b'
```

```
  A wins if b' = b.
```

Advantage: `Adv_Unlink(A) = |Pr[b' = b] - 1/2|`

Theorem: If `H` is modeled as a random oracle, then for all PPT adversaries `A`:

`Adv_Unlink(A) ≤ Adv_PRE(B) + q_H / 2^λ`

where `Adv_PRE(B)` is the advantage of the best preimage-finding algorithm `B` against `H`, and `q_H` is the number of random oracle queries `A` makes.

Proof sketch: Assume A has non-negligible advantage. Then A can distinguish `t_1 = H(username || site_1 || user_id || user_salt)` from `t_random`. In the random oracle model, `t_1` is uniformly distributed unless A queries H on the exact input (`username || site_1 || user_id || user_salt`). But this requires A to know username. If A does not know username, then `t_1` is indistinguishable from random output by the random oracle property.

If A makes `q_H` queries to the random oracle, the probability that any query matches the correct preimage is at most `q_H / 2^λ` (where λ is the entropy of username). Alternatively, if A can distinguish without querying, we can construct B that inverts H with the same advantage.

Caveat: The proof relies on the username having sufficient entropy. Low-entropy usernames (e.g., common first names) reduce λ and make brute-force enumeration feasible. The architecture documents this limitation: username-as-secret is fragile when username entropy is low.

SSO Enumeration Attack

The identity provider stores `hash(user_id || site_id)` as storage keys. The provider knows all `user_id` values and can enumerate public `site_id` values. The provider can compute candidate storage keys and check which exist in its database.

Cost: For n users and m sites, enumeration requires n × m hash computations. This is feasible for moderate values (106 users × 104 sites = 1010 operations—expensive but not impossible for a resourced adversary).

Mitigation: Use keyed HMAC for storage keys, with the key held in a separate security domain (HSM). This raises the cost to include compromise of the HSM. Composition with Blind Database eliminates this attack entirely—the identity mappings are encrypted with keys the operator does not hold.

• • •

C.3 Blind Database: Indistinguishability Analysis

Definition: Operational Blindness Game

```
Game Blind(A, λ):
  Setup:
    1. Challenger generates master_secret ← {0,1}^λ
    2. Challenger generates two plaintext records: m_0, m_1
       where |m_0| = |m_1|

  Challenge:
    3. Challenger flips bit b ⊠ {0, 1}
    4. Challenger computes:
       record_id = H(master_secret || "type" || "discriminator")
       key = HKDF(master_secret, record_id, "encrypt")
       nonce ← {0,1}^192
       ciphertext = AEAD_Enc(key, nonce, m_b, record_id)
    5. Challenger gives A: (record_id, nonce, ciphertext)

  Response:
    6. A outputs bit b'

  A wins if b' = b.
```

Theorem: If `AEAD_Enc` is `IND-CPA` secure (as `AES-256-GCM` and `ChaCha20-Poly1305` are), and `HKDF` is a secure key derivation function in the random oracle model, then:

```
Adv_Blind(A) ≤ Adv_IND-CPA(B)
```

Proof sketch: The `record_id` reveals no information about the plaintext (it is derived from the master secret and type/discriminator, not from the record content). The key is derived via `HKDF` from the master secret, which the adversary does not possess. The ciphertext is produced by an `IND-CPA` secure `AEAD` scheme. Any adversary that distinguishes ciphertexts can be used to break `IND-CPA` security of the underlying `AEAD`.

Access Pattern Leakage

The indistinguishability game above addresses content confidentiality. It does not address access patterns. The server observes:

- Which `record_id` values are accessed

- When each `record_id` is accessed

- How frequently each `record_id` is accessed

- Which `record_id` values are co-accessed (retrieved in the same session)

What the server learns from access patterns:

1. Temporal patterns: Record X accessed every Monday at 9 AM. Record Y always co-accessed with Record X. These patterns can reveal behavioral information even without reading content.

2. Volume analysis: Encrypted blob sizes may leak information about content type.

A 47-byte ciphertext and a 4.7-megabyte ciphertext contain different content. Padding mitigates but does not eliminate this.

3. Frequency distribution: The most-accessed record may correspond to a frequently used resource. Combined with auxiliary information about the user's likely access patterns, frequency matching may be possible.

Formal treatment: Oblivious RAM (ORAM) provides the theoretical solution—the server cannot distinguish any two access sequences of the same length. The canonical construction (Goldreich-Ostrovsky, 1996) achieves this with $O(\log^3 N)$ overhead per access. Practical ORAM constructions (Path ORAM, Ring ORAM) reduce the constant factors but retain polylogarithmic overhead that makes them impractical for general-purpose database workloads at scale.

The Blind Database architecture explicitly accepts access pattern leakage as a tradeoff for practical performance. The claim is not that access patterns are hidden—they are not—but that access patterns without content reveal substantially less than access patterns with content (the status quo).

• • •

C.4 HermesP2P: Sender Anonymity Analysis

Definition: Sender Anonymity Game

```
Game SenderAnon(A, λ):
  Setup:
    1. Network of n nodes, each with public keys
    2. A controls all nodes except the sender and recipient
       (worst case: A controls n-2 of n nodes)

  Challenge:
    3. Challenger selects two candidate senders: S_0, S_1
    4. Challenger flips bit b ⊠ {0, 1}
    5. S_b sends a message to recipient R through a 3-hop
       onion route, choosing relay nodes
    6. A observes all network traffic at all controlled nodes

  Response:
    7. A outputs bit b'

  A wins if b' = b.
```

Analysis: The sender selects three relay nodes for onion routing. If the sender happens to select a relay controlled by A as the first hop, A learns the sender's identity (the first hop sees the sender's network address). The probability of this event is at most $(n-2)/n$ for the first hop.

For a 3-hop route where A controls k of n nodes:

- A learns the sender if the first relay is compromised: probability `k/n`

- A learns the recipient if the last relay is compromised: probability `k/n`

- A learns both (and can correlate) if both first and last relays are compromised: probability `(k/n)²`

Intersection attacks: Over multiple messages, A observes which honest nodes initiate connections temporally correlated with message delivery. If sender S always sends at time T and recipient R always receives at time $T + \Delta$, the correlation strengthens with each observation.

Resistance: Cover traffic (dummy messages sent by all nodes at random intervals) reduces the signal-to-noise ratio of timing analysis. The effectiveness depends on the cover traffic rate relative to real traffic. HermesP2P's gossip protocol provides some inherent cover traffic, as nodes forward messages for the network regardless of whether they are sending their own messages.

What fraction of the network can be adversarial? If A controls more than ⅔ of relay nodes, the probability of route compromise exceeds ½ per message. For practical anonymity, the honest fraction should exceed ½, and ideally exceed ⅔. This is a known result from the anonymity network literature (see Syverson et al., "Towards an Analysis of Onion Routing Security," 2000).

• • •

C.5 Cryptogram: Section Confidentiality Analysis

Security Model

Each cryptogram section is encrypted using asymmetric encryption (X25519 key agreement + ChaCha20-Poly1305) for a specific recipient. The security claim is that the delegator—which routes sections—cannot read any section's contents.

Formally: This reduces directly to the IND-CCA2 security of the authenticated encryption scheme. If the delegator could distinguish two possible plaintexts for a section, it could break the underlying AEAD. The proof is immediate from the construction.

Routing Metadata Leakage

The delegator reads unencrypted routing metadata: which section goes to which service, in what order, at what time. This metadata is not negligible.

What the delegator learns:

- Workflow structure: how many sections, which services participate

- Timing: when each step executes, how long each service takes to respond

- Volume: section sizes (may correlate with content type)

- Patterns: over many workflows, the delegator observes workflow templates—recurring combinations of services that suggest specific transaction types

Attack scenario: A delegator that processes millions of e-commerce workflows can build statistical models: "3-section workflow to PaymentCo, StoreCo, ShipCo is probably a standard purchase." "2-section workflow to PaymentCo and RefundCo is probably a return." The content is hidden. The shape of the workflow is not.

Mitigation: Padding sections to uniform size. Adding dummy sections. Randomizing routing order where the workflow permits. These mitigations increase bandwidth and complexity. They do not eliminate the leakage—they reduce its precision.

Offline Recipient Failure Mode

If a recipient is offline when its section arrives, the delegator must store the section until the recipient becomes available. This creates temporal metadata: the delegator knows which recipients are responsive and which are not, and can observe the delay between section delivery and response.

Error handling: If one party fails mid-workflow, in-flight sections may persist indefinitely. The architecture should specify timeouts and cleanup procedures. Workflow keys should have expiration times after which persistent sections become unrecoverable (crypto-erasure through key expiration).

$$\bullet \ \bullet \ \bullet$$

C.6 Chess: Integrity and Determinism Analysis

Hash Chain Integrity

The integrity claim is straightforward: any modification to any move in the chain produces a hash mismatch that verification detects.

Formally: If H is collision-resistant, then finding two distinct move sequences that produce the same chain of hashes requires finding a collision in H. For SHA-256, the best known collision attack requires approximately 2^{128} operations (birthday bound). This is standard.

The integrity guarantee is: `Pr[A produces a valid chain containing a modified move] ≤ Adv_COLL(H)`

where `Adv_COLL(H)` is the advantage of the best collision-finding algorithm against H.

Determinism Guarantees

The Lisp interpreter must be deterministic: the same code, applied to the same state, must produce the same output on every implementation. This is the foundation of chain verification—a verifier recomputes every state transition and checks that the results match.

Threats to determinism:

1. Floating-point arithmetic. IEEE 754 floating-point operations can produce different results across architectures due to extended precision, fused multiply-add, and different rounding behavior in transcendental functions. Mitigation: Restrict the Lisp subset to integer arithmetic only. Rational arithmetic (as exact fractions) is acceptable. Floating-point is not.

2. Evaluation order. If the language permits side effects, different evaluation orders can produce different results. Mitigation: The Lisp subset is purely functional—no mutation, no I/O, no side effects. Evaluation order does not affect the result.

3. Recursion depth. Different implementations may have different stack limits. A computation that succeeds on one implementation may overflow on another. Mitigation: Specify a minimum recursion depth in the Chess specification. Implementations must support at least this depth.

4. Numeric overflow. If the integer type has bounded precision, overflow behavior must be identical across implementations. Mitigation: Use arbitrary-precision integers. The Lisp subset should not have a fixed integer width.

Sandbox Security

Chess documents contain executable code. The sandbox must prevent that code from accessing the host system. Sandbox escapes are a real and ongoing concern in every sandboxed execution environment.

Known sandbox escape categories:

- Resource exhaustion (infinite loops, memory allocation bombs)
- Side-channel leakage (timing measurements that reveal information about the host)
- Specification ambiguity (behavior that the sandbox spec does not define, leading to implementation-dependent escapes)

Mitigation: The Lisp subset is deliberately minimal—no I/O, no network access, no file system access, no time access except through explicitly provided parameters. Resource limits (maximum computation steps, maximum memory allocation) must be enforced by the interpreter, not by the code. The sandbox boundary is the interpreter itself.

Chain Growth

Long-history documents require verifiers to recompute every state transition from genesis. For a document with n moves, verification is $O(n \times C)$ where C is the cost of executing one move. For long-lived documents, this becomes expensive.

Mitigation: Checkpointing. A checkpoint is a signed state snapshot at a specific move number. Verifiers who trust the checkpoint signer can begin verification from the checkpoint rather than from genesis. The checkpoint does not eliminate the ability to verify from genesis—it provides an optimization for verifiers who trust specific signers. The tradeoff is explicit: you trust the checkpoint signer's computation, or you recompute from scratch.

$$\bullet \ \bullet \ \bullet$$

C.7 Proof of Human: Economic Security Model

This section deliberately does NOT present a cryptographic proof. The Proof of Human component's security is economic, not cryptographic. The claim is that forging a high humanness score is expensive, not that it is computationally infeasible.

Cost Model

The forging cost for a target score s is:

```
Cost(s) ≈ 10^(10s) dollars (order of magnitude)
```

This follows from the logarithmic effort scale: each 0.1 increment in score represents approximately one order of magnitude increase in forging cost.

Assumptions

The cost model assumes:

1. Signal independence. Signals from different providers (email, phone, payment) are independently verifiable. Compromising one signal provider does not reduce the cost of compromising another.

2. Market prices for credentials. Bulk email accounts cost approximately $0.01–$0.10 on underground markets. Verified phone numbers cost approximately $2–$5. Synthetic financial identities cost approximately $50–$200. These are empirical observations from market surveys (see Chapter 7), not proven bounds.

3. No signal provider collusion. If multiple signal providers collude to issue false attestations, the cost model breaks. The mitigation is diversity—using signal providers in different jurisdictions with different incentive structures.

Where the Model Breaks

Stolen credentials + compromised payment instruments: An attacker with access to a stolen identity (name, SSN, address) can open bank accounts, obtain phone numbers, and accumulate signals at costs lower than the individual market prices suggest. The effective cost depends on the attacker's access to identity theft infrastructure.

Score as side channel: The score itself is a signal. Temporal correlation of score changes across sites—"this identity's score increased from 0.2 to 0.3 at time T on Site A, and this identity's score increased from 0.2 to 0.3 at time T on Site B"—could enable probabilistic linking. The mitigation is that scores are not disclosed with full precision or exact timestamps. The leakage is real but bounded.

Signal provider compromise: If the email verification provider is compromised (or is the adversary), email verifications can be generated at zero cost. The architecture's defense is redundancy—no single signal type contributes more than 0.20 to the score, and the highest-value signals require physical-world actions (postal verification, in-person verification) that are expensive to forge at scale.

• • •

C.8 Composition: Multi-Operator Collusion Analysis

Two-Party Collusion Scenarios

SSO + Site collusion: The identity provider knows `user_id` and can compute candidate tokens for all users. A colluding site can confirm which candidate matches its verification hash. This identifies the user on that specific site. The attack requires active cooperation from both parties and scales linearly with the number of users—the provider must compute one candidate token per user per colluding site.

   Mitigation with Blind Database: If identity mappings are stored in a Blind Database, the provider cannot enumerate candidate tokens because it cannot read its own identity mappings. The collusion attack requires the provider to first breach the Blind Database encryption—which requires the user's master secret.

   Delegator + Service collusion: A delegator that colludes with one workflow service can correlate routing metadata (which the delegator sees) with section contents (which the service sees). This reveals workflow details that neither party could learn alone. For example: the delegator knows "this workflow went to PaymentCo, then StoreCo, then ShipCo." PaymentCo knows "this payment was for $47.50." Together: "a $47.50 payment went to StoreCo and then ShipCo."

   Mitigation: Use different delegators for different workflow steps. If the payment step routes through Delegator A and the shipping step routes through Delegator B, no single delegator-service pair sees the complete picture. This increases operational complexity.

N-Party Collusion Bound

Theorem (informal): If all k operators in a workflow collude, they can reconstruct the complete workflow from their combined views. This is a fundamental limitation—if every party you interact with cooperates against you, no cryptographic protocol can help.

   The architecture's defense against collusion is operational, not cryptographic:

   • Distribute operators across jurisdictions

   • Use different organizations for different functions

   • Minimize the number of operators involved in any single workflow

   • Accept that targeted collusion against a specific user is possible; ensure it cannot scale to mass surveillance

• • •

C.9 Attack Surface Summary Table

Component	Honest-but-Curious	Active Adversary	Collusion	Load-Bearing Assumption
Anonymous Identity	Cannot link tokens across sites (ROM assumption)	Can serve modified client code; can deny service selectively	SSO + Site can identify specific users	Username has sufficient entropy
Blind Database	Cannot read stored data (IND-CPA)	Can return wrong data; can deny service	N/A (single operator)	Client holds master secret; AEAD is secure
Proof of Human	Cannot link scores to civil identity	Can issue false attestations	Signal providers can generate cheap signals	Signal independence; market prices for credentials
HermesP2P	Cannot determine sender-recipient pair (if not on route)	Can drop messages; can inject traffic for analysis	First+last relay compromise breaks anonymity	Honest majority of relay nodes
Cryptogram/ Delegator	Cannot read section contents (IND-CCA2)	Can drop sections; can delay workflow	Delegator + Service reveals workflow + one section	AEAD is secure; routing metadata is acceptable leakage
Chess	Cannot modify chain without detection (collision resistance)	Can distribute malicious documents	N/A (no server required)	Interpreter determinism; sandbox containment

Legend:

- *ROM*: Random Oracle Model
- *IND-CPA*: Indistinguishability under Chosen Plaintext Attack
- *IND-CCA2*: Indistinguishability under Adaptive Chosen Ciphertext Attack
- *AEAD*: Authenticated Encryption with Associated Data

Bibliography

Chapter 1: The Architecture of Forgetting

Federal Trade Commission. "Equifax Data Breach Settlement." July 2019. FTC File No. 172-3203. The complaint documented exploitation of an unpatched Apache Struts vulnerability (CVE-2017-5638) exposing PII of approximately 147 million consumers.

United States v. Reality Leigh Winner, Case No. 1:17-cr-00034-JRH-BKE (S.D. Ga. 2017). FBI affidavit details printer steganography, audit log correlation, email metadata review, and geographic matching. Sentenced to sixty-three months—the longest sentence for unauthorized media disclosure under the Espionage Act at the time.

Apple Inc. Removal of VPN applications from China App Store, July 29, 2017. Following MIIT regulations requiring government authorization for VPN services. Tim Cook addressed on Apple Q3 FY2017 earnings call, August 1, 2017. See also: Paul Mozur, "Apple Removes VPN Apps From the App Store in China," *The New York Times*, July 29, 2017.

Statista. "Digital Advertising—Worldwide." 2024. Global digital advertising spending exceeded $600 billion in 2023; estimates range from $602B to $680B depending on market scope. See also: eMarketer/Insider Intelligence, "Worldwide Digital Ad Spending Forecast," 2023.

Facebook (Meta Platforms). Blog post by CTO Mike Schroepfer, April 4, 2018, disclosing that "up to 87 million" Facebook profiles were affected by the Cambridge Analytica data sharing. UK Information Commissioner's Office issued £500,000 fine (maximum under pre-GDPR DPA 1998). U.S. FTC imposed $5 billion penalty, July 2019.

Carpenter v. United States, 585 U.S. ___, 138 S. Ct. 2206 (2018). The Court held (5–4) that accessing seven days of historical cell-site location information constitutes a search under the Fourth Amendment, requiring a warrant supported by probable cause. Opinion by Chief Justice Roberts.

• • •

Chapter 3: Anonymous Identity Architecture

Bellare, Mihir, and Phillip Rogaway. "Random Oracles are Practical: A Paradigm for Designing Efficient Protocols." *Proceedings of the 1st ACM Conference on Computer and Communications Security (CCS '93)*, pp. 62–73, ACM, 1993.

NIST. "Secure Hash Standard (SHS)." FIPS PUB 180-4, August 2015. Specifies SHA-256 with 256-bit preimage resistance.

Camenisch, Jan, and Anna Lysyanskaya. "An Efficient System for Non-transferable Anonymous Credentials with Optional Anonymity Revocation." *Advances in Cryptology—EUROCRYPT 2001*, LNCS vol. 2045, pp. 93–118, Springer, 2001. Foundational work for IBM's Identity Mixer (Idemix).

Alpár, Gergely, and Bart Jacobs. "Credential Design in Attribute-Based Identity Management." *Bridging Distances in Technology and Regulation: Proceedings of the 3rd TILTing Perspectives Conference*, pp. 189–204, 2013. Foundational design work for the IRMA (I Reveal My Attributes) system, later rebranded as Yivi. Maintained by the Privacy by Design Foundation (established 2016). Deployed in Dutch municipal services and healthcare.

Paquin, Christian, and Greg Zaverucha. "U-Prove Cryptographic Specification V1.1." Microsoft Corporation, 2013. Published under Open Specification Promise.

W3C. "Decentralized Identifiers (DIDs) v1.0." W3C Recommendation, July 2022.

W3C. "Verifiable Credentials Data Model v1.1." W3C Recommendation, March 2022.

Jarecki, Stanislaw, Hugo Krawczyk, and Jiayu Xu. "OPAQUE: An Asymmetric PAKE Protocol Secure Against Pre-Computation Attacks." *Advances in Cryptology—EUROCRYPT 2018*, LNCS vol. 10822, pp. 456–486, Springer, 2018. Standardized as RFC 9807.

Bernstein, Daniel J., Niels Duif, Tanja Lange, Peter Schwabe, and Bo-Yin Yang. "High-Speed High-Security Signatures." *Journal of Cryptographic Engineering*, vol. 2, no. 2, pp. 77–89, Springer, 2012. Original Ed25519 paper.

• • •

Chapter 4: The Storage Problem

Boldyreva, Alexandra, Nathan Chenette, Younho Lee, and Adam O'Neill. "Order-Preserving Symmetric Encryption." *Advances in Cryptology—EUROCRYPT 2009*, LNCS vol. 5479, pp. 224–241, Springer, 2009. Introduced OPE and proved IND-CPA security is impossible for order-preserving schemes. See also: Boldyreva, Chenette, and O'Neill, "Order-Preserving Encryption Revisited: Improved Security Analysis and Alternative Solutions," *CRYPTO 2011*, LNCS vol. 6841, pp. 578–595, Springer, 2011 (proves approximately half the plaintext bits leak under the best achievable security notion).

Naveed, Muhammad, Seny Kamara, and Charles V. Wright. "Inference Attacks on Property-Preserving Encrypted Databases." *Proceedings of the 22nd ACM SIGSAC Conference on Computer and Communications Security (CCS '15)*, pp. 644–655, ACM, 2015.

Grubbs, Paul, Kevin Sekniqi, Vincent Bindschaedler, Muhammad Naveed, and

Thomas Ristenpart. "Leakage-Abuse Attacks against Order-Revealing Encryption." *2017 IEEE Symposium on Security and Privacy (SP)*, pp. 655–672, IEEE, 2017.

• • •

Chapter 5: Blind Database Architecture

Popa, Raluca Ada, Catherine M. S. Redfield, Nickolai Zeldovich, and Hari Balakrishnan. "CryptDB: Protecting Confidentiality with Encrypted Query Processing." *Proceedings of the 23rd ACM Symposium on Operating Systems Principles (SOSP '11)*, pp. 85–100, ACM, 2011.

Popa, Raluca Ada, Emily Stark, Jonas Helfer, Steven Valdez, Nickolai Zeldovich, M. Frans Kaashoek, and Hari Balakrishnan. "Building Web Applications on Top of Encrypted Data Using Mylar." *Proceedings of the 11th USENIX Symposium on Networked Systems Design and Implementation (NSDI '14)*, pp. 157–172, 2014.

Grubbs, Paul, Richard McPherson, Muhammad Naveed, Thomas Ristenpart, and Vitaly Shmatikov. "Breaking Web Applications Built On Top of Encrypted Data." *Proceedings of the 2016 ACM SIGSAC Conference on Computer and Communications Security (CCS '16)*, pp. 1353–1364, ACM, 2016. Devastating attack on Mylar's security model.

Goldreich, Oded, and Rafail Ostrovsky. "Software Protection and Simulation on Oblivious RAMs." *Journal of the ACM*, vol. 43, no. 3, pp. 431–473, 1996. Foundational ORAM construction.

Keybase. Client-side cryptographic identity and storage platform. Acquired by Zoom Video Communications, May 2020. Service subsequently deprecated.

Lund, Joshua. "Technology Preview: Sealed Sender for Signal." Signal Blog, October 29, 2018. Technical description of Signal's sender anonymity feature.

Krawczyk, Hugo. "Cryptographic Extraction and Key Derivation: The HKDF Scheme." *Advances in Cryptology—CRYPTO 2010*, LNCS vol. 6223, pp. 631–648, Springer, 2010. HKDF specification and ROM security proof.

• • •

Chapter 7: Proof of Human Architecture

Back, Adam. "Hashcash—A Denial of Service Counter-Measure." Technical report, August 2002. Original computational proof-of-work proposal for spam deterrence, first described in 1997.

Davidson, Alex, Ian Goldberg, Nick Sullivan, George Tankersley, and Filippo Valsorda. "Privacy Pass: Bypassing Internet Challenges Anonymously." *Proceedings on Privacy Enhancing Technologies*, vol. 2018, no. 3, pp. 164–180, 2018. Cloudflare's anonymous token protocol for bot filtering.

Worldcoin Foundation. "Worldcoin Whitepaper." 2023. Biometric proof-of-personhood using iris scans; centralized orb-based enrollment. Developed by Tools for Humanity; whitepaper published by the Worldcoin Foundation. For critique, see Gebru and Torres (2024).

Gebru, Timnit, and Émile P. Torres. "The TESCREAL Bundle: Eugenics and the Promise of Utopia through Artificial General Intelligence." *First Monday*, vol. 29, no. 4, April 2024. Critical analysis of the ideological frameworks underlying AI-driven biometric identity projects including Worldcoin.

Google. "reCAPTCHA v3." Developer documentation. Behavioral risk scoring without interactive challenges; assigns scores based on observed user behavior patterns.

Anderson, Ross. *Security Engineering: A Guide to Building Dependable Distributed Systems*. 3rd ed. Wiley, 2020. Underground market pricing data for credential fraud economics.

Monrose, Fabian, and Aviel D. Rubin. "Keystroke Dynamics as a Biometric for Authentication." *Future Generation Computer Systems*, vol. 16, no. 4, pp. 351–359, 2000.

Goldwasser, Shafi, Silvio Micali, and Charles Rackoff. "The Knowledge Complexity of Interactive Proof Systems." *SIAM Journal on Computing*, vol. 18, no. 1, pp. 186–208, 1989. Foundational definition of zero-knowledge proofs.

Chaum, David. "Blind Signatures for Untraceable Payments." *Advances in Cryptology—CRYPTO '82*, edited by David Chaum, Ronald L. Rivest, and Alan T. Sherman, pp. 199–203, Plenum Press, 1983.

Camenisch, Jan, and Anna Lysyanskaya. "An Efficient System for Non-transferable Anonymous Credentials with Optional Anonymity Revocation." See Chapter 3 entry.

Englehardt, Steven, and Arvind Narayanan. "Online Tracking: A 1-million-site Measurement and Analysis." *Proceedings of the 2016 ACM SIGSAC Conference on Computer and Communications Security (CCS '16)*, pp. 1388–1401, ACM, 2016. DOI: 10.1145/2976749.2978313.

• • •

Chapter 8: The Metadata Problem

Hayden, Michael V. Remarks at Johns Hopkins University Foreign Affairs Symposium ("The Price of Privacy: Re-Evaluating the NSA"), April 1, 2014. "We kill people based on metadata." Made publicly, on video, in defense of NSA collection programs.

United States v. Reality Leigh Winner, Case No. 1:17-cr-00034-JRH-BKE (S.D. Ga. 2017). See Chapter 1 entry for full citation.

Electronic Frontier Foundation. "DocuColor Tracking Dot Decoding Guide." October 2005. Decoded the Xerox DocuColor yellow-dot pattern encoding printer serial number, date, and time. The technology was developed by Xerox and Canon in the mid-1980s and first publicly reported in 2004.

• • •

Chapter 9: HermesP2P Architecture

Dingledine, Roger, Nick Mathewson, and Paul Syverson. "Tor: The Second-Generation Onion Router." *Proceedings of the 13th USENIX Security Symposium*, pp. 303–320, 2004.

van den Hooff, Jelle, David Lazar, Matei Zaharia, and Nickolai Zeldovich. "Vuvuzela: Scalable Private Messaging Resistant to Traffic Analysis." *Proceedings of the 25th Symposium on Operating Systems Principles (SOSP '15)*, pp. 137–152, ACM, 2015.

Tyagi, Nirvan, Yossi Gilad, Derek Leung, Matei Zaharia, and Nickolai Zeldovich. "Stadium: A Distributed Metadata-Private Messaging System." *Proceedings of the 26th Symposium on Operating Systems Principles (SOSP '17)*, pp. 423–440, ACM, 2017.

Langley, Adam. "Pond." Technical design document, 2012–2014. Experimental forward-secure, transport-agnostic messaging system. Discontinued.

Briar Project. "Briar: Secure Messaging, Anywhere." Open-source peer-to-peer encrypted messaging for activists. Uses Tor for transport.

Piotrowska, Ania M., Jamie Hayes, Tariq Elahi, Sebastian Meiser, and George Danezis. "The Loopix Anonymity System." *Proceedings of the 26th USENIX Security Symposium*, pp. 1199–1216, 2017. Mix network with Poisson cover traffic and tunable latency-anonymity tradeoff.

Murdoch, Steven J., and George Danezis. "Low-Cost Traffic Analysis of Tor." *2005 IEEE Symposium on Security and Privacy (S&P '05)*, pp. 183–195, IEEE, 2005.

Danezis, George, and Ian Goldberg. "Sphinx: A Compact and Provably Secure Mix Format." *2009 IEEE Symposium on Security and Privacy*, pp. 269–282, IEEE, 2009.

Rogaway, Phillip, and Thomas Shrimpton. "Cryptographic Hash-Function Basics: Definitions, Implications, and Separations for Preimage Resistance, Second-Preimage Resistance, and Collision Resistance." *Fast Software Encryption (FSE 2004)*, LNCS vol. 3017, pp. 371–388, Springer, 2004.

Bernstein, Daniel J. "ChaCha, a Variant of Salsa20." ECRYPT Stream Cipher Project Report, 2008. See also: IETF RFC 8439, "ChaCha20 and Poly1305 for IETF Protocols," June 2018.

IETF. RFC 8446, "The Transport Layer Security (TLS) Protocol Version 1.3," August 2018. Forward secrecy via ephemeral key exchange.

• • •

Chapter 11: Cryptogram/Delegator Architecture

Yao, Andrew C. "Protocols for Secure Computations." *23rd Annual Symposium on Foundations of Computer Science (FOCS '82)*, pp. 160–164, IEEE, 1982. Foundational work on secure multi-party computation.

Shamir, Adi. "How to Share a Secret." *Communications of the ACM*, vol. 22, no. 11, pp. 612–613, 1979.

Costan, Victor, and Srinivas Devadas. "Intel SGX Explained." *IACR Cryptology ePrint Archive*, Report 2016/086, 2016. Comprehensive analysis of Intel SGX architecture and threat model.

Van Bulck, Jo, Marina Minkin, Ofir Weisse, Daniel Genkin, Baris Kasikci, Frank Piessens, Mark Silberstein, Thomas F. Wenisch, Yuval Yarom, and Raoul Strackx. "Foreshadow: Extracting the Keys to the Intel SGX Kingdom with Transient Out-of-Order Execution." *Proceedings of the 27th USENIX Security Symposium*, pp. 991–1008, 2018.

Katz, Jonathan, and Yehuda Lindell. *Introduction to Modern Cryptography*. 3rd ed. CRC Press, 2020. Definition 3.22 (IND-CPA security); Theorem 3.23 proves that IND-CPA security implies security for multiple encryptions.

Bernstein, Daniel J. "Curve25519: New Diffie-Hellman Speed Records." *Public Key Cryptography (PKC 2006)*, LNCS vol. 3958, pp. 207–228, Springer, 2006.

Bernstein, Daniel J., Tanja Lange, and Peter Schwabe. "The Security Impact of a New Cryptographic Library." *LATINCRYPT 2012*, LNCS vol. 7533, pp. 159–176, Springer, 2012. NaCl/libsodium constant-time implementation.

Sabt, Mohamed, Mohammed Achemlal, and Abdelmadjid Bouabdallah. "Trusted Execution Environment: What It Is, and What It Is Not." *2015 IEEE Trustcom/BigDataSE/ISPA*, pp. 57–64, IEEE, 2015. DOI: 10.1109/Trustcom.2015.357.

Murdock, Kit, David Oswald, Flavio D. Garcia, Jo Van Bulck, Daniel Gruss, and Frank Piessens. "Plundervolt: Software-based Fault Injection Attacks against Intel SGX." *2020 IEEE Symposium on Security and Privacy (SP)*, pp. 1466–1482, IEEE, 2020.

Menezes, Alfred J., Paul C. van Oorschot, and Scott A. Vanstone. *Handbook of Applied Cryptography*. CRC Press, 1996. Forward secrecy is defined in Section 12.2 (Classification and framework).

Lindell, Yehuda. "Secure Multiparty Computation (MPC)." *Communications of the ACM*, vol. 64, no. 1, pp. 86–96, 2021. Survey of practical MPC.

• • •

Chapter 12: The Distribution Problem

See Chapter 1 entry for Apple China VPN removal.

• • •

Chapter 13: Chess Architecture

Yarvin, Curtis, Philip Monk, Anton Dyudin, and Raymond Pasco. "Urbit: A Solid-State

Interpreter." Tlon Corporation, 2016. Deterministic computing platform with identity-bound execution.

Benet, Juan. "IPFS—Content Addressed, Versioned, P2P File System." arXiv preprint arXiv:1407.3561, 2014. Content-addressing for distributed storage.

Dolstra, Eelco, Merijn de Jonge, and Eelco Visser. "Nix: A Safe and Policy-Free System for Software Deployment." *18th Large Installation System Administration Conference (LISA '04)*, pp. 79–92, USENIX, 2004. Reproducible builds through functional package management.

Ingalls, Daniel H. H. "The Smalltalk-76 Programming System: Design and Implementation." *Proceedings of the 5th ACM SIGACT-SIGPLAN Symposium on Principles of Programming Languages*, pp. 9–16, ACM, 1978. Image-based persistence—code and state in a single artifact.

NIST. "Secure Hash Standard (SHS)." FIPS PUB 180-4, August 2015. See Chapter 3 entry. SHA-256 collision resistance (128-bit birthday bound).

Rogaway, Phillip, and Thomas Shrimpton. See Chapter 9 entry for hash-function basics.

Bernstein, Daniel J., Niels Duif, Tanja Lange, Peter Schwabe, and Bo-Yin Yang. See Chapter 3 entry for Ed25519 paper.

• • •

Chapter 15: Implementation Roadmap

Jarecki, Stanislaw, Hugo Krawczyk, and Jiayu Xu. See Chapter 3 entry for OPAQUE citation.

NIST. "Post-Quantum Cryptography Standardization." ML-KEM (FIPS 203) and ML-DSA (FIPS 204), August 2024.

Biryukov, Alex, Daniel Dinu, and Dmitry Khovratovich. "Argon2: New Generation of Memory-Hard Functions for Password Hashing and Other Applications." *2016 IEEE European Symposium on Security and Privacy (EuroS&P)*, pp. 292–302, IEEE, 2016. Winner of the Password Hashing Competition (2015).

Krawczyk, Hugo. See Chapter 5 entry for HKDF citation.

• • •

Appendix C: Formal Security Analysis

Syverson, Paul, Gene Tsudik, Michael Reed, and Carl Landwehr. "Towards an Analysis of Onion Routing Security." *Proceedings of the Workshop on Design Issues in Anonymity and Unobservability*, pp. 96–114, Springer LNCS vol. 2009, 2000.

Goldreich, Oded, and Rafail Ostrovsky. See Chapter 5 entry for ORAM citation.

Glossary

Terms are defined as used in this book. Some terms have different meanings in other contexts.

• • •

Anonymous Identity An authentication architecture where each user receives a different, unlinkable token for each service they use. The tokens are cryptographically derived from the user's credentials combined with site-specific identifiers. No party can correlate tokens across sites without possessing secrets held only by the user's client.

Blind Database A storage system where the operator cannot read the data it stores. Clients encrypt data before upload using keys the server never possesses. The server provides availability—storing and returning records on request—without the capability to interpret content. Also called "operationally blind storage."

Chess A document format for self-validating applications. A Chess document contains executable code (in a minimal Lisp dialect), application state, and a cryptographically signed hash chain of state transitions. Any device can verify the document's integrity and provenance without contacting external authorities.

Cryptogram A structured document containing encrypted sections, each readable only by its intended recipient. Used to coordinate multi-party workflows where no single intermediary should see all information. The payment processor sees payment details; the shipper sees the address; neither sees what the other sees.

Crypto-Erasure Destroying data by discarding the encryption keys rather than the ciphertext. The encrypted data remains on disk but becomes computationally indistinguishable from random noise. Useful when physical deletion is impractical or when deletion must be provable.

Delegator A routing service that coordinates cryptogram workflows without reading their contents. The delegator receives encrypted fragments, forwards them to designated recipients based on routing metadata, and accumulates responses—all without possessing decryption keys. A blind courier.

Ephemeral Designed to disappear. Ephemeral data exists only for the duration of its immediate use, then is discarded or becomes unrecoverable. Ephemeral messaging leaves no logs. Ephemeral workers self-destruct after completing their task. The opposite of persistent.

Good Police Work Principle The architectural principle that mass surveillance queries should be structurally infeasible while targeted investigation of specific suspects remains possible. The architecture enforces what legal process is supposed to enforce: investigation requires a hypothesis before it begins. Named throughout the book as a design constraint that distinguishes privacy-preserving architecture from anti-law-enforcement architecture.

Hash Construction The cryptographic mechanism underlying anonymous identity. A one-way function combines user credentials with site identifiers to produce site-specific tokens. The same user produces different tokens for different sites. The tokens cannot be reversed to recover the inputs or correlated without knowledge of those inputs.

HermesP2P A peer-to-peer messaging architecture where no central server accumulates metadata. Messages route through intermediate nodes using onion encryption. Each node knows only its immediate neighbors in the routing path. Messages are ephemeral; the network retains nothing after delivery.

Honest-but-Curious Operator A trust model where operators are assumed to follow protocols correctly but cannot be trusted to resist reading data they can access. The architecture removes temptation by removing capability. An honest-but-curious operator cannot read what it cannot decrypt, cannot log what it never receives.

Humanness Score A numerical value (0.0 to 0.99) representing accumulated evidence that an identity belongs to a human rather than a bot. The score reflects effort to establish—email verification, payment instruments, behavioral patterns over time—without revealing the specific signals. Higher scores are exponentially harder to forge.

Move In Chess, a single state transition in an application's history. A move contains the hash of the previous state, the operation performed, the hash of the resulting state, and a cryptographic signature from the authorized actor. The sequence of moves forms an unbroken, verifiable chain.

Onion Routing A technique for anonymous communication where messages are wrapped in layers of encryption, one for each relay node. Each node decrypts one layer, learns only the next destination, and forwards. No node except the sender knows the complete path. Used in HermesP2P for metadata protection.

Operational Blindness The condition where an operator cannot interpret the data it handles. Distinguished from formal zero-knowledge proofs, which provide mathematical guarantees about information leakage. Operational blindness acknowledges that side channels exist (access patterns, timing, volume) while ensuring content remains unreadable.

Perfection Fallacy The rhetorical pattern of attacking an improvement by pointing to remaining vulnerabilities as though the improvement created them. Takes the form: "Your system does not protect against X, therefore it is useless." The response: does the status quo protect against X? If not, the criticism is not an argument against the improvement. Used throughout the book to frame honest assessment of limitations.

Proof of Human (PoH) A system for demonstrating humanness without biometric capture or identity disclosure. Signals accumulate over time—verification events, behavioral patterns, economic stake—and convert to a score. The score attests to humanness; the underlying signals are not retained or exposed.

Site-Specific Token The identifier that a user presents to a particular service under anonymous identity. Derived from the user's credentials and the site's identifier through the hash construction. Stable across sessions for that site, unlinkable to tokens the same user holds on other sites.

Trust Boundary The explicit statement of what a system component must be trusted for and what it need not be trusted for. Example: the User Service must be trusted for availability (being online when needed) but need not be trusted for confidentiality (the blind database ensures it cannot read mappings).

User Service The identity provider in the anonymous identity architecture. Facilitates authentication by providing values needed for token derivation. Stores identity mappings in a blind database so that even the User Service operator cannot correlate user activity across sites.

Also by Jeremy McEntire

The Cage and the Mirror

Why organizations systematically destroy the information they need most. A formal theory of institutional blindness, built from the same structural logic that governs the systems in your hands.

Uncommon Leadership

Everything you've been told about leadership, delivered with complete sincerity. A 490-page masterclass in the conventions that keep organizations functioning exactly as they are.

Applied Synthesis

A course in higher-order thinking disguised as a textbook. Fourteen chapters on developing the cognitive processes that institutions measure out of existence, taught through a fictional student's portfolio that demonstrates what the chapters describe.

City of Mercy

A detective mystery set in San Francisco's Tenderloin. A killer on the loose in the city's downtrodden center. Atmospheric, morally unsettled, and not interested in giving you an easy answer.

Per Ardua

www.ingramcontent.com/pod-product-compliance
Lightning Source LLC
Chambersburg PA
CBHW051206200326
41519CB00025B/7026